MOUNTAIN BIKE!
Texas and Oklahoma

MOUNTAIN BIKE!
Texas and Oklahoma

A GUIDE TO THE CLASSIC TRAILS

SECOND EDITION

CHUCK CYPERT

Menasha
Ridge
Press

Library of Congress Cataloging-in-Publication Data:
Cypert, Chuck.
Mountain bike! Texas and Oklahoma/Chuck Cypert—2nd ed.
p.   cm.
Rev. ed. of: Mountain biking Texas and Oklahoma. 1st ed. c1995.
Includes index.
1. All terrain cycling—Texas—Guidebooks.
2. 1. All terrain cycling—Oklahoma—Guidebooks.
3.—Texas—Guidebooks.
4. Oklahoma—Guidebooks.
I. Title: Texas and Oklahoma.
II. Cypert, Chuck. Mountain biking Texas and Oklahoma.
III. Title
GV1045.5.T4 C7 1995
7.96.6'3'09764—dc21
20020213

Photos by the author unless otherwise credited
Maps by Steven Jones and Jeff Goodwin
Cover and text design by Suzanne Holt
Cover Photo by Dennis Coello

Menasha Ridge Press
P.O. Box 43673
Birmingham, Alabama 35243
www.menasharidge.com

All the trails described in this book are legal for mountain bikes. But rules can change—especially for off-road bicycles, the new kid on the outdoor recreation block. Land access issues and conflicts between bicyclists, hikers, equestrians, and other users can cause the rewriting of recreation regulations on public lands, sometimes resulting in a ban of mountain bike use on specific trails. That's why it's the responsibility of each rider to check and make sure that he or she rides only on trails where mountain biking is permitted.

CAUTION

Outdoor recreational activities are by their very nature potentially hazardous. All participants in such activities must assume the responsibility for their own actions and safety. The information contained in this guidebook cannot replace sound judgment and good decision-making skills, which help reduce risk exposure, nor does the scope of this book allow for disclosure of all the potential hazards and risks involved in such activities.

Learn as much as possible about the outdoor recreational activities in which you participate, prepare for the unexpected, and be cautious. The reward will be a safer and more enjoyable experience.

CONTENTS

Dedication viii
Map Legend ix
Ride Location Map x–xi
List of Maps xii
Acknowledgments xiv
Foreword xvii
Preface xix
Build Trails xxiv
Ride Recommendations for Special Interests xxvi

INTRODUCTION 1

Trail Description Outline 1
Abbreviations 2
Ride Configurations 3
Topographic Maps 3
Trail Etiquette 4
Hitting the Trail 7
And Now, a Word about Cellular Phones… 9

OKLAHOMA 11

1 Old Military Road Trail—Talihina 12
2 Oklahoma "Ankle Express" Trail—Greenleaf State Park 16
3 Turkey Mountain Park Trails—Tulsa 20
4 Lake McMurtry Trails—Stillwater 23
5 Benny's Trail—Guthrie 27
6 Arcadia Lake Trail—Arcadia Lake 30
7 NuDraper Mountain Bike Park—Stanley Draper Lake 33
8 Clear Bay Trail—Lake Thunderbird State Park 37
9 Bluff Creek Trail—Lake Hefner 40
10 Roman Nose State Park Trail—Lake Watonga 43

TEXAS   49

NORTH TEXAS   52

11   Northshore Trail—Grapevine Lake   52
12   Knob Hills Trail—Grapevine Lake   57
13   Horseshoe Trail—Grapevine Lake   61
14   L. B. Houston Nature Trail—Dallas   64
15   Arbor Hills Nature Preserve Mountain Bike Trail—Plano   67
16   Boulder Park Trail—Dallas   76
17   Windmill Hill Nature Preserve Trail—DeSoto   74
18   DORBA Trail—Cedar Hill State Park   77
19   Rowlett Creek Nature Preserve Trails—Garland   81
20   Sister Grove Park Trail—Lake Lavon   84
21   Erwin Park Trail—McKinney   88
22   Johnson Branch Trail—Ray Roberts Lake State Park   92
23   "The Breaks" at Bar-H Ranch—Saint Jo   **95**

CENTRAL TEXAS   100

24   Fossil Rim Wildlife Center—Glen Rose   100
25   Cedar Brake Trail—Dinosaur Valley State Park   104
26   The Seven Mile Loop—Cleburne State Park   108
27   Cameron Park Trails—Waco   112
28   Barton Creek Greenbelt—Austin   115
29   Emma Long Motorcycle Park—Austin   119
30   Walnut Creek Trails—Austin   122
31   Muleshoe Bend Trail—Bee Caves   126
32   Bluff Creek Ranch—Warda   129
33   Rocky Hill Ranch—Smithville   133
34   Wolf Mountain Trail—Pedernales Falls State Park   137
35   McAllister Park Trails—San Antonio   140
36   Flat Rock Ranch—Comfort   143

EAST TEXAS AND THE GULF   148

37   Bonham State Park Trail—Bonham   149
38   Tyler State Park Trail—Tyler   151
39   Lake Bryan Trails—Bryan   155
40   Double Lake Park Mountain Bike Trail—Coldspring   158
41   Memorial Park Trails—Houston   161
42   The Anthills/Terry Hershey Park—Houston   164
43   Jack Brooks Park Trail—Hitchcock   167
44   North Padre Island—Padre Island National Seashore   170

TEXAS PANHANDLE   177

   45 Big Loop MTB Trail—Copper Breaks State Park Trail   178
   46 Mae Simmons Park Trail—Lubbock   181
   47 Caprock Canyons Trailway—Quitaque   184
   48 The "GSL" and Capitol Peak Trails—Palo Duro Canyon State Park   187

WEST TEXAS   193

   49 San Angelo State Park Trails—San Angelo   194
   50 X-Bar Ranch—Eldorado   199
   51 Glenn Springs and Black Gap—Big Bend National Park   203
   52 The Old Ore Road—Big Bend National Park   207
   53 The Monk's Trail—Crazy Cat Arroyo   212
   54 Gilbert's Trail (The Southside)—Franklin Mountains State Park   216
   24 The Sunset Loop—Franklin Mountains State Park   220

Afterward   225
Glossary   227
Index   239
About the Author   257

DEDICATION

(Because that's what it is)

Imagine you are in a building that is engulfed in flames. There is a man running down an upstairs hallway in the midst of the blaze. He wears a masked helmet and a big canvas coat. All you can hear over the roar of the fire is his breathing, as he sucks air from a tank on his back. Behind the mask is a face of total concentration, eyes focused. Charging down, burning bits of building falling all around like glowing leaves, he heads straight into a wall of flames.

He bursts through the blaze into a spray of fire hoses. The water instantly turns to steam when it hits him, boiling and hissing and trailing like a fog. Pausing painful seconds to get drenched, he moves on.

At the street is a family, completely panicked, watching their home and their lives be consumed by disaster. Their eyes fix on him with terrified but hopeful looks, looks you and I never want to know. As the fireman reaches them he rips open his coat and there, nestled safely inside, is a baby. A tiny, precious child.

He passes infant to its mother, who collapses tearfully into the father's arms. They fall to the ground sobbing thankful prayers. Though the fireman can't quite hear their words, he understands them well enough; he has heard them before.

With a quick nod to the ambulance crew he goes back to his job. Despite the miserable scene ahead, a grin flickers across his face for an instant. Two seconds later, this face is set with a stoic look that says everything about who he is and what he does.

This book is dedicated to firefighters and paramedics everywhere. Thank you for your sacrifices and your bravery.

AMERICA BY MOUNTAIN BIKE MAP LEGEND

Ride trailhead	Steep grade	Optional trailhead	
Primary bike trail	Direction of travel	(arrows point downhill)	Optional bike trail	Restricted area	Hiking trail

Interstate highways (with exit no.)	US routes	State routes	Other paved roads	Unpaved, gravel, or dirt roads (may be 4WD only)

Covell Blvd.

US Forest Service roads	Cities	Towns or settlements	Dam	Lake	River, stream, or canal

Asheville ◉   Linville ◉

0   ½   1

MILES

Approximate scale in miles   True north   Public Lands*   International border   State border

TOPANGA ST. PK.

✈ Airport

Ski Area

Orchard

▲ Campground (CG)

≡ Cattle guard

Spring

Park

Cliff, escarpment, or outcropping

Drinking water

Power Plant

Fire tower or lookout

Food

Gate

House, shelter, or cabin

Lodging

Mountain or butte

Mountain pass

Mountain summit
3312 (elevation in feet)

Rest room

✗ Mine

Museum

Observatory

Park office or ranger station

Picnic area

Sno-Park

Power line or pipeline

Ranch or stable

Swimming Area

Transmission towers

Tunnel or bridge

*Remember, private property exists in and around our national forests.

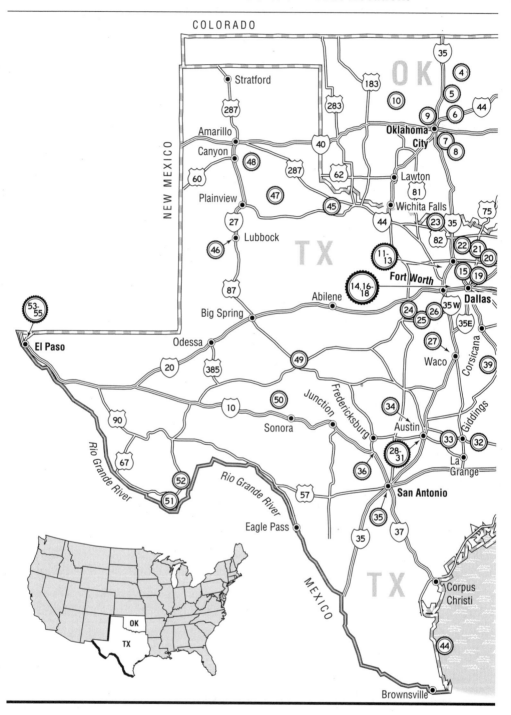

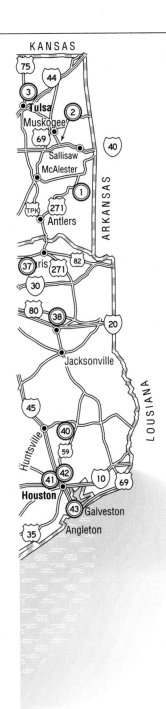

LIST OF MAPS

1 Old Military Road Trail—Talihina 13

2 Oklahoma "Ankle Express" Trail—Greenleaf State Park 17

3 Turkey Mountain Park Trails—Tulsa 21

4 Lake McMurtry Trails—Stillwater 25

5 Benny's Trail—Guthrie 28

6 Arcadia Lake Trail—Arcadia Lake 31

7 NuDraper Mountain Bike Park—Stanley Draper Lake 34

8 Clear Bay Trail—Lake Thunderbird State Park 38

9 Bluff Creek Trail—Lake Hefner 41

10 Roman Nose State Park Trail—Lake Watonga 44

11 Northshore Trail—Grapevine Lake 53

12 Knob Hills Trail—Grapevine Lake 58

13 Horseshoe Trail—Grapevine Lake 61

14 L. B. Houston Nature Trail—Dallas 65

15 Arbor Hills Nature Preserve Mountain Bike Trail—Plano 68

16 Boulder Park Trail—Dallas 71

17 Windmill Hill Nature Preserve Trail—DeSoto 75

18 DORBA Trail—Cedar Hill State Park 78

19 Rowlett Creek Nature Preserve Trails—Garland 82

20 Sister Grove Park Trail—Lake Lavon 85

21 Erwin Park Trail—McKinney 89

22 Johnson Branch Trail—Ray Roberts Lake State Park 93

23 "The Breaks" at Bar-H Ranch—Saint Jo 96

24 Fossil Rim Wildlife Center—Glen Rose 101

25 Cedar Brake Trail—Dinosaur Valley State Park 105

26 The Seven Mile Loop—Cleburne State Park 109

27 Cameron Park Trails—Waco 113

28 Barton Creek Greenbelt—Austin 116

29 Emma Long Motorcycle Park—Austin 120

30 Walnut Creek Trails—Austin 123

31 Muleshoe Bend Trail—Bee Caves 127

32 Bluff Creek Ranch—Warda 132

33 Rocky Hill Ranch—Smithville 134

34 Wolf Mountain Trail—Pedernales Falls State Park 138

35 McAllister Park Trails—San Antonio 141

36 Flat Rock Ranch—Comfort 144

37 Bonham State Park Trail—Bonham 150

38 Tyler State Park Trail—Tyler 152

39 Lake Bryan Trails—Bryan 156

40 Double Lake Park Mountain Bike Trail—Coldspring 159

41 Memorial Park Trails—Houston 162

42 The Anthills/Terry Hershey Park—Houston 165

43 Jack Brooks Park Trail—Hitchcock 168

44 North Padre Island—Padre Island National Seashore 171

45 Big Loop MTB Trail—Copper Breaks State Park Trail 179

46 Mae Simmons Park Trail—Lubbock 182

47 Caprock Canyons Trailway—Quitaque 185

48 The "GSL" and Capitol Peak Trails—Palo Duro Canyon State Park 190

49 San Angelo State Park Trails—San Angelo 194

50 X-Bar Ranch—Eldorado 200

51 Glenn Springs and Black Gap—Big Bend National Park 204

52 The Old Ore Road—Big Bend National Park 209

53 The Monk's Trail—Crazy Cat Arroyo 213

54 Gilbert's Trail (The Southside)—Franklin Mountains State Park 217

55 The Sunset Loop—Franklin Mountains State Park 221

ACKNOWLEDGMENTS

"Texan by choice, not by chance"

To my mom for giving me life, "Thank you for birthing me. I have so much fun, and I love you so much, let's go over to the Railhead and eat some ribs. And have a couple of beers. OK, you have tea. I'll do Shiner Bock."

Heartfelt respect and love to my roomie, Kennis Ketchum. She is half the reason I can finish a project like this. "If you are unfortunate enough to precede me to the grave I have a warning for you; the cockatiel is history. Straight into the newspaper classifieds as soon as you are in the ground. I'm thinking medical research." OK, I'm just kidding, she knows I would never harm an animal. I'm just tired of it squawking incessantly and eating my photographs.

I love my home club, the Dallas Off-Road Bicycle Association (DORBA), but I am mighty fond of my new away-from-home club, the Oklahoma Earth-bike Fellowship (OEF). I have to gush; these are some trail monsters, both groups. I strongly urge you to get involved with your local mountain bike club to meet some folks and get right with your dirt. I have had so much fun over the years and I have so many wonderful pals and I cannot thank them all enough for what they have given me.

I see the OEF in the same light I saw DORBA a few years ago: a lot of semi-fringe folks putting together superior single-track. Some of them have tattoos and earrings, and their intensity might frighten some riders. They are top-shelf human beings. They care about the dirt, and it ain't because they have fancy bikes. It is because they understand. They understand the beauty of trail, and they love that dirt more than they love their bikes. What a concept! I am UP FOR THAT.

In a slightly different vein, the DORBA seems (to me) to include a lot more mainstream people than before. A lot of the members are average folks who love the woods. There are still lots of bike hippies like me around, but the people I see at club meetings and out building stuff are like your next door neighbor or something. They are almost normal. It's weird, but I love it. I never thought mountain biking would be anything but a fringe interest, something that only the sickest of cyclists would enjoy. I was wrong. Nowadays, the average mountain biker has a job and a nice car and a bike with two-to-four inches of travel in the rear. That used to be so extreme.

I want to thank everyone who has a life and still finds time to make cool places for me to ride. To all the clubs I have failed to mention here, in Oklahoma and in Texas, thank you for the hard work. Lurve yer trails, man. Send me an e-mail, let's ride!

To Armond Schwartz, of Spokes for Folks, "Armond, you have done so much good for kids in Dallas. You've made so many old ruined bikes look new, and sent good bikes to good homes. I can deal with this my brother; it is way special to get a bike when you are a kid. I know you understand this. And thanks to Cindy (mom) for giving you that. And thank you to all the volunteers who have helped with this project."

To Jim and Rhonda Hoyt of the Richardson Bike Mart, "Thank you for all the cool bikes you loaned me while I was working on this book. I'm not sure I could have better friends. And for the bikes you let me buy, and for buying my books, and for just generally being really fine folks and a major credit to the local cycling community. There ain't a better shop I have ever been in. I have never walked away pissed off, about anything."

To Ken Smith (AKA Woody, Woods, Wooder, Woodword, Woodman, Woodmont, Woodlet, Woodpuppy, Woodster, Woodmeister, Woodmonster, or just plain Wood) at the same Richardson Bike Mart, "Dude you are the reason I love that shop so much. I have never met such a patient and thoughtful person in a bike shop. And that is saying something, Woodly, considering some of the folks I know. You da man."

To Lance Armstrong, "Thank you for being another American winner of the Tour de France. 'There is only one, you know.' They hate it over there when we win that race, and I will always love you for that. And for all that other stuff you have done. For the Lance Armstrong Foundation, for living your life, and for being so brave. A gracious thank you. You are a Texas hero, as much as Davy Crockett or Sam Houston, to me. And you were born here, they just got here as fast as they could."

To Carlos Santana, and to Mark Knoppfler. "Y'alls music does something for my soul, something akin to what mountain biking does for my mind. Thank you both." And to SRV, "I remember where I was when I heard yer chopper went down. I barely knew who you were back then. Now I love you like I love my bikes."

And lastly to the Urban Legends website, "Thank you for all the hard work you have obviously put into running down all those silly rumors. Y'all got it goin' on, and y'all are welcome down here in Texas any time."

Respectfully,

Charles Buddy Cypert, Jr.
Dallas, November 2001
"2OLD2CRASH"
www.home.mindspring.com/~ccypert
ccypert@mindspring.com

Recommended contacts:

International Mountain Bicycling
  Association (IMBA)
1121 Broadway, Suite 203
P.O. Box 7578
Boulder, CO 80306
(303)545-9011
(888)442-4622
www.imba.com

Lance Armstrong Foundation
P.O. Box 161150
Austin, TX 78716-1150
(512)236-8820
www.laf.org

Milagro Foundation
P.O. Box 9125

San Rafael, CA 94912
www.santana.com/milagro

Spokes for Folks
221 West Calorado Boulevard
Suite 630
Dallas, Texas 75208
(214)890-8960
www.spokesforfolks.org

Soka Gakkai International
"Victory over Violence"
www.sgi-usa.org

Urban Legends Reference Pages
www.snopes.com

FOREWORD

Welcome to *America by Mountain Bike*, a series designed to provide all-terrain bikers with the information they need to find and ride the very best trails around. Whether you're new to the sport and don't know where to pedal, or an experienced mountain biker who wants to learn the classic trails in another region, this series is for you. Drop a few bucks for the book, spend an hour with the detailed maps and route descriptions, and you're prepared for the finest in off-road cycling.

My role as editor of this series was simple: First, find a mountain biker who knows the area and loves to ride. Second, ask that person to spend a year researching the most popular and very best rides around. And third, have that rider describe each trail in terms of difficulty, scenery, condition, elevation change, and all other categories of information that are important to trail riders. "Pretend you've just completed a ride and met up with fellow mountain bikers at the trailhead," I told each author. "Imagine their questions, be clear in your answers."

As I said, the editorial process—that of sending out riders and reading the submitted chapters—is a snap. But the work involved in finding, riding, and writing about each trail is enormous. In some instances our authors' tasks are made easier by the information contributed by local bike shops or cycling clubs, or even by the writers of local "where-to" guides. Credit for these contributions is provided, when appropriate, in each chapter, and our sincere thanks goes to all who have helped.

But the overwhelming majority of trails are discovered and pedaled by our authors themselves, then compared with dozens of other routes to determine if they qualify as "classic"—showcasing that area's best in scenery and cycling fun. If you've ever had the experience of pioneering a route from outdated topographic maps, or entering a bike shop to request information from local riders who would much prefer to keep their favorite trails secret, or know how trying it is to double- and triple-check data to be positive your trail info is correct, then you have an idea of how each of our authors has labored to bring about these books. You and I, and all the mountain bikers of America, are the richer for their efforts.

You'll get more out of this book if you take a moment to read the Introduction explaining how to read the trail listings. The "Topographic Maps" section will help you understand how useful topos will be on a ride, and will also tell you where to get them. And though this is a "where-to," not a "how-to" guide, those of you who have not traveled the backcountry might find "Hitting the Trail" of particular value.

In addition to the material above, newcomers to mountain biking might want to spend a minute with the Glossary, page 227, so that terms like *hardpack, singletrack,* and *waterbars* won't throw you when you come across them in the text.

Finally, the tips in the Afterword on mountain biking etiquette and land-use controversy might help us all enjoy the trails a little more.

All the best.

Dennis Coello
St. Louis

PREFACE

"Every time I see an adult on a bicycle, my faith is restored in the human race."
—H.G. Wells

"George, George, George of the jungle.
Watch out for that tree!
Watch out for that...TREE!"

—Unknown

This is where I get to be yer Mom. If you like to shred and jump off buildings then you are probably not one of my friends. I don't shred and I don't get big air. Gave it up. When I was ten, and my Schwinn Sting-Ray finally gave out.

Now, I don't want to seem negative, I am actually a very positive person. I just don't believe in being loud and/or abusive. To trails, or to people. Where I live and ride you have to take care not to damage anything. The trails here are very sensitive. I receive e-mails from wacko anti–mountain bike nuts who have a point sometimes. This ain't no Mountain Dew commercial, brothers and sisters. This is a sustainable recreational activity, bordering on and completely at ease with being a sport. If we are smart.

Mountain biking is a privilege, not a right. Don't go around laying down 30-foot-long skid marks. It chews the crap out of the trail, causing erosion, and it looks really bad. You know all those stair-step holes on the descents and turns? Locked-brake skidding is what creates them. Now, I know you gotta ride hard and live free and all that, but freedom has a price tag: responsibility. I like to think that I ride like it matters. Riding my bikes may not matter to anyone but me, but that is the way I approach my art. On or off the pavement.

Don't ride in the mud. That makes the trail wider and deeper, and pretty soon instead of an 18" path you have one four feet wide. Don't cut the trail; meaning don't take shortcuts. Why are you out here if you don't want to savor every inch? Don't cut your own trail; meaning don't knock over trees and move things around to make it easier for your wimpy little legs to get through some techie bit. We build this stuff to be challenging because we enjoy honing our skills. If you can't ride it, walk it. No shame in that. Otherwise leave it as alone as you possibly can. It belongs to my trail-nazi pals and me, because we made it.

I wasn't there when this shot was taken, somewhere along the trails at Lake Murray,. but I'm guessing Greg is about to meet Mr. de Zaster. That rock is in a bad spot. Photo by Marcel Slootheer.

I love my trails, but I also love my machines. I like weird old stuff that nobody else has. I have bikes that are twenty-plus years old, and I still ride them. I will keep all my bikes forever—until I die. "Why does a person need several bikes?" you're thinking. "He can only ride one at a time, right?" What kind of total nonsense is that? Are you gonna go play eighteen holes of golf with one club? No, fool, yer gonna drag out whatever you need from yer bag. 'Cause yer prepared. That's what I'm talkin' about!

What I'm saying is take care of your machine. Don't break things off it unless you really are one of the bad-ass racers who just go THAT hard. Don't jump a fine steed off some thirty-foot drop just to see if you can make it. This ain't the North Shore and you ain't Crazy Dan. All those injuries and broken bones you earn being a daredevil will visit you when you're my age. I for one want to live to ride another day; my motto is "2OLD2CRASH," and my bikes are too valuable to me to hurt them.

Having a good bike is such a pleasure. But don't go overboard. You don't need to spend thousands of dollars to ride any of these trails. If you start on a $200 bike you got at Wal-Mart, then more power to you. In today's dollars that's equivalent to a Schwinn Sting-Ray. Go get yerself some. But understand that a better bike will

Unfortunately this trail is not included in this edition. It resides on Army land, way out west in Oklahoma, and any Oklahoma rider with a lick of mountain bike sense knows exactly where this shot was taken: the beautiful Wichita Mountains and the evil 12 Miles of Hell. Photo by Chris Knarr (with Marcel's camera).

make you a better rider. However, you hit the point of diminishing returns pretty quick at the bike shop. Pretty soon you have spent about twice what you really need to lay out just to ride for fun. Of course, it is always nice to have something to grow into, a little extra up your sleeve, and I have had all manner of mountain bikes. Beginner bikes, mid-range bikes, and custom ones I built.

I only recently got a real mountain bike. I rode rigids for too many years, being the retro-grouch I am. My wrists and butt are too old for that now. On my new Ibis Ripley, I can see straight on a fast downhill. I used to be blinded at speeds above 20 mph. I have a bike that squishes on both ends now. No DH/FR fifty pounds of crap, but I am quite happy. I don't need six inches in the rear and eight in the front because I, personally, would look stupid on something like that. Everybody knows I ain't jumpin' off nuthin' taller than a tequila bottle. Patron Añejo, preferably.

My Ripley is a super sweet machine, everything I hoped for and more. Who says an aluminum soft-tail is foolish? Hell, they make race car suspension stuff from aluminum, and I ain't ridin' near that hard. It's the best climbing bike I ever rode—mighty sweet. (Thank you Scot Nicol and John Castellano. And Roger and Doug, you maniacs tortured me until I just about expired the moment I saw it. Next, an Ibis Single Malt. Next year, maybe, or for my 50th birthday, no hurry.)

I ride a rigid Breezer Lightning, when I can. I stole it from Steve Patterson long ago. It is light and sweet and it is pure featherweight pleasure. True to its name it is a "breeze in the woods." Steve knows bikes, and I'll bet he is still sorry I got that beautiful machine out of his shop. (It came to a good home, my brother.)

Sometimes I ride an old Schwinn Cimarron that I bought from Ken Smith (AKA Woody—everybody knows Woody, he works for Jim Hoyt over at the Richardson Bike Mart). I built it up from a frame and lots of mail order catalogs. It has fenders and racks and weighs a good forty pounds. I love this bike—four water bottle cages! (Thanx Woods.)

And then I have fine road bikes: a Ron Cooper that knows every back road in Texas, a Schwinn Paramount that was brazed by a lady named Betty (it still tries to kill me occasionally), and an old Schwinn Prelude that I got from an ex. I set it up with a fixed gear. It's my beater-bike and will do things to your shins that will make you cuss.

I always have a few others hanging around. One of my favorites is an old Specialized RockHopper total assault-vehicle commuter bike I built from my first mountain bike. The "M1A1 Main Battle Bike." Sometimes I ride it to work, when I feel like punishing the automorons.

I always wear a helmet. I saw a motorcycle rider die once. His hair was perfect (except for the left side), but his helmet was at home and he died. Plus, I have lost dear friends. Some had gone for a quick ride on an easy trail, but left their helmets in the car. DO NOT DO THIS. I might ride on the beach or on my driveway without a brain bucket, but you won't see me do that anywhere else. I don't want to have to move in with my mom and spend the rest of life being spoon-fed. Her cats would probably…well, never mind.

When I go for a ride over a mile from home I always carry a patch kit (with tire tools) and a pump and two tubes, and at least one cheesy tool of some sort. I always either know where I am or have a real map that I know how to use. I know first-aid techniques, and I'd love to put a tourniquet on your leg. But then your parents will want to see my medical license, and I don't have one.

Yes, you can look at the maps in this book and find an alternate route, but I am writing about the trails I like. Do you want to ride with me or not? I gave up on GPS, figuring few of you would have one. I am a map nut and I drew maps for you but there might be a mistake or two in them or in some of the text. Nothing crucial, I promise, but have some wits about you when you go out on these trails. If you don't know your way around try to keep some sort of running tally of how far and in approximately what direction you have been going.

Again. Don't ride in the mud. I know it doesn't matter if you live in British Columbia or somewhere, but this is Texas and we have something here worse than the blistering summer heat, fire-ants, and I-35 construction project all rolled into one. Let's call it, hmmmm, how about *erosion?* Our trails are somewhat fragile. When fools abuse them, we all lose. Don't be an idiot, go to the gym or get your road bike out when the trails are wet. Or, I'll feed you to my mom's cats.

OK, I'm not yer mom any more. Get out there and play with your friends. Be home in time for supper. And wash behind your ears, for your mom's sake. And wear clean underwear, just in case…you know the old story.

> *"Work to eat, eat to live, live to ride, ride to work"*
> —Unknown commuter

BUILD TRAILS

"Do right and risk the consequences."
—Sam Houston, frontier statesman

Trails are about getting on the bicycle. And just ripping it up and screaming through the trees and jamming. I'm up for that. Trails are eating fresh redfish while you watch the moon rise over the gulf, down on Padre. Or while you have scrambled eggs and bacon and enjoy the morning sun peeking over the Winding Stair up in the Ouachitas. Trails are Stevie Ray's licks for Hendrix's "Little Wing." Trails are those little chocolate sprinkles in your cappuccino, and fresh dry clothes when you are out on a long camping trip.

Trails are what you make of them. I say you may as well go for the gusto, because trails are also something else. Trails are also about getting off the bike. And looking around and noticing things. And relishing the woods. And making it happen.

Do you know the difference between a shovel and a sharpshooter? Do you know the difference between a mattock and a pickax? Do you know what a french-drain or a rolling sloping grade is? Do you care? You should care. You should care about dirt. You are made of dirt. Did you ever notice how everyone's skin is the color of dirt? Think about it, there are people colored the white-tan of caliche, there are folks the color of all shades of sands and clays, and some as dark as black gumbo mud. Dirt is good; trail dirt is mixed with blood and pain, and pain is life. And life is where we are.

Where are you on trail day? Sleeping? We are building trails, and we're damn good at it. We can sleep tomorrow. If you haven't had the pleasure of making a trail happen then you are spending way too much time on the bicycle. Don't bitch because you have to drive so far to a good trail. That means you need to make trails happen closer to home. And don't cry if you don't like those two really bad mud holes in that one corner, because if you are just riding it you are not helping like you should be. Come on out sometime. It ain't easy, nope, but it sure is sweet. What we call "gravy" down here in the South. Build it and then bitch about it. Mo betta.

Trails can happen anywhere, maybe in your backyard. I mean, have you looked? Is there a corner back there the dogs have destroyed or something? Is there a place on the edge of town where everybody rides? Is there a place you always thought looked really prime? Make it legal. Get married to the idea. And then pat yourself on the back fifty times a day for having intestinal fortitude. Then become a trail-nazi like me and my pals. It could happen.

I know people who have trails in their backyards. But that is and will always be an oxymoron. Normally you and I will have to con somebody else into letting us have a try at building a trail on their property. Find these people, the land is out there. Trails can be where you least expect them. There may be a few acres of land that you can't build anything useful on. Give it to the county. Let the kids have it. Make it a park or something beneficial for property values in the neighborhood.

Trails are places where we share time with the land. Trails are places we respect and cherish. Trails are part of us because we make them happen. You can't have a trail without having a relationship with the person who cares for the land. There is very little public land in my state, most is private. People who own land and don't want it trashed often want it held in a public trust of some sort so you and I benefit from it's existence. (As Austin Powers would say… "YEAH BABY!") These are the people you want as friends and allies in the struggle to keep trails open and to keep opening trails. Don't let it all turn into 7-11 and Home Depot. (Two establishments I patronize on a regular basis).

Do not ride where riding is not allowed. Do not ride when riding is not allowed. Do not ride if you are interfering with traffic. Do not ride without a helmet and the appropriate preparation and proper gear.

DO RIDE WHERE riding is allowed. DO RIDE WHEN riding is allowed. RIDE and DO NOT interfere with traffic. RIDE and HELP make trails happen. RIDE and ENJOY trails you have helped happen. RIDE and LAUGH at your friends when they crash. RIDE and hassle people without helmets. RIDE and RIDE and RIDE. And BUILD.

BUILD relationships with the people who manage all that beautiful land out there where you live. BUILD trails on it when you can. Love the land. Be the trail. Make "The Woods" a precious and essential part of your life.

Ride. Build. Love. Enjoy. Pain. Life. Blood. Sweat. Tears. Wind. Sky. Skin. Rain. Trees. Sun. Peace. Ride…

RIDE RECOMMENDATIONS
FOR SPECIAL INTERESTS

"This ain't the Little Washita, General.
Them ain't defenseless women and children down there.
Them are war braves, Sioux and Cheyenne.
You go down there General, iff'n you got the nerve."

— Dustin Hoffman, Muleskinner "Little Big Man"

I have been on every trail in this book. I however cannot claim that I have seen every inch of every trail in every park. Get real. But I have a pretty good eye for what I think the average rider can relate to. I will endeavor to now enter a section that gives you a rough idea of what might be a suitable gradation of the trails contained herein, divided into some relevant categories. Writing this part was sort of fun. I'm goofy like that.

No Sweat Trails: These are trails that are very easy, you can probably ride them on a single-speed cruiser bike. There will be nothing in the way of serious technical skills or fancy equipment required to enjoy an afternoon on any of them. There aren't that many anyway, most of the good ones are paved and therefore not in this book. These are beginner level or below.

14	L.B. Houston Nature Trail	47	Caprock Canyons Trailway
24	Fossil Rim Wildlife Center		

95/95 Trails: These are trails where 95% of my readers will be able to ride 95% of the terrain. Anyone with beginner level mountain bike skills and a dependable steed can enjoy these. Wear your helmet, bring water and your patch kit.

6	Arcadia Lake Trail	35	McAllister Park Trails
13	Horseshoe Trail	37	Bonham State Park Trail
15	Arbor Hills Nature Preserve Trail	39	Lake Bryan Trails
19	Rowlett Creek Nature Preserve Trails (west)	40	Double Lake Park Mountain Bike Trail
24	Fossil Rim Wildlife Center	42	The Anthills/Terry Hershey Park
31	Muleshoe Bend Trail		

Skills and Chills Trails: On these trails you need to be able to ride. I mean really ride. None are extremely hard, but beginners should work on their bike handling and survival skills before tackling one. These are for more, experienced riders who can go hard without getting scared or hurt. I mean no insult, I'm just trying to be realistic here.

4	Lake McMurtry Trails	21	Erwin Park Trail
7	NuDraper Mountain Bike Park	24	Fossil Rim Wildlife Center
9	Bluff Creek Trail	25	Cedar Brake Trail
12	Knob Hills Trail	30	Walnut Creek Park Trails
17	Windmill Hill Nature Preserve Trail	34	Wolf Mountain Trail
		41	Memorial Park Trails
19	Rowlett Creek Nature Preserve Trails (east)	46	Mae Simmons Park Trail
		54	Gilbert's Trail (The Southside)
20	Sister Grove Park Trail		

Mr. Bustyerass de Zaster Trails: These are fairly hard trails that Joe Average will not enjoy. If you have a real bike, and you have been around long enough to know some tricks, these are for you. Pack in some nutrition, plenty of liquids, your tools, and maybe an extra tube..

3	Turkey Mountain Park Trails	29	Emma Long Motorcycle Park
5	Benny's Trail	30	Walnut Creek Park Trails
8	Clear Bay Trail	32	Bluff Creek Ranch
10	Roman Nose State Park Trail	33	Rocky Hill Ranch
11	Northshore Trail	36	Flat Rock Ranch
16	Boulder Park Trail	38	Tyler State Park Trail
18	DORBA Trail	43	Jack Brooks Park Trail
22	Johnson Branch Trail	45	Big Loop MTB Trail
23	"The Breaks" at Bar-H	48	The "GSL" and Capitol Peak Trails
24	Fossil Rim Wildlife Center		
26	The Seven Mile Loop	49	San Angelo State Park Trails
27	Cameron Park Trails	50	X-Bar Ranch
28	Barton Creek Greenbelt	53	The Monk's Trail

Scenic Rides: I threw this in because some trails are so inspiring to see that I think it is important to get the word out. Know your sport, have your bike in tune, and be ready for several hours in the woods before you go here. These are rides to take a camera on.

24	Fossil Rim Wildlife Center	48	The "GSL" and Capitol Peak Trails
36	Flat Rock Ranch		
44	North Padre Island	50	X-Bar Ranch
45	Big Loop MTB Trail	51	Glenn Springs and Black Gap
47	Caprock Canyons Trailway	52	The Old Ore Road
		55	The Sunset Loop

Epic Rides: These rides are just nuts. Totally ridiculous. I started to call this section "death rides" but the publishers thought that was not a great idea. These are rides to try when you are tired of everything mundane. They are typically in remote areas where there is no hope of rescue. You should not go here unless you have your last affairs in order, and are not bothered by the idea of death or serious injury while in pursuit of your love of riding really hairy places. Best of the best, don't apply unless you have some skins on the wall.

1	Old Military Road Trail	51	Glenn Springs and Black Gap
2	Oklahoma "Ankle Express" Trail	52	The Old Ore Road
44	North Padre Island	55	The Sunset Loop

MOUNTAIN BIKE!

Texas and Oklahoma

INTRODUCTION

*"I do believe God had good intentions when he created man.
He was so disappointed in the monkey."*

—Mark Twain

TRAIL DESCRIPTION OUTLINE

Below are descriptions of what the headings in the following chapters mean. I have tried to maintain a realistic approach, and it is my greatest desire to keep you happy, healthy, and on the trail.

Ride number: What is the true existential reason for numbering, anyway?

Ride name: What the signs in the park call it, and hopefully what the locals call it as well.

Length/configuration: The orientation of the trail (whether a loop, or lollipop, or out-and-back, or whatever), what kind of trail (single-track or double-track, typically), and how far in miles each lap is (or each leg of a trip, with the total specified as well).

Aerobic difficulty: How hard the trail is on your legs and lungs. Easy means easy and hard means hard.

Technical difficulty: How hard the trail is as it relates to riding skills. Beginner-level means easy and expert-level means hard.

Scenery: Whether there is anything but dirt and trees to look at. If I say bring your camera, humor me. You got to cut me some slack at some point.

Special comments: Whatever popped into my mind as I was writing. Whether riding the trail in question requires a fee, or asking permission for admission, or if there are reasons to note specific things about the ride.

Story: The description passage telling what you will see and experience as you ride, and maybe some asides on history or local "induhviduals." In these sections I will try to ride you through the trail with my words; things I felt when I was there.

General location: What is the nearest town or landmark.

Elevation change: How far in feet it is from the highest point of the trail to the lowest. I may even speculate about how severe the elevation "delta" is, in other words whether the changes of elevation are impressive or maybe just barely noticeable. I may even mention a loose overall total climbing figure for riding the whole enchilada.

Season: When it is OK to ride. If there are special considerations, such as hunting season closures, I try to mention that here. I will also repeatedly tell you to stay off certain trails if they are sensitive to damage from being ridden shortly after rainfall.

Services: If you can get a drink, or go potty, or find a pay phone. And if there is camping or whatever else in the vicinity.

Hazards: What presents the biggest threat to your happiness, or survival in some cases. Some obvious stuff that you might not think about too, like dangerous plants or reptiles that surely live there.

Rescue index: How to get found if you screw the pooch, and the likelihood of that happening. I just about always had a phone and tried it for a reference on whether they work out there, wherever. How far it is to the hospital also shows up here a lot.

Land status: Who owns it. Who manages it, or lives on it, or otherwise should be respected as an authority.

Maps: Who has 'em. Where to find 'em. And if they are any good.

Finding the trail: How to find the trailhead, and from which direction you will return. In many cases I left it at that and told you to carry a map to find your way around the trail if it was questionable.

Sources of additional information: The players. Who runs the place, who knows about the place, any local clubs or bike shops that might be nice to know about.

Notes on the trail: Whatever else seemed relevant after I had written the chapter. I often throw in some kudos to local groups that are involved with maintenance or construction of this trail. Sometimes I tell you a sordid story of my past experiences in the area. Sometimes I just bitch.

> *"Pain is life is pain is life is pain is life."*
>
> *Chuck Cypert*

ABBREVIATIONS

The following road-designation abbreviations are used in *Mountain Bike! Texas and Oklahoma:*

CR	County Road	IH	Interstate Highway (a Texas
FR	Farm Route		designation different from
FM	Farm-to-Market Road		Internstate)
	(a Texas designation)	IR	Indian Route
FS	Forest Service Road	US	United States highway
I	Interstate		

State highways are designated with the appropriate two-letter state abbreviation, followed by the road number. Example: WI 33 = Wisconsin State Highway 33.

RIDE CONFIGURATIONS

Combination: This type of route may combine two or more configurations. For example, a point-to-point route may integrate a scenic loop or an out-and-back spur midway through the ride. Likewise, an out-and-back may have a loop at its farthest point (this configuration looks like a lollipop with a stem attached; the stick is the out-and-back, the candy is the terminus loop). Or a loop route may have multiple out-and-back spurs and/or loops to the side. Mileage for a combination route is for the total distance to complete the ride.

Loop: This route configuration is characterized by riding from the designated trailhead to a distant point, then returning to the trailhead via a different route (though perhaps by continuing along a circuitous trail) without doubling back. You always move forward across new terrain but return to the starting point when finished. Mileage is for the entire loop from the trailhead back to trailhead.

Out-and-back: A ride where you will return on the same trail you pedaled out. Although this might sound far more boring than a loop route, many trails look very different when pedaled in the opposite direction.

Point-to-point: A vehicle shuttle (or similar assistance) is required for this type of route, which is ridden from the designated trailhead to a distant location, or endpoint, where the route ends. Total mileage is for the one-way trip from the trailhead to endpoint.

Spur: A road or trail that intersects the main trail you're following.

Ride Configurations contributed by Gregg Bromka

TOPOGRAPHIC MAPS

The maps in this book, when used in conjunction with the route directions present in each chapter, will in most instances be sufficient to get you to the trail and keep you on it. However, you will find superior detail and valuable information in the 7.5 minute series USGS topographic maps. Recognizing how indispensable these are to bikers and hikers alike, many bike shops and sporting goods stores now carry topos of the local area.

But if you're brand new to mountain biking you might be wondering "What's a topographic map?" In short, these differ from standard "flat" maps in that they indicate not only linear distance but elevation as well. One glance at a topo will show you the difference: "Contour lines" are spread across the map like dozens of intricate spider webs. Each contour line represents a particular elevation, and at the base of each topo a particular "contour interval" designation is given. Yes, it sounds confusing if you're new to the lingo, but it truly is a simple and wonderfully helpful system. Keep reading.

Let's assume that the 7.5 minute series topo before us says "Contour Interval 40 feet," that the short trail we'll be pedaling is two inches in length on the map, and

and that it crosses five contour lines from its beginning to end. What do we know? Well, because the linear scale of this series is 2,000 feet to the inch (roughly 2 3/4 inches representing 1 mile), we know our trail is approximately 4/5 of a mile long (2 inches × 2,000 feet). But we also know we'll be climbing or descending 200 vertical feet (5 contour lines × 40 feet each) over that distance. And the elevation designations written on occasional contour lines will tell us if we're heading up or down.

The authors of this series warn their readers of upcoming terrain, but only a detailed topo gives you the information you need to pinpoint your position exactly on a map, steer yourself toward optional trails and roads nearby, plus let you know at a glance if you'll be pedaling hard to take them. It's a lot of information for a very low cost. In fact, the only drawback with topos is their size — several feet square. I've tried rolling them into tubes, folding them carefully, even cutting them into blocks and photocopying the pieces. Any of these systems is a pain, but no matter how you pack the maps you'll be happy they're along. And you'll be even happier if you pack a compass as well.

In addition to local bike shops and sporting goods stores, you'll find topos at major university and some public libraries where you might try photocopying the ones you need to avoid the cost of buying them. But if you want your own and can't find them locally, contact:

USGS Map Sales
Box 25286
Denver, CO 80225
(800) ASK USGS (275-8747)

VISA and MasterCard are accepted. Ask for an index while you're at it, plus a price list and a copy of the booklet *Topographic Maps*. In minutes you'll be reading them like a pro.

A second excellent series of maps available to mountain bikers is that put out by the U.S. Forest Service. If your trail runs through an area designated as a national forest, look in the phone book (white pages) under the United States Government listings, find the Department of Agriculture heading, and then run your finger down that section until you find the Forest Service. Give them a call and they'll provide the address of the regional Forest Service office, from which you can obtain the appropriate map.

TRAIL ETIQUETTE

Pick up almost any mountain bike magazine these days and you'll find articles and letters to the editor about trail conflict. For example, you'll find hikers' tales of being blindsided by speeding mountain bikers, complaints from mountain bikers about being blamed for trail damage that was really caused by horse or cattle traffic, and cries from bikers about those "kamikaze" riders who through their antics threaten to close even more trails to all of us.

The authors of this series have been very careful to guide you to only those trails that are open to mountain biking (or at least were open at the time of their research), and without exception have warned of the damage done to our sport through injudicious riding. All of us can benefit from glancing over the following International Mountain Bicycling Association (IMBA) Rules of the Trail before saddling up.

1. *Ride on open trails only.* Respect trail and road closures (ask if unsure), avoid possible trespass on private land, obtain permits and authorization as may be required. Federal and state wilderness areas are closed to cycling.

2. *Leave no trace.* Be sensitive to the dirt beneath you. Even on open trails, you should not ride under conditions where you will leave evidence of your passing, such as on certain soils shortly after rain. Observe the different types of soils and trail construction; practice low-impact cycling. This also means staying on the trail and not creating any new ones. Be sure to pack out at least as much as you pack in.

3. *Control your bicycle!* Inattention for even a second can cause disaster. Excessive speed can maim and threaten people; there is no excuse for it!

4. *Always yield the trail.* Make known your approach well in advance. A friendly greeting (or a bell) is considerate and works well; startling someone may cause loss of trail access. Show your respect when passing others by slowing to a walk or even stopping. Anticipate that other trail users may be around corners or in blind spots.

5. *Never spook animals.* All animals are startled by an unannounced approach, a sudden movement, or a loud noise. This can be dangerous for you, for others, and for the animals. Give animals extra room and time to adjust to you. In passing, use special care and follow the directions of horseback riders (ask if uncertain). Running cattle and disturbing wild animals is a serious offense. Leave gates as you found them, or as marked.

6. *Plan ahead.* Know your equipment, your ability, and the area in which you are riding—and prepare accordingly. Be self-sufficient at all times. Wear a helmet, keep your machine in good condition, and carry necessary supplies for changes in weather or other conditions. A well-executed trip is a satisfaction to you and not a burden or offense to others.

For more information, contact IMBA, P.O. Box 7578, Boulder, CO 80306; (303) 545-9011.

Additionally, the following Code of Ethics by the National Off-Road Biking Association (NORBA) is worthy of your attention.

1. I will yield the right of way to other non-motorized recreationists. I realize that people judge all cyclists by my actions.

2. I will slow down and use caution when approaching or overtaking another and will make my presence known well in advance.

3. I will maintain control of my speed at all times and will approach turns in anticipation of someone around the bend.

4. I will stay on designated trails to avoid trampling native vegetation and minimize potential erosion to trails by not using muddy trails or shortcutting switchbacks.

5. I will not disturb wildlife or livestock.

6. I will not litter. I will pack out what I pack in, and pack out more than my share if possible.

7. I will respect public and private property, including trail use and no trespassing signs; I will leave gates as I found them.

8. I will always be self-sufficient and my destination and travel speed will be determined by my ability, my equipment, the terrain, and present and potential weather conditions.

9. I will not travel solo when bike-packing in remote areas.

10. I will leave word of my destination and when I plan to return.

11. I will practice minimum impact bicycling by "taking only pictures and memories and leaving only waffle prints."

12. I will always wear a helmet when I ride.

Worthy of mention are the following suggestions based on a list by Utah's Wasatch-Cache National Forest and the *Tread Lightly!* program advocated by the National Forest Service and Bureau of Land Management.

1. *Study a forest map before you ride.* Currently, bicycles are permitted on roads and developed trails which are designated bikes permitted. If your route crosses private land, it is your responsibility to obtain right-of-way permission from the landowner.

2. *Stay out of designated wilderness areas.* By law, all vehicles, including mountain bikes are not allowed.

3. *Stay off of roads and trails "put to bed."* These may be resource roads no longer used for logging or mining, or they may be steep trails being replaced by easier ones. So that the path returns to its natural state, they're usually blocked or signed closed to protect new vegetation.

4. *Keep groups small.* Riding in large groups degrades the outdoor experience for others, can disturb wildlife, and usually leads to greater resource damage.

5. *Avoid riding on wet trails.* Bicycle tires leave ruts in wet trails. These ruts concentrate runoff and accelerate erosion. Postponing a ride when the trails are wet will preserve the trails for future use.

6. *Stay on roads and trails.* Riding cross-country destroys vegetation and damages the soil. Resist the urge to pioneer a new road or trail, or to cut across a switchback. Avoid riding through meadows, steep hillsides or along stream banks and lakeshores because the terrain is easily scarred by churning wheels.

7. *Always yield to others.* Trails are shared by hikers, horses, and bicycles. Move off the trail to allow horses to pass and stop to allow hikers adequate room to share the trail. Simply yelling "Bicycle!" is not acceptable.

8. *Control your speed.* Excessive speed endangers yourself and other forest users.

9. *Avoid wheel lock-up and spin-out.* Steep terrain is especially vulnerable to trail wear. Locking brakes on steep descents or when stopping needlessly damages trails. If a slope is steep enough to require locking wheels and skidding, dismount and walk your bicycle. Likewise, if an ascent is so steep that your rear wheel slips and spins, dismount and walk your bicycle.

10. *Protect waterbars and switchbacks.* Waterbars, the rock and log drains built to direct water off trails, protect trails from erosion. When you encounter a waterbar, ride directly over the top or dismount and walk your bicycle. Riding around the ends of waterbars destroys their effectiveness and speeds erosion. Skidding around switchback corners shortens trail life. Slow down for switchback corners and keep your wheels rolling.

11. *If you abuse it, you lose it.* Mountain bikers are relative newcomers to the forest and must prove themselves responsible trail users. By following the guidelines above, and by participating in trail maintenance service projects, bicyclists can help avoid closures that would prevent them from using trails.

12. *Know your bicycle handling limitations.*

You get the drift. So that everyone can continue riding our bikes through some of our country's most beautiful places, I urge you to follow the codes above and not be the "one bad apple" that spoils it for the rest of us.

HITTING THE TRAIL

Once again, because this is a "where-to," not a "how-to" guide, the following will be brief. If you're a veteran trail rider these suggestions might serve to remind you of something you've forgotten to pack. If you're a newcomer, they might convince you to think twice before hitting the backcountry unprepared.

Water: I've heard the questions dozens of times. "How much is enough? One bottle? Two? Three?! But think of all that extra weight!" Well, one simple physiological fact should convince you to err on the side of excess when it comes to deciding how much water to pack: a human working hard in 90° temperature needs approximately ten quarts of fluids every day. Ten quarts. That's two and a half gallons—12 large water bottles, or 16 small ones. And, with water weighing in at approximately 8 pounds per gallon, a one-day supply comes to a whopping 20 pounds.

In other words, pack along two or three bottles even for short rides. And make sure you can purify the water found along the trail on longer routes. When writing of those routes where this could be of critical importance, each author has provided information on where water can be found near the trail—if it can be found at all. But drink it untreated and you run the risk of disease. (See *Giardia* in the Glossary.)

One sure way to kill the protozoans, bacteria, and viruses in water is to boil it. Right. That's just how you want to spend your time on a bike ride. Besides, who wants to carry a stove or denude the countryside stoking bonfires to boil water?

Luckily, there is a better way. Many riders pack along the inexpensive and only slightly distasteful tetraglycine hydroperiodide tablets (sold under the names Potable Aqua, Globaline, and Coughlan's, among others). Some invest in portable, lightweight purifiers that filter out the crud. Unfortunately, both iodine *and* filtering are now required to be absolutely sure you've killed all the nasties you can't see. Tablets or iodine drops by themselves will knock off the well-known *Giardia*, once called "beaver fever" for its transmission to the water through the feces of infected beavers. One to four weeks after ingestion, *Giardia* will have you bloated, vomiting, shivering with chills, and living in the bathroom. (Though you won't care while you're suffering, beavers are getting a bum rap, for other animals are carriers also.)

But now there's another parasite we must worry about—*Cryptosporidium*. "Crypto" brings on symptoms very similar to *Giardia*, but unlike that fellow protozoan it's equipped with a shell sufficiently strong to protect it against the chemical killers that stop *Giardia* cold. This means we're either back to boiling or on to using a water filter to screen out both *Giardia* and crypto, plus the iodine to knock off viruses. All of which sounds like a time-consuming pain but really isn't. Some water filters come equipped with an iodine chamber, to guarantee full protection. Or you can simply add a pill or drops to the water you've just filtered (if you aren't allergic to iodine, of course). The pleasures of backcountry biking—and the displeasure of getting sick—make this relatively minor effort worth every one of the few minutes involved.

Tools: Ever since my first cross-country tour in 1965 I've been kidded about the number of tools I pack on the trail. And so I will exit entirely from this discussion by providing a list compiled by two mechanic (and mountain biker) friends of mine. After all, since they make their livings fixing bikes, and get their kicks by riding them, who could be a better source?

These two suggest the following as an absolute minimum:

tire levers
spare tube and patch kit
air pump
Allen wrenches (3, 4, 5, and 6 mm)
six-inch crescent (adjustable-end) wrench
small flat-blade screwdriver
chain rivet tool
spoke wrench

But, while they're on the trail, their personal tool pouches contain these additional items:

channel locks (small)
air gauge
tire valve cap (the metal kind, with a valve-stem remover)
baling wire (ten or so inches, for temporary repairs)
duct tape (small roll for temporary repairs or tire boot)
boot material (small piece of old tire or a large tube patch)
spare chain link
rear derailleur pulley
spare nuts and bolts
paper towel and tube of waterless hand cleaner

First-aid kit: My personal kit contains the following, sealed inside double Ziploc bags:

sunscreen
aspirin
butterfly-closure bandages
Band-Aids
gauze compress pads (a half-dozen 4" × 4")
gauze (one roll)
ace bandages or Spenco joint wraps
Benadryl (an antihistamine, in case of allergic reactions)
water purification tablets / water filter (on long rides)
moleskin / Spenco "Second Skin"
hydrogen peroxide, iodine, or Mercurochrome (some kind of antiseptic)
snakebite kit

Final considerations: The authors of this series have done a good job in suggesting that specific items be packed for certain trails—raingear in particular seasons, a hat and gloves for mountain passes, or shades for desert jaunts. Heed their warnings, and think ahead. Good luck.

Dennis Coello

AND NOW, A WORD ABOUT CELLULAR PHONES . . .

Thinking of bringing the Flip-Fone along on your next off-road ride? Before you do, ask yourself the following questions:

- Do I know where I'm going? Do I have an adequate map? Can I use a compass effectively? Do I know the shortest way to civilization if I need to bail out early and find some help?

- If I'm on the trail for longer than planned, am I ready for it? Do I have adequate water? Have I packed something to eat? Will I be warm enough if I'm still out there after dark?

- Am I prepared for possible injuries? Do I have a first-aid kit? Do I know what to do in case of a cut, fracture, snakebite, or heat exhaustion?

- Is my tool kit adequate for likely mechanical problems? Can I fix a flat? Can I untangle a chain? Am I prepared to walk out if the bike is unrideable?

If you answered "yes" to *every* question above, you may pack the phone, but consider a good whistle instead. It's lighter, cheaper, and nearly as effective.

If you answered "no" to *any* of these questions, be aware that your cellular phone does little to reduce your risks in the wilderness. Sure, being able to dial 911 in the farthest corner of the White Mountains sounds like a great idea, but this ain't downtown, friend. If disaster strikes, and your call is routed to some emergency operator in Manchester or Bangor, and it takes a while to figure out which ranger, sheriff, or search-and-rescue crew to connect you with, and you can't tell the authorities where you are because you're really not sure, and the closest they can come to pinpointing your location is a cellular tower that serves 62 square miles of dense woods, and they start searching for you but dusk is only two hours away, and you have no signaling device and your throat is too dry to shout, and meanwhile you can't get the bleeding stopped, you are out of luck. I mean *really* out of luck.

And when the battery goes dead, you're on your own again. Enough said.

Jeff Faust
Author of Mountain Bike! New Hampshire

OKLAHOMA

Oklahoma. Where the wind comes sweeping down the plain. I said it in the first book and I'm gonna say it again; I grew up here. Until I turned twelve, anyway. I had my first bicycle (a gold Schwinn Sting-Ray) and my first girlfriend here (prettiest girl in the 7th grade at Del Crest Junior High in 1969). I wonder what ever happened to that girl? The bike finally broke from repeated ramp jumps over trash cans. But I digress. My sordid past is not why we are here, it's my sordid present.

Our 46th state is wide open in a "trails" sense. There are some monster mountain bike clubs and the head guy over all the state parks is a cyclist. I met John Ressmeyer at a bike club meeting one night, at Lake Thunderbird (at the restaurant out by the Clear Bay Trail). This gentleman would put a mountain bike trail in every state park in Oklahoma, if he could find riders in the area to help keep them useable. If nothing else comes of this book, I would be happy if just two people read it and wanted to get involved and become trail stewards. That is, of two new trails. I would go smiling to my grave with the knowledge that I helped two new trails be born.

If you know me you know that I'm not about shredding; I'm about oozing along and listening to the birds and checking out the trees. The state of Oklahoma has some mighty terrain, some stunning parks, and some dedicated trailnuts. This is a very good thing. People, get out there and get involved and help make it happen. You may not realize this, but there is probably greater potential for new trails up there in the Indian Nation than in Texas, where mountain bikers are loved (for the most part).

The western part of the state is a lot of rock out in the open; there ain't that many trees. There are some real mountains, though. And there are some great trails up in some of those mountains, but I did not put them in this book. The famous "12 Miles of Hell" race course is superb, someplace you'd never want to crash. However, with the ongoing war on terror, it is no longer OK to just run out to Fort Sill and wander around. And I understand why the Army didn't want the ride profiled here. Hopefully, someday soon, we will again be able to just run over there and have fun, and nobody will get nervous. I'd recommend you check out my bud Mike Thompson at the "Mud, Sweat, & Gears" bike shop in Lawton and see what's going on. They will still have the annual race.

Tom Steed Lake (Great Plains State Park) has a couple of trails that the locals race on. If you know the trail it's pretty groovy, but I couldn't find my way around. I apologize to the people who care deeply about every trail I missed, but I can't write 'em up if I can't find my way. And I am reasonably good at keeping found, so to speak. I can't send Joe Normal out there to get lost.

There just aren't enough people to keep things up in the more remote areas of Oklahoma. There's probably no more than a handful of mountain bikers in most of these counties. Two or three guys can get burned out really quick, if it's just them helping and everyone else enjoying. If I can get one person from western Oklahoma to get involved with the guys who build this stuff, then I'll have done something good. You Oklahomans out there have some frighteningly marvelous terrain, and hopefully new trails will be blazed in the future; maybe at Quartz Mountain or a new one in the Wichitas.

As for the east, hell, there are miles of trail that you can hike-a-bike on. Some only get cut once a year, right before a race. They could really use some help. I need that other trail steward to help in eastern Oklahoma.

I didn't get to enjoy Kaw Lake up near Ponca City because it was solid bugs. I went 2.5 miles, used my loppers until they gave out, had a flat, and I finally lost the scent. It was raining anyway, so I didn't mind turning around. There is some fine terrain around that lake; I'll bet the trail is sweet when it is in prime condition. I'm sorry I missed it.

And there are others. Like Lake Murray in Ardmore. I will ride that. But if you don't know your way around, it's a bunch of tough rocks that call up every millimeter in your suspension. There are rumors that the David Boren Hiking Trail at Broken Bow might open up, which is one of the prettiest lakes in the whole state. OK, somebody from southern Oklahoma needs to jump in here— now I need three folks. I'm beggin' ya. We need bodies.

Oklahoma. Probably a lot prettier than Texas, square mile for square mile. All it needs are a few more people who don't mind walking around in the ticks and clipping branches or running a mower. Don't forget your bug spray. And I am still waiting for a home remedy that cures a chigger bite.

RIDE 1 · Old Military Road—Talihina

AT A GLANCE

Length/configuration: A 7-mile point-to-point single-track; a 14-mile round-trip the way I'm going to tell it.

Aerobic difficulty: Very difficult. This is 1,000 feet of

RIDE 1 • Old Military Road Trail

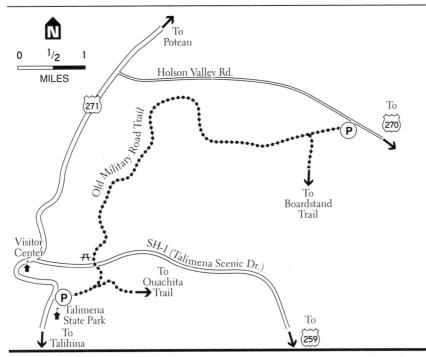

elevation in 7 miles, meaning one technical opportunity for disaster for every 50 feet of trail. This is not a beginner trail.

Technical difficulty: There isn't another trail with more tricky bits that I know of. Again, beginners, stay away from this ride.

Scenery: A beautiful forest, full of birds and bees and quiet. The whole area around the Winding Stair is part of the Ouachita National Forest, a truly gorgeous southern forest.

Special comments: This is a hiking trail, so you should behave yourself and mind your manners. I've never seen a hiker out there in the woods, but don't do anything annoying to them or the horseheads. Be nice, say hello, and live to ride these wonderful woods again.

This is easily my favorite trail in the whole state of Oklahoma. But then, I'm weird. This is a hard ride, full of grunting output and hike-a-bike. When you have developed your mountain biking and survival skills and are ready to be tested, it's time to visit the Winding Stair. The ride is very technically challenging, the climbs are hard, and the conditions are sufficiently severe that you will need to be on your toes and have your body and bike well tuned. If you don't, you're going to suck wind and feel like dying. The damn ticks are gonna eat you either way, it doesn't matter what you do.

This is me as I start to ride the Old Military Road. Within an hour that stupid grin was gone. The Old Military bugs ate me, it got really hot, and then, as usual, I ran out of water.

The Old Military Road was built in 1832 to connect Fort Smith in Arkansas with Fort Towson near the Red River in Oklahoma. It was used to convey troops and supplies between military installations of the day and also saw the passage of various Native American tribes being relocated by the government to the Indian Territories in Oklahoma. Built during the administration of President Andrew Jackson, it was traveled by several figures of regional historical significance. Along the road you might have met some people who went on to fame, people like old Sam Houston, the first President of the Republic of Texas, or the 12th President of the United States of America, General Zachary Taylor.

The Old Military Road Trail is a tough rocky hiking path connecting Talimena Scenic Drive, up on Winding Stair Mountain, with the trailhead, located on Holson Valley Road. This place can nearly grow over in the summer, but it is fairly well marked by white or blue rectangular blaze marks painted on the trees along the trail every 100 yards or so. Keep your eyes in scan-mode, going from the trail to the trees and back constantly. That way you will not get lost; at least, not too lost. I wandered a little the first time I rode here, but anyone with a lick of sense will be able to stay on the proper route.

What you do is follow the single-track west out of the parking lot at the trailhead. In a mile or so you will find where the Boardstand Trail forks off to the left. Keep going, cross the creeks and roads you find, and follow the blazes until you are at the picnic grounds up on top of the Winding Stair. Take a break, and then head back. This is a really cool ride. Stop along the way and take some pictures, and think about history. It makes us who we are.

The trail crosses several active gravel roads, so take care to look for automobile traffic before blasting across any of them. In several places you will see that you are riding on old double-track. Take heed; this is very old double-track, indeed—like 170 years old. These sections are pieces of the Old Military Road, and if you listen really carefully you can almost hear the sound of wagons bouncing and crunching along, ferrying bullets and beans to the soldiers at Fort Towson.

The Ouachita Forest is huge, stretching far into Arkansas, all tall pine trees and rocks. This trail is pretty typical of those in the Ouachitas, very rideable in nearly all weather conditions, but treacherous when wet. These rocks are covered with lichens and moss and are as dangerous as anything you can ride. You will spend some time walking your bike across loose-rock creek beds, no matter how good you are technically, and you may meet cattle along some sections. When you reach the trailhead on Talimena Scenic Drive, hang a right and go a short distance over to Dead Man's Vista; the overlook there is a nice place to have a break when the area is blessed with clear weather. Don't sit up there if there is lightning anywhere in sight.

General location: Eastern Oklahoma, near Talihina.

Elevation change: Let's call it 1,000 feet.

Season: Not much fun in the rain. The trail is generally OK but the rocks are as slick as—well, as they can be. Hunting season is suicide. Figure that late September through the first of the year, roughly, this place is off-limits.

Services: Nothing. Barely a place to park. Load up in one of the small nearby towns before you hit the trailhead.

Hazards: Oh my friends, we've got hazards for you. This place is so remote and lonely that you won't meet anyone else. I've ridden or hiked here probably half a dozen times, and I have never seen a soul. The trail surface is rock outcroppings and loose rock, terrifying in a rainstorm. The creeks can swell and be extremely dangerous to cross in a heavy rain. There are more bugs than you can feed in a month, and ticks and chiggers make the summer a hell on earth. You could easily step on a snake here without trying. Doesn't this sound like fun? Not yet? There is also the occasional equestrian to steer around. Now how do you feel?

Rescue index: Low. You ain't getting out of here without a pal. I doubt a cell phone is much use except for maybe in a few spots, and you will be way far out in the woods, a long drive from help. It is possible to catch the roads back to where you parked once you make it up to the picnic grounds, if you are too cooked to return on the trail. Go right (north) on the pavement in front of the picnic area, then right (east) at the visitor center, then right (south) at Holson Valley Road and you'll be at your car in 30 to 40 minutes.

Land status: U.S. Forest Service hiking trail. Be nice.

Maps: The rangers have some that are OK; check either at the visitor center on the highway or at the trailhead kiosk.

Finding the trail: The Winding Stair Visitor Center is located a few miles east of Talihina, Oklahoma, on US 271 at the exit for Talimena Scenic Drive (OK 1). From there proceed east on US 271 to the exit for the next pavement, Holson Valley Road. Turn right (south) and go a couple of miles until you see the sign for the trailhead. Turn right (west) and the parking lot is right there. The trailhead kiosk has a sign-in list (so they know to look for you if you don't come back) and usually has maps. Ride up the hill and then back, and use lots of bug spray before you start. It is also possible to start at Talimena State Park and take the hiking trail up to the top of the hill and then over onto the Military Road (see below).

Sources of additional information:

Ouachita National Forest
P.O. Box 1270
Hot Springs, AR 71902
(501) 321-5202
www.fs.fed.us/oonf/ouachita.htm

Choctaw Ranger District
HC 64, Box 3467
Heavener, OK 74937
(918) 653-2991

Kiamichi Ranger District
P.O. Box 577

Talihina, OK 74571
(918) 567-2326

Talimena State Park
P.O. Box 318
Talihina, OK 74571
(918) 567-2062

Oklahoma Earthbike Fellowship
(OEF)
P.O. Box 2320
Oklahoma City, OK 73101-2320
www.okearthbike.com

Notes on the trail: Yes, the town is Talihina and the road is Talimena. Don't ask, I don't know. The last time I was over here I couldn't ride at all because a monster ice storm the previous winter had covered the trail in fallen timber. I have heard, and read on the Internet, that the Boy Scouts have it cleared and the Old Military Road Trail is ready to use. You might want to call ahead and ask the rangers about trail conditions before you head way out here. Additionally, the U.S. Forest Service, in their infinite wisdom, has proposed opening a bunch of the nearby Ouachita Trails to bikes. You can't ride a lot of it because it is too hard, but it's just a thought. That means you are probably OK to ride the trail up from Talimena State Park to the picnic grounds on the Winding Stair, and then on to the Old Military Road and back. Check it out; that's the way to do this trail. Ask at the visitor center or state park.

RIDE 2 · Oklahoma "Ankle Express" Hiking Trail —Greenleaf State Park

AT A GLANCE

Length/configuration: Two major loops. Up to 18 miles total. Laugh if you want, but I say this is a 4–6 hour ride.

Aerobic difficulty: Harder than you probably want. Hard in every dimension. The climbs don't want you there, the rocks love human skin, and the bugs like anything with warm blood.

Technical difficulty: Harder than you probably can handle. Hard. No-BS hard. You'll be walking some unless you are a trials rider like Hans Rey or somebody with a lot more suspension travel than me.

RIDE 2 • Oklahoma Ankle Express Trail

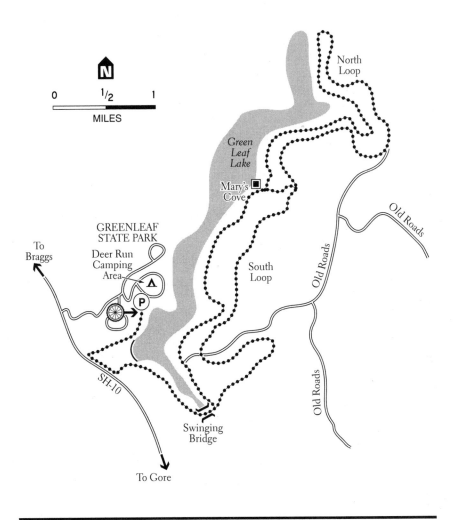

Scenery: The most beautiful part of a beautiful state. This is a sweetly forested trail, along a scenic lake. This ride would probably be especially stunning in the fall. Definitely bring a camera.

Special comments: Bring an extra tube and a derailleur. And a lunch. Don't do this one alone, don't do this one for fun, and don't do this one without a commitment to pain.

I rode here with a half-dozen guys on rain-slick rocks. Everybody crashed three or four times, as far as I know, and in the end the body count was huge. Several shins, some forearms, two flat tires, two bikes (both with broken rear derailleurs), at least one hand, and both my wrists. And we only rode about half of it. This is a monster ride that will eat your heart, suck your legs, melt your lungs, break your bike, and twist every joint in your body. What a blast! Let's do another lap, Trail Man. That one was EPIC!

Thank you, Trail Man, whoever and wherever you are. You do good trail, dude, major good. I especially like the water bars you put on the down parts of the upper loop. Well done. Trail Man has kept this one of the premier hiking trails in the state of Oklahoma. But this is also a monster bike trail. Just be nice to the folks who forgot their bikes, one of them might be Trail Man. It would be major bad karma to be mean to someone who puts this kind of backbreaking work into the rocks and dirt of eastern Oklahoma. I'll kick your butt if I ever catch you on the trail being mean to a hiker. I ain't kidding. I'm one of them.

Large rock outcrops, all covered with moss and lichens; quick, serious, technical places about every 54.5 yards; steaming climbs; and blinding downers. It is like a Goya painting, so try your best not to get hurt. Greenleaf is a six-hour brush with death. Your adrenal glands may take a while to recover and your shins and forearms will be there with those little scratch-marks, just to remind you. The hanging bridge is really cool, probably the least wicked part of the whole trail.

But hey, this ain't no stinking Mountain Dew commercial with jumps and skids and ripping. This is a mountain bike ride on the wild side, a ride in the woods to keep you honest. Don't think you are just passing through and don't care about this place. Love this place; doing so minimizes the long-term damage to bods and bikes. I am into karma; ride here like you don't care if you get hurt, because you will. Pay your dues and pick your ticks, you'll get both. Everybody does.

The lakeside loop is fairly flat, slippery, off-camber, and tricky, all the way out to Mary's Cove. After that the primitive loop is hard, maybe not worth the effort if it is grown over. The upper loop will suck your lungs until they are empty and hurt like stepping on a nail. Then it will hand you all the dangerous downhill quick-stop "look out for that turtle" dips and creeks you can handle, with six more thrown in for fun. The switchbacks will injure someone in your group, so don't ride alone. Carry your tools and tubes and a lunch. You can't ride here without preparation. Not if you intend to stay alive.

General location: About 3 hours east of Oklahoma City, Oklahoma, near Braggs.

Elevation change: Maybe 120 to 150 feet all together. Several times.

Season: I probably would not recommend riding in deer season. Unless you like buckshot. Summer can be brutal, with the bugs and all. Other than that, any weekend is good.

Services: The park has fine camping facilities, with showers and water and potties, all that. Pack in any other stuff you might want out on the trail.

Hazards: Riding here is enough to fill in all the blanks in the hazard category. Bugs (you will find a tick or fifty), maybe some poison ivy, a snake or five, crashing on your head, crashing on your arm, crashing on your shoulder...you get the idea.

Rescue index: Bad—bad to the point of not likely. Don't ride alone.

Land status: Oklahoma Tourism and Recreation Department state park.

Maps: The rangers have a mighty fine one; ask or check at the trailhead kiosk.

Finding the trail: This trail is well marked with signs and blue blaze marks on the trees. There appear to be two schools of thought here, the "start in the park" school, and the "start near the hanging bridge" school. I am going to start you from inside the park because the trailhead there is the easiest to find. Just make sure that if you go ride this with the OEF folks, you know where they are starting.

Greenleaf State Park is located on the east side of OK 10, three miles south of Braggs and about nine miles north of Gore. Stop at the kiosk by the ranger station and grab a map. The trailhead is well marked, located just west of the Deer Run camping area.

Sources of additional information:

Greenleaf State Park
Route 1, Box 119
Braggs, OK 74423
(918) 487-5196
www.touroklahoma.com/Pages/cabin
4.html

Oklahoma Tourism and Recreation
Department
Division of State Parks

2401 N. Lincoln Boulevard
Oklahoma City, OK 73105
(405) 521-3411
www.otrd.state.ok.us

Oklahoma Earthbike Fellowship
(OEF)
P.O. Box 2320
Oklahoma City, OK 73101-2320
www.okearthbike.com

Notes on the trail: This is a very, very cool ride. Get on the trail and follow the blue blazes until you have wound around to the highway bridge. Go south over the bridge and cut back to your left toward the lake. Follow the blue blazes until you are at the hanging bridge. Just across the bridge the trail splits and the loop starts. A sign there warns of the dangers of being stupid. To the left takes you along the lake with a return from the right. Once you are way out on the eastern sections of the trail it splits again, near Mary's Cove. To the left takes you onto the primitive area outer loop; to the right takes you up on the ridge and eventually west, back to the hanging bridge. Retrace the steps that got you here and you will be back at the trailhead in a mile or so.

In parts of Oklahoma the trails are erased during certain seasons of the year because there are nowhere near enough people to work on trails and keep them useable. I went looking for other trails in places people told me to go, and I still had a hard time finding them sometimes. I cannot recommend rides to you if I can't even find them. This one was ridden late in the summer and was easy to follow, but I had guides and an awesome map. I have to warn you that on this ride you will find bugs, and plenty of other threats, but you can't call yourself a well-rounded Oklahoma mountain biker until you have ridden Greenleaf. It is one of the best rides around for hundreds of miles. I'd call it the Womble Trail of Oklahoma. Truly epic. (Womble Trail is a few hundred miles east of here, near Hot Springs, Arkansas, and is in the opinions of many the finest single-track within 500 miles of Dallas.)

RIDE 3 · Turkey Mountain Park Trails—Tulsa

AT A GLANCE

Length/configuration: A confusing maze of tough single-track, sweet if you know your way. There are probably 15 miles of trail packed in here, if you know where to find them. Just go wander, but bring a Camelbak full of water and an extra PowerBar.

Aerobic difficulty: Hard in plenty of places. Loose, steep, long climbs, not a beginner trail anywhere in sight. There is more than 200 feet of climbing if you ride it all. This place is an agonizing misery of pain, sometimes. I love it.

Technical difficulty: All you can stand and more. This is a hard bunch of trails, hard to stay found on and hard to negotiate. This is, again, not a beginner trail. There's a lot of hike-a-bike, lots of loose rock, and lots of tortuous single-track. What fun!

Scenery: The views from the bluffs over the Arkansas River are worth working for. The view of downtown Tulsa is cool from the power lines. The rest is just tricky technical riding, so don't let your eyes or mind wander.

Special comments: This is a pretty amazing place. There are more murderous miles of tricky single-track and steep double-track than you will likely find anywhere else in urban Oklahoma. There is stuff here you probably can't ride—I know I always walk some—and hike-a-bike is the way to survive. But this is definitely one of the best trails in Oklahoma or Texas.

Monstrous trails. That is the only thing I can think to say. This is a lot of hard riding, technical and dangerous. There are miles of trails on both sides of the power lines that bisect the property here. As far as I can tell this place has basically two trail areas, the bluff side and the YMCA/Pepsi plant side. At least that is how I know it; the locals probably have fancier names than that.

This place is a spider-web maze of single-track. It is easy to get lost, but you are in a pretty contained piece of property and can only wander far enough to find yourself down by the Pepsi plant with 300 feet of loose delta ahead, between you and your car. Remember where the power lines are, they cut this place in two. Remember that you cannot ride down the bluff to the river (as far as I know) or across any paved roads. Remember that if you hit civilization, over by the YMCA and the Pepsi plant, you have to turn around. This way you will know which direction you have to go to find the car.

If you've been here before, note that they moved the parking area, so now you no longer have the lot at the top of the hill and you park farther south. Down

RIDE 3 • Turkey Mountain Park

more toward 71st Street on Elwood. Thank you, City of Tulsa and local bike clubs and shops, this place is top-shelf.

General location: On the east side of the Arkansas River in Tulsa, Oklahoma.

Elevation change: My maps show about 300 feet of available delta. You and I will get most of that at least twice in a day of exploring.

Season: This place is pretty durable; I have ridden here the day after substantial rains more than once. That does not mean you won't find mud if it has rained,

A bunch of the OEF gang at Turkey Mountain. This trail is worthy, a ride with pride. Thank you mountain bikers of Tulsa. Photo by Marcel Slootheer.

and please do not punish the dirt. Stay on the rock or wait until tomorrow. Still, considering the traffic and races, this place is dependable.

Services: Parking. Maybe a chemical toilet. Nothing else. Tulsa is just across the river, so bring what you will need.

Hazards: Dying from crash-related injuries is at the top of my list. Poison ivy, loose trail surfaces, tight trees, and big roots. This is an easy place to get hurt. There are technical-till-ya-puke trails out there boys and girls, so go get some.

Rescue index: Medium-high; this place has lots of survivors. Bring your cell phone and know where you are, and they'll come find you. The maps on T-Town Bicycles' website are nice—carry one with you and know where you are. Please?

Land status: City of Tulsa Parks and Recreation park.

Maps: Check with T-Town Bicycles, they have it going on.

Finding the trail: I love this. Turkey Mountain is on Elwood Street, just like Elwood Blues in the movie. From 71st Street North, just on the west side of the Arkansas River, turn north on Elwood, and you will find the new parking area on your right (east) at the signs for Turkey Mountain Urban Wilderness. The trails are north of you, so leave the parking lot and grab some single-track. If you know your way around, or have a lick of sense, you can have some great fun out here. Just remember whether you are on the river side of the power line or the YMCA/Pepsi plant side. If you hit pavement, you may ride up and find your car, or you may head back into the woods and then try to ride the jeep trail up, under the power lines. Pass the burned out old Ford truck and climb that hill, if you've still got the legs.

Sources of additional information:

T-Town Bicycles, Inc.
1660-B East 71st Street
Tulsa, OK 74136
(918) 492-8696
http://www.t-townbicycles.com/

Tom's Rivertrail Bicycles, Inc.
6861 South Peoria
Tulsa, OK 74136
(918) 481-1818

Tulsa Parks and Recreation
Tulsa City Hall
200 Civic Center
Tulsa, OK 74103
(918) 596-2100
www.cityoftulsa.org/GI/depts/
   parks.ihtml

Notes on the trail: There are miles of trail here that I have never been able to find, at least not twice. I have been lost every time I have ridden Turkey Mountain, but it is all contained in an area of reasonable dimensions. I would just ramble northward, taking the various forks to the right, and enjoy an afternoon. You will wind around on the bluff until you pop out by the power lines. Cross onto more single-track and ride until you find the Pepsi plant and then the YMCA area. There are markers in a few places, but just remember this: Once you cross the power lines and leave the bluff area, you will ride downhill to the creek, and then have to find your way back up the hill to get to the car. There are miles of trail here, and as far as I can tell it is all open to bikes, but I can't ride lots of it. There is tough, rocky, loose terrain in these trees. When, and if, you survive, you will find yourself by the ponds. The power lines and the old jeep trail are near, to the east. You have to go south a ways, climbing steadily, and once you are on top of the hill you have a fairly easy ride, either more woods or on the pavement, back to the car. What a monster ride this place is.

RIDE 4 · Lake McMurtry Trails — Stillwater

AT A GLANCE

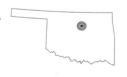

Length/configuration: Four separate trails, each of 3 to 7 miles in length, mostly loops of solid single-track, totaling over 25 miles of riding if you hit it all.

Aerobic difficulty: The sand can be brutal here; it gets powdery. There are some climbs that are touch-and-go, but nothing beyond what any mid-range rider can handle. This is one of those places with several nice sections requiring decent outputs of horsepower, though, and if you don't think it's tough enough, try shaving a few minutes on your next lap. Ha ha ha.

Technical difficulty: There are probably a few sections along these trails where you and I will be walking. Most of it is very rideable. Considering all the rock gardens and little techie bits. This is not exactly a beginner trail, but anybody with moderate skills should be able to survive.

Scenery: There is actually some very pretty terrain around Lake McMurtry; I'd bring a camera if I were you.

Special comments: This is a fee area, $5 a day per headset. Annual passes are available—ask the rangers or the bike shop.

Four-four-four trails in one! Groovy. When I was here long ago, Mary Cash from Cooper's Bicycles kept telling me they were going to build some mighty trail here. And she called it, even back then; a total of nearly 25 miles of fine single-track, one piece of which has evolved into the local race loop. Great trails; you should try riding it all in one day (like I failed to do).

I met so many nice people here. Mary set me up with a guy named Dennis who showed me around the race loop, the southeast loop. Another kind soul named Paul let me follow him and try to keep up without having a coronary. We went around the northwest and southwest loops. I didn't try the northeast loop due to reports that it was pretty much like Vietnam in terms of weeds and tree limbs.

In order to try and organize this for you I will talk about the loops the way the locals do: the northeast, southeast, southwest, and northwest. Their lengths vary, but all are around seven miles, either ridden as a loop or out-and-back. Each has a subtly different flavor, and the locals generally refer to the "east side" or "west side" of the lake. To paraphrase my buddy Paul, the west is more Oklahoma and the east is more Arkansas. The park areas are organized that way too: the West Recreation Area and the East Recreation Area.

Northeast: Like I said earlier, I was a wimp and didn't ride here. Judging from the other loops I am sure it has some loose sand and some tight trees, and tends toward overgrown in the middle of the year. I am told it is an out-and-back single-track. The maps make it look like there might be some delta out there, probably the full 50 feet.

Southeast: The Race Loop. Expect the unexpected on this fast single-track stretch. It is cut in places by short cattle-guard bridges that join the local pastures. These things scare me—I mean, they're easy, but all day I knew I would crash on one. I finally got a pretty good endo, out of sight of my riding partner Dennis. Lots of good small jumps, lots of places to get trick air. The terrain here is fairly flat but the trail winds up and down through some creeks and there are slight climbs. A fun trail, no lung bursting is required to ride here, but if you ain't tired after a lap then you ain't riding hard enough.

Northwest: A little more in the way of challenges, technically. In fact, this may be the best trail, if you like techie stuff. Rock gardens, tricky climbs of reasonable duration, tight conditions, and lots of sand. This is probably the hardest trail to the average pair of legs. You will cross and follow some old double-track; watch for the trail signs and you'll get the whole can of beans. This is an enjoyable place to let your suspension keep you alive.

Southwest: Shorter than the others, typically ridden as an out-and-back. More sand, more tight single-track in the trees, not so much climbing, but enough to

RIDE 4 • Lake McMurtry Trails

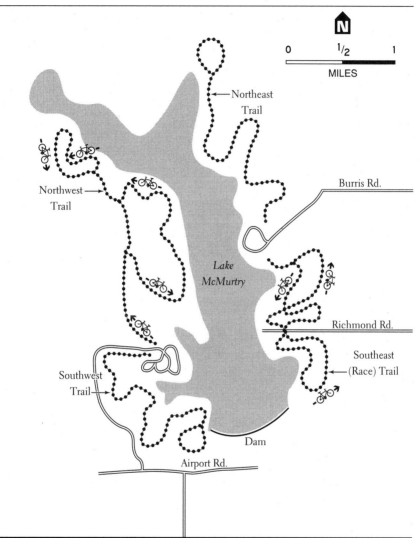

make you sweat. We took the pavement back to my camp because I was cooked. I'm not in that great condition—you should try chasing the locals every day for a week and doing as many miles as possible every day, while driving back and forth across the state. It ain't no thang, but it wears on you after a while.

General location: Northwest of Stillwater, Oklahoma, a few miles.

Elevation change: Not all that much overall, maybe 50 feet from stem to stern.

Season: Mostly all year, the sand drains well after a rain. Don't get out there in the mud, please.

Services: Camping, parking, potties, drinking water, and the occasional pay phone. Anything else will have to follow you in from town.

Hazards: I didn't see any, but there is probably some poison ivy out here. The mosquitoes get around pretty good, too. There are lots of tree roots, soft sand, and places to reacquaint yourself with Mr. Bustyerass de Zaster. There are enough techie bits to put me on my guard, but you might want to be careful and not overcook anything. When you cross a paved road you can be sure it is active. Stop, look, listen.

Rescue index: This depends on where you ride. The Race Loop gets quite a bit of traffic, but the rest is going to see only a few cyclists in a month. I'd bring your phone and a map. The location is not all that remote, but it ain't Times Square either.

Land status: Stillwater Parks, Events, and Recreation city park.

Maps: The rangers will give you a decent one, just ask.

Finding the trail: There are two main places people start from.

Eastern trails: Go six miles north of Stillwater on US 177 and then six west miles on Burris Road. Turn left (south) at the stop sign and you will see the sign for the East Recreation Area entrance. Enter the area and go to the picnic shelter and park. The southeast trail starts just east of the parking area; look for the sign. The northeast trail starts north of the parking area; back up the pavement, and look for the trailhead sign.

Western trails: From three miles west of Stillwater on OK 51, go north on Redland Road. Redland Road ends at Airport Road; turn left (west) and go to the next paved road north, where you will see the signs for the West Recreation Area. Follow the road until you reach the ranger station, pay, and ask them where to park. The trailhead for the northwest trail is right across the road from the ranger station, plainly marked with a sign. The trailhead for the "southwest" trail is just south, on the other side of the paved road that brought you here, and it's well marked.

Sources of additional information:

Stillwater Red Dirt Pedalers
  Bicycle Club
P.O. Box 2614
Stillwater, OK 74076
(405) 372-2525
www.reddirtpedalers.com

Cooper's Bicycle Center
220 South Main Street

Stillwater, OK 74074
(405) 372-2525

Stillwater Parks, Events, and
  Recreation
315 East 9th Avenue
Stillwater, OK 74074
(405) 747-8070
www.stillwater.org/parksandrec/

Notes on the trail: You'll get busted for riding here if you don't pay. People kept telling me that. Don't cheat, and if you live nearby buy the annual pass (it's something like $25). Otherwise, stop in and give 'em your $5 before you ride. Don't make any enemies for the rest of us. This place is way too cool to jeopardize for your own puny personal gains.

RIDE 5 · Benny's Trail—Guthrie

AT A GLANCE

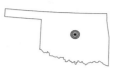

Length/configuration: 2.5-mile loop of glorious Oklahoma single-track, built with an emphasis on clever surprises.

Aerobic difficulty: Some medium-hard patches; nothing like monster climbs, but go chase those OEF guys and see what you think.

Technical difficulty: This is where things get interesting. This place is about all you can do with 15–20 acres of densely wooded central Oklahoma dirt. There are some places where you will use your skills, or hit something if you don't have any. There are a few places to relax, but mostly you need to pay close attention and look up the trail.

Scenery: Kind of a neat little area of thick trees, but we are here to ride, not to look for pretty butterflies.

Special comments: This ride is on private property. It is not exactly a secret, but it is a place where you need to respect the fact that you can't just go do whatever you want. I am going to tell you about Benny's, but not exactly where it is. You will have to schmooze some of my OEF pals to get to enjoy it.

If there are two **V** trees Benny has not built trail through then I will eat your pedals. And I'm quite confident that my culinary future is secure.

This place is cool. It is a mountain bike playground, and Benny wants you to come enjoy his trail. But be on your best behavior, and don't do anything inconsiderate or idiotic. This land is home to Benny and his family, and you will be honored with the feeling that it is your home too, if you treat it that way. Just as long as you understand that we ride here because he is a mountain biker who really likes his fellow bikers. Help us stay in his good graces by not being disrespectful. Don't throw trash on the ground, don't show up unannounced with a bunch of rowdy pals, and don't change any of the lines. They are fabulous. And don't ride here if the trail is muddy. Does any of this sound familiar? It should. These are the normal trail rules, the world according to me. I don't claim credit for them, they are just good common sense. Somebody had to teach me these things, too.

This is one of those fine Oklahoma trails where much thought has gone into making you work. Through hard work we reap benefits. Through the appreciation of fine trail we gather insights. You can learn some things out here, and you can gain a whole new respect for quick gear shifts and narrow handlebars. I always trim mine a centimeter or two when I build a new bike, just for places like this. Get ready for tight, sneaky turns and everything Benny can think of to throw at you. Evil little challenges and unexpected threats. These things put hair on your

RIDE 5 • Benny's Trail

chest, make you think. I'll quote Star Trek's Worf here: "That which does not kill us makes us stronger." (Though he probably wasn't the first to say so.)

Hook up with the OEFers, and get on a piece of property that most people have never heard of. A piece of property with the blood, sweat, and tears of the guy who built it. A place where you can soar like an eagle, or crash like a turkey.

General location: Near Guthrie, Oklahoma.

Elevation change: Not bad, maybe 30 to 40 feet, but repeated.

Season: Any time it is dry enough to ride, if you have the proper connections.

My pal Marcel, one of many fine folks who helped me with this book. I think if you cut this guy he would bleed mountain bikes. Thanx dude, you and your OEF pals are some quality induhviduals and I hope we can ride again real soon.

Services: Parking. A trail. That's it, cowboys.

Hazards: Poison ivy and mosquitoes are the most notable. Crashing or skinning a forearm or knee are not far behind.

Rescue index: Medium-high. You aren't running around this place without people knowing you are there. But you are a good ways from town and rescue personnel, just the same. A cell phone is probably useless.

Land status: Private property. Open only to the friends of the OEF.

Maps: Forget it.

Finding the trail: Hey, guess what? In keeping with the tradition began in the first edition, this trail is a secret and I am not going to reveal its exact location. Make friends with my friends in the OEF, and I'll let them show you.

Sources of additional information:

Oklahoma Earthbike Fellowship (OEF)
P.O. Box 2320
Oklahoma City, OK 73101-2320
www.okearthbike.com

Notes on the trail: This guy has worked hard to make this a fun place to ride. It is also one of the best-kept secrets in Oklahoma. I don't want hooligans going out here and trashing the place and then asking if they can use his bathroom. Or get a jump for their dead battery. Get on the inside, make friends, and then maybe you can ride here when you want to. And don't go knocking on his door at 6:30 some Sunday morning asking to use the phone. He doesn't have one.

RIDE 6 · Arcadia Lake Trail—Edmond

AT A GLANCE

Length/configuration: This is a point-to-point single-track trail of about 7 miles, giving a 14 mile total if you eat the whole can of chili.

Aerobic difficulty: Fairly gentle, this is a good 95/95 beginner trail.

Technical difficulty: Many sections are tight and twisty, especially the area near the Project Office, but this is an easy trail. The hardest part of riding it is contending with the deep sand that plagues much of it. The creek crossing at Spring Creek is tricky, but mostly because the approach and exit are usually very powdery.

Scenery: The woods here are nice; it's quiet and there's a lot of wildlife. Hello? We are here to ride.

Special comments: There is a fee of $7 to enter the park and ride from there. If you start at the Project Office the fee is $3, on the honor system. Don't cheat—that's a really cheesy thing to do. If you can't afford the fee then come to a workday sometime and bring your bike. The rangers might let you in for nothing under those circumstances.

This is one of the first Oklahoma trails I ever rode. That was years ago, when I was working on the first edition of this book. The trail hasn't changed all that much; some new single-track has been added over the years, and I still find this a groovy, fun place to ride.

Just about anyone can enjoy riding here. The trail is gentle, there are no monster climbs or great technical challenges, but the caveat is that it can get really sandy if there hasn't been any rain in a while. I'm talking ankle-deep powder—one of the softest trails in the state, sometimes. And that creek crossing over by Edmond Park is touch-and-go, the water can get deep enough to give you fits but is usually shallow enough to ride through.

If you start by the lake Project Office, you get some really nice flat single-track for a couple of miles and then you're in the City of Edmond parks, Edmond and Spring Creek. Down by Spring Creek Park is where the steepest sections are. This part probably has the trickiest parts, from a technical standpoint. The part

RIDE 6 • Arcadia Lake Trail

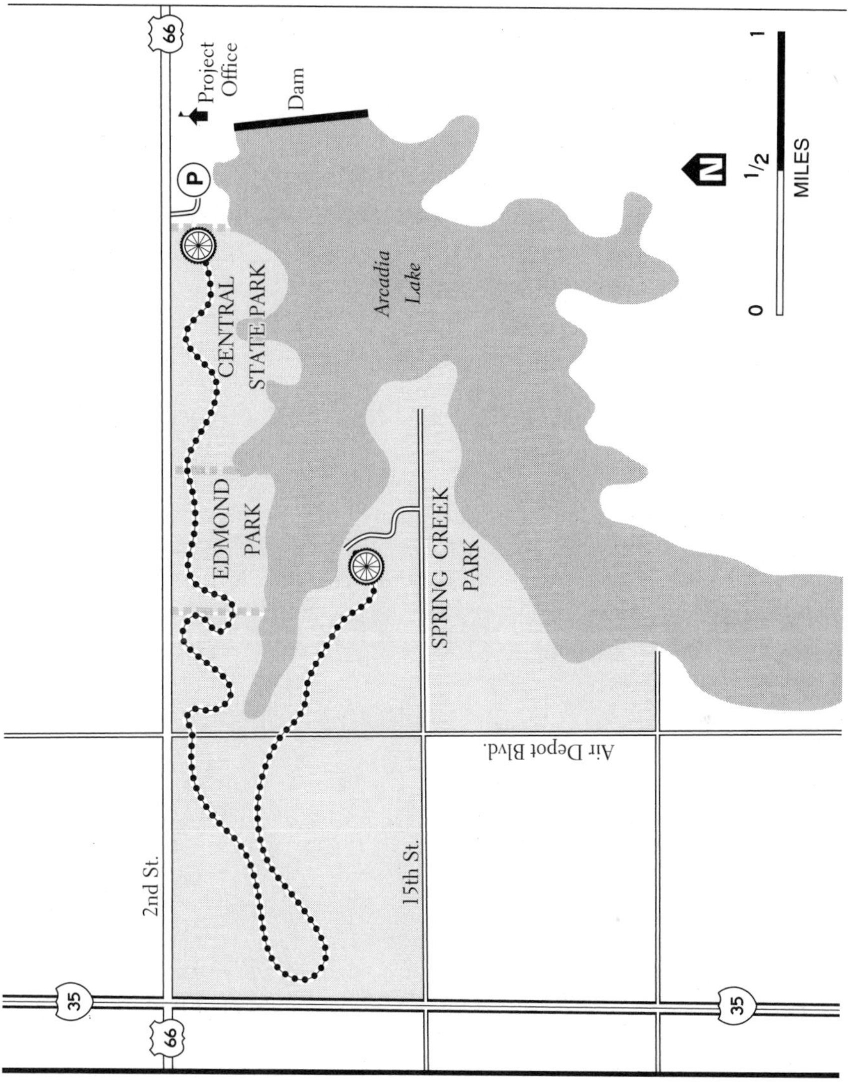

66

Project
Office

Dam

P

N

1/2

MILES

1

0

CENTRAL
STATE PARK

Arcadia
Lake

EDMOND
PARK

SPRING CREEK
PARK

Air Depot Blvd.

2nd St.

15th St.

35

66

35

known as Burnout Hill is probably the hardest, and might be beyond the abilities of some riders. Walk it if you're scared.

A fast, fun trail, well worth the price of admission. Well maintained and well designed, this place gets lots of riders. Be careful blowing through the trees because some of the curves are blind and many of the braking zones are very soft. Keep your wits about you and be nice to the other trail users. I think you can get an annual pass from the rangers, somewhere in the neighborhood of $20. Again, don't cheat the rangers out of their entry fee. That's not honorable. Check with the OEF folks about workdays and group rides—they're a great bunch.

General location: Near Arcadia, Oklahoma, about half an hour north of Oklahoma City.

Elevation change: Not a whole lot, but more than you might think. Maybe 60 feet, all told.

Season: You can ride here all year (there are no hunters). This trail is usually rideable a day or two after rain. It is pretty sandy, so it drains well. Check with the OEF; somebody usually posts trail conditions in their newsgroup if the weather has been nasty.

Services: Camping, showers and potties, water, and the occasional pay phone. If you need any other supplies, grab them before you head over to the lake because there are no stores nearby, as far as I know.

Hazards: I'd be careful on blind curves, because this place gets lots of traffic. There might be some poison ivy up under the trees, and I promise there are plenty of mosquitoes and even the occasional tick. Keep on the lookout for snakes; I figure there are a few in the vicinity. The conditions on this trail are often such that the sand gets real powdery, so be careful blasting around turns. And be careful when you cross roads—many of them are active and will carry automoron traffic.

Rescue index: High. Lots of people use this trail, and you're very close to civilization on most of the trail here.

Land status: Army Corps of Engineers lake dotted with City of Edmond parks.

Maps: The rangers have a decent one, just ask.

Finding the trail: From I-35, just north of Oklahoma City, take the US 66/2nd Street exit and go east for a few miles to the Arcadia Lake Project Office. Park in the lot there (on weekends I'm told it's OK to use the Employee Parking area, but don't take their spots during the week), and you will see the fee honor box and trailhead sign. Pay. Jump on the single-track and ride through Central State Park and Edmond Park until you get to the end of the trail, near the entrance to Spring Creek Park. Turn around and retrace your steps back to the Project Office. The trail is well established and fairly well marked; very easy to follow. Forks and branches you find may be explored, because all trails eventually converge into the main trail.

Sources of additional information:

City of Edmond
100 East First Street
Edmond, OK 73034
(405) 348-8830
www.ci.edmond.ok.us/index.html

Arcadia Lake
Project Office
9000 East 2nd Street
Arcadia, OK 73007
(405) 359-4570

Central State Park—(405) 359-4574

Edmond Park—(405) 359-4575

Spring Creek Park—(405) 359-4577

Scissortail Campground—(405) 359-4576

Oklahoma Earthbike Fellowship (OEF)
P.O. Box 2320
Oklahoma City, OK 73101-2320
www.okearthbike.com

Notes on the trail: This trail is in many places a stone's throw from old Route 66, the Great American Highway and the Mother Road of Jack Kerouac fame. You can see eagles in the winter, sometimes, and there are lots of nice spots in the park for picnics and camping. Enjoy the trail, and respect other trail users. Keep on rollin'!

RIDE 7 · NuDraper Mountain Bike Park —Stanley Draper Lake

AT A GLANCE

Length/configuration: Three main loops, about 12 miles total.

Aerobic difficulty: Most of it is fairly flat, and none of it has any serious climbing, but this place can be a workout if you go like a hellhound hammerdog. Otherwise, this is 95/95; most people can ride most of this trail.

Technical difficulty: There's some hairy stuff out there in them trees. The majority of it is fairly straightforward, but there are jumps and stunts and man-made challenges. Anyone of moderate skills can ride this trail. I would not be too proud to walk the scary parts, though, if I were you. I did. The green loop is fairly easy, the yellow a little more challenging, but the red loop has some very interesting pieces.

Scenery: Don't be looking around. Keep your eyes on the dirt in front of you; that's the only scenery that matters here.

Special comments: It amazes me when I imagine how the OEF managed to squeeze 12 miles of great single-track out of 180 acres of Oklahoma red sand. Hey, if you've got a lick of sense you'll join this club and get your butt involved. This is an amazing piece of property brought to us by an even more amazing group of individuals. Thanks, y'all.

A jump-a-mile, fun-fun-fun trail, you can't beat this place for sheer enjoyment. Gosh, these OEF folks are just monsters. They build some superb, sweet, smart single-track. As I heard it, a guy named James Perry built most of this. Way to go, James, you da man.

The OEFers will blow around this place on their single-speed bikes like they don't need gears. And you really don't need to shift on most of this, but give me my nine cogs anyway. I like the sound an XT rear derailleur makes when I click those shifters. But this is a place where a single-speed bike makes perfectly good sense to me. It doesn't have that much elevation delta; a few creek beds are kind of steep, but it's all very rideable and they make it look natural to fly around here on one gear. Go ahead, try to keep up with them. You'll be doing some serious air sucking.

RIDE 7 • Nu Draper Mountain Bike Park

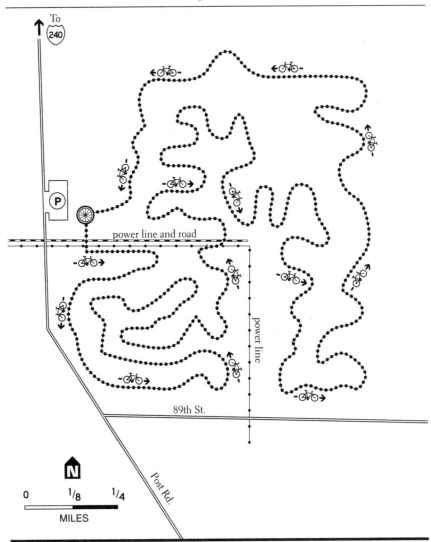

The old Draper trail was fun, but this place is like a giant mountain bike playground. You like air? Get yourself some. You like tricky bits? They've got those too. The V-Coaster is a rush, sort of a "northshore-style" bridge, and the drop is much steeper than the approach. The Big Dawg? Hell, I got scared and tried to walk it. I would have been much better off just riding over into it and holding on; it's too hard to walk unless you just throw your bike down there. And Tierra de Loco is about as crazy as dirt can get.

The Mountain Bike Park at Stanley Draper Lake, aka NuDraper. A fun trail that deserves to be in the great state of Oklahoma, and a tribute to the efforts of local mountain bike clubs. Photo by Marcel Slootheer.

What a great place to ride! Parts can get sort of soft and sandy at times, but this trail will usually hold you. If you're lucky enough to ride here a day or two after the rain has packed the surface, you can just let the bike fly. Ride it, love it, help take care of it. Don't go laying down any 30-foot skidmarks and we can still be pals. This place is a monument to what a bunch of smart and respectful mountain bikers can get from the system when they obey the rules.

General location: Midwest City, Oklahoma, over on the north side of Stanley Draper Lake.

Elevation change: Not much, maybe 50 feet.

Season: All year long. Don't ride in the rain if you can help it, but a day or two later it's often gorgeous, at least in summer. During the wetter months it can be pretty muddy, so don't ride here when the dirt is wet enough to fly up and stick to your bike. Abuse it and I'll abuse you.

Services: Picnic tables, chemical toilets, and parking. Drag whatever else you need in from town.

Hazards: Getting in over your head and hitting one of the trees that provide dense cover here. Or losing it in one of the turns because of the sand. Most people ride a sort of counterclockwise loop, but it's not out of the question to find a rider coming at you, so be careful of that. The few bits that are really technical deserve respect; some are steep and have stuff at the bottom that requires adept braking and careful handling of the machine.

Rescue index: Medium-high. This park is not that far from town and gets a lot of traffic. A cell phone is probably a good idea here. Most of the trails are often near the power lines, and it's easy to find your way to the parking lot from there. And the whole place is confined by paved roads.

Land status: Official Oklahoma City Parks and Recreation Department "Mountain Bike Park." Very cool.

Maps: Check the OEF webpage; they have a nice one posted there.

Finding the trail: This is the tricky part. I'm sure that if you know what you're doing, getting here is a piece of cake, but I always get lost. The roads around Stanley Draper Lake are weird, some go through and some don't. Some get you onto the highway and some don't. I'll pretty much quote from the OEF website here.

From Oklahoma City, go east on I-240 to the Douglas Road exit. Go north on Douglas Road to the light at 74th Street and turn right (east). Go east on 74th to Post Road and turn right (south). Follow Post Road south not quite a mile, and the trailhead parking lot is on the east side of Post Road. Pull in, take a deep breath, and follow the trail south, toward the power lines. Ride the various marked loops until you can't stand yourself any longer or until you're back at the parking lot. Then go home and plan your next ride here.

Sources of additional information:

Oklahoma Earthbike Fellowship
(OEF)
P.O. Box 2320
Oklahoma City, OK 73101-2320
www.okearthbike.com

Oklahoma City Parks and Recreation
Department
420 W. Main, Suite 210
Oklahoma City, OK 73102
(405) 297-3882
www.okc- cityhall.org/Parks/
index.html

The Bicycle Store
336 N.E. 122nd Street
Oklahoma City, OK 73114
(405) 752-8402
or
6066 S. Western Avenue
Oklahoma City, OK 73139
(405) 634-8080

Pro Bike, Inc.
5820 N.W. 63rd Street
Oklahoma City, OK 73132
(405) 721-6707

Notes on the trail: My helmet is off to the OEF. They have done more in the last five or so years than any other mountain bike club for hundreds of miles. They're smart, they work within the system with intelligence and effective public relations, and they love to build fun trails. You people are groovyness in human form. Keep up the great work. And thank you.

RIDE 8 · Clear Bay Trail—Lake Thunderbird State Park

AT A GLANCE

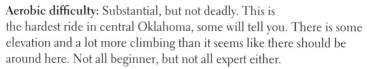

Length/configuration: Counterclockwise single-track loop of about 8 miles.

Aerobic difficulty: Substantial, but not deadly. This is the hardest ride in central Oklahoma, some will tell you. There is some elevation and a lot more climbing than it seems like there should be around here. Not all beginner, but not all expert either.

Technical difficulty: There are some nice challenges here. The turns are tight and abrupt in a lot of places, and some climbs are short but steep. Much of this trail is loose rock and sand. Still, I think most people can ride this.

Scenery: A really beautiful area, but another place to watch the trail and not the birds and bees.

Special comments: What a fabulous trail-thank you to the Bicycle League of Norman/Oklahoma Earthbike Fellowship consortium. Y'all have busted some major buns doing this place up. This facility has really grown up in a terrific way. When I was here before it was a baby trail. Now it's a burn-your-lungs-out "real" mountain bike trail. Well done!

People who are from around here will tell you that this is the best of the local trails. I would be a fool (or a worse fool than normal, anyway) if I found some way to disagree with them.

When I rode here I was with about a dozen of the locals. Guys and gals who built this thing and know every square inch. I tried to follow them for a lap without bursting a lung, but it was tough. There is more elevation delta here than anywhere around these parts, and this is another mighty fine and well thought out piece of Oklahoma dirt. I agree, there ain't a better one, not for many miles.

After our ride we went to a Bicycle League of Norman club meeting over at the restaurant at one end of the trail, the famous Clear Bay Cafe. In spite of busily stuffing my face with Suzie's BBQ brisket the·whole time I was there, I was lucky enough to meet the guy who's the head of the Oklahoma Parks and Recreation Department. What a stroke of luck. John Ressmeyer is a fine human being, and he would love to put a mountain bike trail in every state park in Oklahoma. The problem is that there aren't enough volunteers out there to maintain what he would let us have. Bummer. Severe bummer. There are some mighty parks under his control, and y'all that live around them could be champs. All it takes is some flagging tape, a chainsaw, and some loppers. Oh, yeah, and a commitment. Think of the possibilities, they're practically endless. All it takes is doin'.

Oh yeah, the Clear Bay Mountain Bike Trail. Back to the ride. Some of it is soft, the turns will make you either use your brakes too hard or let your skills rule

RIDE 8 · Clear Bay Trail

and throw caution to the wind. You'll probably get bit either way. This place was designed by nefarious and evil people. Mean mountain bikers with an eye for the challenges to "make it or die trying." The climbs are more than you expect, look for bits of lung as you go. I promise you, they are out there (the climbs, I mean). This whole trail is about as good as I have seen, long enough in miles that you have to plan your attack, but close enough to the world that they can get a medical chopper in to extract you if you find yourself having a yard sale, posthumously.

General location: Lake Thunderbird State Park, east of Norman, Oklahoma.

Elevation change: A lot more than you might expect, probably almost 100 feet from top to bottom.

Season: Year-round, unless it has been raining. The soil here is sandy and I think it will dry in a day or three after a rain. Please, do not ride on it when it's wet. You are not helping our situation if you abuse our privileges. After all, mountain biking is a privilege and not a right.

Services: Drinking water, toilets and showers, great camping. There's a nice restaurant near one end of the trail. There's a pay phone at the ranger station, near the entrance to the Clear Bay area. There are beer stores on the way, in case you need supplies.

Hazards: Oh, I'd imagine there's a ton or two of poison ivy along this trail, probably some snakes—pretty typical stuff. The other hazards are riders going the wrong way and the generally loose conditions along many sections of this trail. Trees, roots, and deadfalls are all to be expected, and the technical spots are to be respected as potentially dangerous.

Rescue index: Medium. This trail gets a fair amount of traffic, but once you're out there in the trees it's pretty tough to know exactly where you are in relation to the parking area and roads. Take your cell phone.

Land status: Oklahoma Tourism and Recreation Department state park.

Maps: Not readily available, but I'm sure that will change soon. Check the club websites.

Finding the trail: From Norman, Oklahoma, go about 13 miles east on OK 9 to the entrance to the Clear Bay area. Turn left (north) and follow the park road until you reach the Turkey Pass camping area. The trailhead is just south of Turkey Pass, plainly marked with a kiosk. You may park here or over by Turkey Pass in the lot next to the trash dumpster. Enter the trail and follow the signs. You will do a counterclockwise loop and end up back where you started. Hopefully.

Sources of additional information:

Lake Thunderbird State Park
Route 4, Box 277
13101 Alameda Drive
Norman, OK 73026-8605
(405) 360-3572
www.touroklahoma.com/Pages/state
parks/parks/ltspbig.html

Oklahoma Tourism and Recreation
Department
Division of State Parks
2401 N. Lincoln Boulevard
Oklahoma City, OK 73105
(405) 521-3411
www.otrd.state.ok.us

Bicycle League of Norman (BLN)
5016 Deerhurst Drive
Norman, OK 73072
www.bicycleleague.com/index.htm

Oklahoma Earthbike Fellowship
(OEF)
P.O. Box 2320
Oklahoma City, OK 73101-2320
www.okearthbike.com

Al's Bicycles
562 West Main
Norman, OK 73069
(405) 364-8787

Buchanan Bicycles
561 Buchanan Street
Norman, OK 73069
(405) 364-5513

Miller's Cycling
215 West Boyd
Norman, OK 73069
(405) 360-3838

Notes on the trail: Another fantastic piece of property brought to life and kept healthy by great Oklahoma mountain bike clubs. I strongly urge you to get involved with the clubs in your area; they're where the dirt comes from, and they can always use another pair of hands.

RIDE 9 · Bluff Creek Trail—Oklahoma City

AT A GLANCE

Length/configuration: A counter-clockwise loop of single-track measuring slightly less than 4 miles long.

Aerobic difficulty: Some, not real bad. A beginner can ride most of this trail, and walk the rest.

Technical difficulty: This is where things get interesting. There are some tricky bits here. This place was built to be a challenge, and it's a marvelous ride. It won't make you too fearful, but it will keep you thinking about braking, and weight distribution, and being in the correct gear. (Unless you are Marcel or James or Chris, or one of those other guys with no gears.)

Scenery: It's a nice ride, here along the creek. The trees and dirt are not for casual examination, though, so watch the trail and where your front wheel is going.

Special comments: Another fine example of the efforts of an awesome mountain bike club. People, this is about doing what's exciting and right with a parcel of property most people in the city had abandoned and forgotten about. Good job, and thank you to everyone who has helped build and maintain this cool trail.

This is another place I chased the OEFers on their single-speed bikes. Again, I prefer gears, but riding with these people makes me sure I will build a single-speed bike one of these days. There's no reason someone in reasonable physical condition cannot enjoy riding here without any shifting. It actually makes for a nice rhythm, I'm told—you just sail along and focus on the approaches to the steep parts. There's something to be said for simplicity. Simplicity of machine and of trail design.

You spend your time here winding around and through the creek, hopping tree roots, and leaning the bike through the turns. It's a moderate trail, not too hard, but certainly no piece of cake. On one of the creek crossings it took me three attempts to succeed in climbing the exit. And I had to hit a couple of trees—it just didn't seem like I was doing this place up right if I didn't get a little blood outside of my body.

Boys and girls, this is a fun trail. A trail to be explored and mastered, so go for your best time. Just don't do the brainless brake-lock skidding that the average moron loves. This trail is very durable if it's not abused. Don't ride like an idiot,

RIDE 9 • Bluff Creek Trail

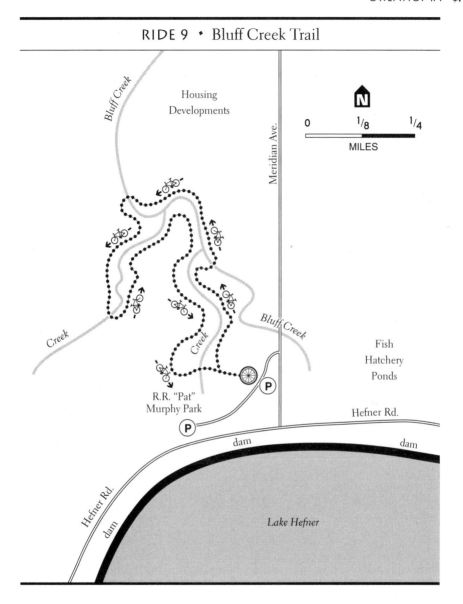

and we will all enjoy the trail here for many years to come. And don't ride here if the trail is wet.

The trailhead is adjacent to R.R. "Pat" Murphy Park, just north of the dam at Lake Hefner. There is a kiosk marking where to start, but otherwise the trail has no signage. You don't need it, unless you get to wandering around and don't follow the accepted loop. Don't cut the trail, because it may be impossible to tell which direction to travel if you cut across between two segments. It winds around a lot. Most people ride counter-clockwise, but oncoming traffic is not out of the question. And this place gets lots of traffic. It's practically in the middle of town, after all.

This thing was forgotten and abandoned when the OEF took it under their wing. Now they have one of the best city trails you will find anywhere right here. God bless 'em, one and all. You people do good trail.

General location: Northwestern Oklahoma City, Oklahoma.

Elevation change: Not much, maybe 30 feet.

Season: Barring extremely wet conditions, this is a year-round ride. The trail is normally OK a few days after rains in the summer, but prolonged periods in the winter will see it too slimy to use. Please don't abuse it by riding when it is wet; you're not helping if you do so. You're just being a self-centered jerk, and I hope you have to drag your bike a mile back to the parking lot.

Services: Parking. That's it. There's a water fountain and chemical potty next door, at R.R. "Pat" Murphy Park.

Hazards: There's plenty to hit on this trail. There are lots of trees and roots to watch out for. There are some deadfalls to get over and many steep but short climbs/drops through the creek. Poison ivy and the occasional snake lurk here, and the surface can get loose and soft after a lot of riding. Watch for people going the other way; there are a lot of riders and hikers that use this trail.

Rescue index: High. You are in the middle of town and there are people through here just about every day. A cell phone is a good idea, so carry one with you. This is one of those trails where you can leave your patch kit and pump in the car because you're never more than a mile (as the crow flies) from the parking lot.

Land status: Oklahoma City Parks and Recreation Department park.

Maps: Not yet, but I understand it is being handled. Can you say GPS? Check the OEF website.

Finding the trail: From the intersection of West Hefner Road and North Meridian Avenue in Oklahoma City (just north of the dam at Lake Hefner), go north on Meridian about 100 yards and turn left (west) into the entrance to R.R. "Pat" Murphy Park. In another 50 yards or so you will find the parking area, near the trailhead kiosk. Ride west past the kiosk and to where the trails fork. Go right, down to the creek, and follow the trail until you return to the main fork. Retire east to the parking area after as many laps as you can stand.

Sources of additional information:

Oklahoma Earthbike Fellowship
(OEF)
P.O. Box 2320
Oklahoma City, OK 73101-2320
www.okearthbike.com

Oklahoma City Parks and Recreation
Department
420 W. Main, Suite 210
Oklahoma City, OK 73102
(405) 297-3882
www.okc-cityhall.org/Parks/
index.html

Pro Bike, Inc.
5820 N.W. 63rd Street
Oklahoma City, OK 73132
(405) 721-6707

The Bicycle Store
336 N.E. 122nd Street
Oklahoma City, OK 73114
(405) 752-8402
or
6066 S. Western Avenue
Oklahoma City, OK 73139
(405) 634-8080

Notes on the trail: Another smart, well-conceived, perfectly enjoyable piece of fine Oklahoma single-track. All of you who ride here should stop along the trail sometime, take a drink and a deep breath, and think about the people behind the scenes who are making places like this happen. There ain't no finer folks, anywhere. You could be one of them. It's so easy—just sign up and then pay some dues. What a country! God Bless America.

RIDE 10 · Roman Nose State Park Trail —Lake Watonga

AT A GLANCE

Length/configuration: About 7 miles of single-track in a winding "figure-8" loop.

Aerobic difficulty: Pretty darned hard. Though it doesn't have a lot of elevation, it does have some hard climbs. They may not be over 200 meters in length, but they will make some of us puke. I ain't sayin' who.

Technical difficulty: Pretty darned hard. There is major equestrian traffic on this trail and they do tend to chew it up some. Nothing is worse on a good mountain bike trail than horses. They have caused some erosion that will make your ride here heroic in spots. This ain't no beginner ride. This is a good hard trail.

Scenery: It's actually kind of nice out here, unless the temperature is 100+ and there ain't a cloud in sight. From up on the bluff (at the overlook) the sun looks mighty fine going down, all orange and red and gauzed with clouds. I would definitely rate this place high for visual pleasure when the conditions are right.

Special comments: A hard ride, technical, steep, and loose. Many people have met Mr. de Zaster here. I can hear him calling me sometimes, but I ignore him because he's much slower than I am and can't catch me. Usually.

The local trail crew, Team Body Bag, will probably laugh at me for putting so much drama into this profile, but I think this place is hard. The climbs are not notable by Oklahoma standards, but it is a piece of work. Broken and exposed rock, sand, steep techies, tree roots; I think you get the picture. I saw "rose rocks" here, and I haven't seen those since I was a kid. (Rose rocks are these really cool, and painful, little sandstone formations; they are round and once you see one you will understand the name.)

The dirt is not going to be nice to you if you wander out here in wet conditions. You'll be sorry. The trail becomes an oozing mess of soft slippery mud so slimy that

RIDE 10 • Roman Nose State Park Trail

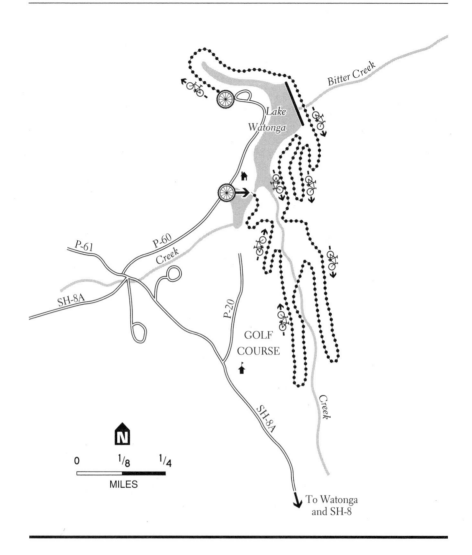

it's unrideable. Some of the surface here is broken rock, but most of it is dirt. There are lots of other trail users, from hikers and joggers to the occasional equestrian. Other than maps out on the trail in one or two places, there isn't much in the way of trail markings at present, but the single-track is well established and you should have no problem staying on track. The climbs are tough and the downhills will really get your respect. A lot of the trail is exposed, out on the prairie or up on the bluff, but there are some nice sections in the trees. Many of the turns are tight and lean you right up against red cedar trees. These sections are usually loose and covered with marbles, so be careful and don't get in over your head.

More loyal members of the Oklahoma Earthbike Fellowship. This batch is hammering the dirt out at Roman Nose State Park right after it opened. Just pickin' and grinnin'.

I highly recommend the food at the General Store—you oughtta stop by for a glass of iced tea at the very least. There are some nice places to have a picnic after your ride, and the locals often come and camp and do night rides. I think they also run a race or two here every year. Considering the amount of traffic this place sees, I'd have to say it has held up well. There has been a substantial amount of work done by various clubs—you'll see evidence of their handiwork in the form of bridges and various landscaping modifications that have been put in to keep the trail alive.

Right after I finished the first edition of this guidebook the OEF came up with this trail. I am dreadfully sorry I didn't get it in the first time, but here it is now. This is another fine example of the hard work of local mountain bike clubs— clubs working on the system from the inside—to score and maintain a totally sustainable launch point for your mountain bike skills and imagination. What a tremendous piece of red dirt!

General location: Northwest of Oklahoma City, Oklahoma, about an hour-and-a-half.

Elevation change: There is over 100 feet of delta here, according to the maps. You will consume several hundred feet in the course of riding a lap here, altogether.

Season: Not when it is wet. Just completely get over it—this place makes some of the worst red Oklahoma mud. When it's dry you can get it on. A blazing 100° day is not the best choice here your first time, either. Call ahead, or get on the web and ask around for conditions if there's any doubt.

My pal Chris, another mountain bike monster from the OEF, and a cactus flower along the trails at Roman Nose State Park. You are definite dork material if you live up there and don't get out with these folks. Photo by Marcel Slootheer.

Services: Camping, food, drinks, showers, and rest rooms.

Hazards: There is plenty to fear around this trail. Lots of stuff to get a flat tire from, lots of technical challenges that can be dangerous. The equestrians are another hazard, so don't run into any of them. The trail surface is loose in many areas and the terrain here is very difficult. There is poison ivy here, but it's only a problem if you're really allergic.

Rescue index: Medium-high. You are near enough to civilization to get rescued if you need it; bring your cell phone. There's a fair amount of traffic on this trail, probably some riders every day.

Land status: Oklahoma Tourism and Recreation Departments state park.

Maps: Check the OEF website, they have a good one.

Finding the trail: Watonga, Oklahoma, is about an hour and a half northwest of Oklahoma City. From Watonga go north on OK 8 for a couple miles to OK 8A, and turn left toward the park, following the signs. In a few miles you will pass the pro shop for the golf course; keep going and follow signs for the General Store. Park somewhere around the General Store so you can come back and have a burger later. Follow the pavement north until it ends at the turnaround near the camping area. Put your bike over the gate at the end of the road and go up the hill. Follow the obvious trail as it winds to your right and around the lake. You will cross the spillway and enter the steeper sections. Once you are down in the creek, you'll need to cross over, and then you can hang a right and go back to the car or hang a left onto the outer sections of the loop. Here you will find the hardest climbs and the most demanding terrain. Follow the trail until you're back at the creek. Now you may cross and head back to the car by catching the trail to the right.

Sources of additional information:

Roman Nose Resort Park
Route 1
Watonga, OK 73772
(580) 623-4215 Park Office
(800) 892-8690 Reservations
www.touroklahoma.com/Pages/
    resort5.html

Oklahoma Earthbike Fellowship
    (OEF)
P.O. Box 2320
Oklahoma City, OK 73101-2320
www.okearthbike.com

Notes on the trail: This park is named after Cheyenne Chief Henry Roman Nose. He owned some of the land here long ago, and lived near the trailhead. I think he is actually buried not far away. The last time I was here I helped with a workday, trimming trees and stuff like that. I get a real good feeling from how hard the OEF folks work at keeping their trails alive. They have done a fine job with this trail, and it's a tribute to what can happen when a dedicated club flexes its muscles. Good show, and thank you all.

TEXAS

"On Earth, as it is in Texas."

—Unknown

*"If I owned Hell and Texas, I'd rent out Texas
and live in Hell."*

—General Philip H. Sheridan
(King of the Carpetbaggers)

Texas, the Lone Star State. A few words about Texas and Texans are in order at this point. I moved to Texas in 1969, from Oklahoma, and I am still a "damn Yankee" to my friends who were born south of the Red River. It's just a joke. We Texans love to see ourselves as a cut above the average American. We like to rib folks from other states for not being Texans. As soon as you open your mouth to reveal an accent, or lack thereof, it happens; we know, and will proceed to identify you as "a foreigner." The best way to respond is to ignore us. Just play along, someday you will meet a Texan where you live and you can turn the tables. Otherwise you won't meet friendlier and more honest folks anywhere. I promise.

Though I cannot claim Texas as a birthright, I have a special answer when someone asks me where I'm from; I'm from Dallas. That one word says it all. People don't ask if you mean Dallas, Texas, because they know there is only one "Big D." Dallas and Texas are famous worldwide, though some of that may be infamy. To live here is to fall in love with the heritage, if you can ignore the heat.

The name Texas allegedly comes from some old word *tejas*, for "friendly." The name was applied to a tribe of Indians the original Spanish explorers met early in their travels through this part of North America. The Spaniards were impressed with the Native Americans' friendliness and openness. So, we all know what happened to those tribes, eh? Maybe this being friendly stuff ain't all it's cracked up to be? But, the original meaning still applies to Texans today, which you will discover if you just relax and ignore the "everything is bigger in Texas" bit.

Texas became part of the United States on December 29, 1845, as the 28th state. The Republic of Texas existed independently for 10 years prior. This probably explains the native habit of seeing our state as slightly larger than life. Texans declared independence from Mexico on March 2, 1836. And then we won our war, with the assistance of many early frontiersmen such as Tennessee native David Crockett and Louisiana gentleman Jim Bowie. These two died in the war. They caught bullets at a church down in San Antonio around March 6, 1836.

Everyone has heard of the Alamo. Most people know about the massacres that occurred that spring, but few non-natives are aware of all the other battles that were fought. There was a lot of Texan and American blood spilled winning our independence from Mexico. To this day, we are a very proud people and some of us have extremely long memories, though our relationship to our southern neighbor is amicable now.

Until the late 1800's Texas was mostly wide-open land. Earlier than that pockets of the state were populated by Indians and outlaws. Many areas figure prominently in historic gunfights. After the War for Southern Independence (a.k.a. Civil War, War Between the States, or War for State's Rights) the ranchers used barbed wire to fence in huge areas. This spelled the end of roaming free on the land, for the most part. Though today, mountain bikers are at no loss for terrain to tackle, with a wealth of trails clustered about Dallas and scattered throughout the state.

Words of caution: Watch for poison ivy and snakes. Just about any area where a trail runs under a canopy of hardwoods there is poison ivy, poison oak, or poison sumac. If your skin reacts to these plants, learn what they look like. They are VERY common on shaded trails. Snakes are also fairly common. I have seen poisonous ones just about everywhere I've been in Texas; I promise you they are out there. Rattlesnakes, copperheads, and especially cottonmouth water moccasins are a definite threat on trails in Texas. Rattlers ain't that bad—I kinda like the little beasts—but moccasins will chase you down and try to bite you. If you see a snake, and you are not a herpetologist, leave it alone. Just try to spot them. If you stop on the trail for a break, look where you are stepping before getting off the bike. One time a friend of mine nearly stepped right into a pile of water moccasins because he wasn't watching his step. It wouldn't have been pretty, I promise you, so be alert. I ain't biting your leg to suck the poison out.

The weather is another worthy opponent of the Texas mountain biker. Storms blow in with a sudden fury. In an hour or two a fluffy cloud on the horizon can turn into a monster hailstorm, and there may be nowhere to hide. Think about it, this is Texas. Always keep an eye tuned to the sky. As Texans are fond of saying "if you don't like the weather, wait a few minutes and it will change."

It never gets real cold in most parts of the state, but the panhandle gets some pretty severe winter weather just about every year. To quote another Texas axiom "there is nothing between Amarillo and the Canadian border but a barbed-wire fence, and the top two strands are down." The heat in summer months is deadly, carry plenty of water with you to the trailhead. Have at least two quarts if you want to ride any distance in July.

Please realize that much of the land where trails are built is fairly delicate. Stay on the trail, don't cut. Don't ride if the trail is muddy. Be careful, and keep locked-brake skidding to a minimum. The main enemy of Texas mountain bikers is EROSION. The worse an area is abused, the more of it washes away in the next rain. Famed trails elsewhere in the country have been closed because of negligent users. Let's keep Texas land managers from having to do the same. Carry your trash out with you. There are slobs out there who figure "they pay people to clean this up." No they don't you moron, people who care pick up your trash. Our paycheck is a ride with no trash. Ride responsively. Think about the future. This attitude is what has helped us gain access to the land. This attitude is also what mountain biking and true mountain bikers are all about. Amen.

NORTH TEXAS

My home. I almost hate living in Dallas, with the crushing throng of urban sprawl. All that noise and everything, but the local trails still make it all worthwhile. I think you'll have to agree that the smorgasbord of flavored dirt available to riders in this area will make everybody happy, not just me.

Make no mistake—there are places here that will help you forget the city. Once you have a few miles of these trails in your head you'll stop thinking about traffic and melt into the woods. This is no an accident. There are a lot of folks out there who have spent many an hour to make these places exactly as wonderful as I have described them. A place out of time, or maybe just a place away from the Metromess, but something to cherish just the same.

The terrain here ranges from real flat to pretty hairy. You can come into my neighborhood and have any kind of ride you want. Do you just want to ooze along, or do you want to hammer? We've got it all, thanks to locals who care about that sort of thang. Let's all raise our glasses of Guinness and toast DORBA, because even though some of them drink Coors Light, they are nonetheless the core of local mountain biking. Real people, doing real things for the mountain biking enthusiasts in the area. And beyond. Bloody hell—I love y'all.

RIDE 11 · The Northshore Trail—Grapevine Lake

AT A GLANCE

Length/configuration: About 9 miles of point-to-point single-track with a mile or so of decrepit old pavement. An 18-mile round-trip. Lots of sand, some clay, and some gumbo.

Aerobic difficulty: Easy to medium-hard. The eastern section is called the "easy side" but don't let that fool you; there are still plenty of places with short tricky climbs. And the western section isn't called the "hard side" for nothing. It's as good a workout as you will find in this part of Texas.

RIDE 11 • Northshore Trail

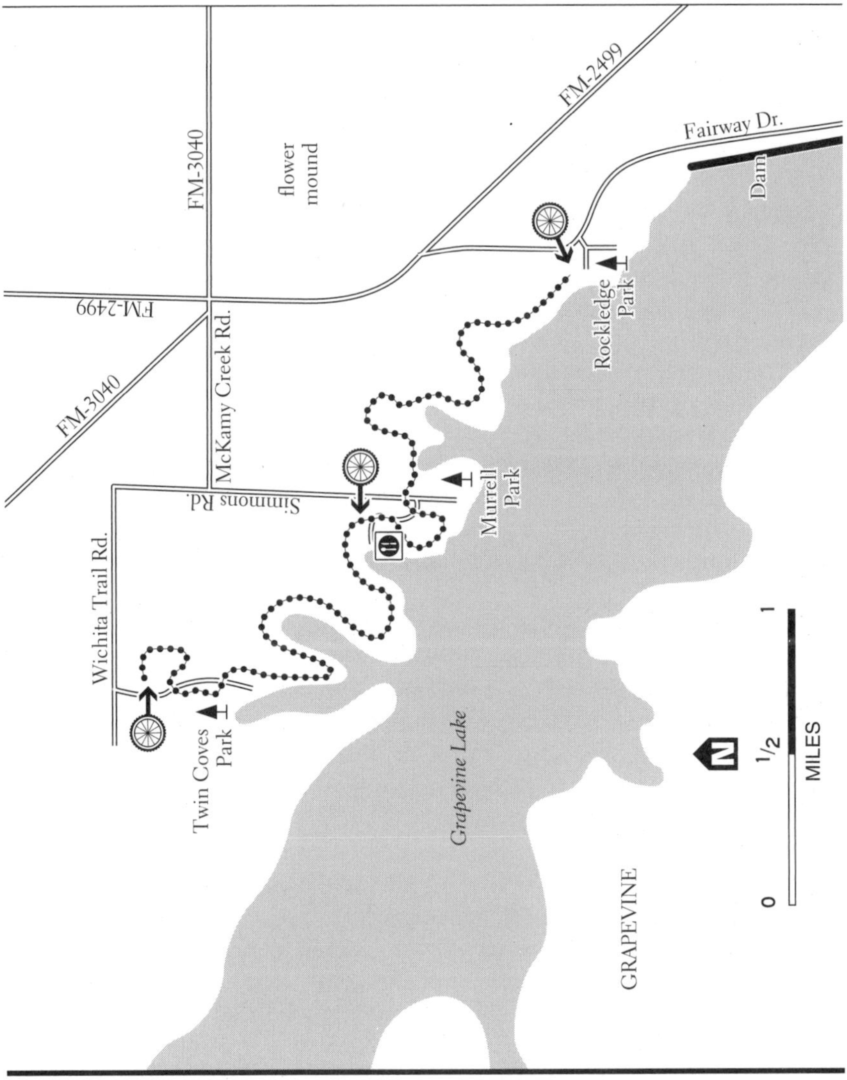

FM-2499

Fairway Dr.

FM-3040

flower mound

Dam

FM-2499

Rockledge Park

FM-3040

McKamy Creek Rd.

Murrell Park

Simmons Rd.

Wichita Trail Rd.

Twin Coves Park

Grapevine Lake

N

1/2   MILES

1

0

GRAPEVINE

Technical difficulty: Short climbs that are loose or grown up with rock gardens, loose sand, and tight bumpy turns are why this trail has claimed lots of skin from riders over the years. This isn't the hardest trail I have ridden, but it's right up there on a hot Texas summer afternoon.

Scenery: There are some nice spots on the eastern end that take you down by the water, or up on the bluffs along the lake. The western parts are mostly in the trees, so you had better watch the trail and not the scenery.

Special comments: This place gets probably a thousand riders in a good week. It gets almost overgrown with ragweed in the summer. A bell on your bike does not look silly here. Use it on the blind curves to let oncoming riders know you're there.

This is Mecca, the trail people think of when they talk about north Texas. Most folks just call it Lake Grapevine, but there are two other nice trails on Grapevine Lake. Still, this is the only trail some local riders have ever seen.

This place has just about everything. The eastern area, from the dam to Little Pete's, is sandy and loose in most places. There are a few easy sections along the lake where you might think the riding is easy. There are some climbs, and there's even a mile or so of pavement you have to use, which created the popular conception that this is the easy end. Only short stretches of the "easy side" could in a pinch be considered beginner level. Parts of the "easy side" are butt-crunchers; not as extreme as you can find here, but enough to make most people breathe hard. And some cry like a little girl. Waaah.

The western parts, from Little Pete's over to Twin Coves Park, are pretty darn serious. Soft sand, ankle-deep and powdery, mixed in with rock gardens of exposed sandstone. And then there are the technical spots. I don't care who you are or where you're from, this is technical like it oughtta be. Short, steep climbs that will challenge you to find the line. I promise you, I have ridden every piece of the Northshore at one time or another in my life, but seldom all in the same day. It is that kind of trail—always new and always a piece of work.

This place changes every year. There are sections that used to be extremely difficult but have become rideable. There are sections I used to be able to ace that are now so tough it often takes me three or four tries to get it right. And even then the result may or may not be reproducible. You need short explosive outbursts of ability and control to come away bragging. Of course, those same bursts of brilliance sometimes convince the bike to slam you to the ground and leave part of your knee or elbow there for posterity.

Not a good place for testing your new pedals. But a great place to learn a new bike, once you have it all working together and dialed in. And always a great place to ride if you haven't been here in a while.

If you think that's blood roaring in your ears, take a look upwards. It's just the continuous stream of jet aircraft coming or going from the airport. If you start hearing peacocks, keep going. There really are peacocks here, so you don't have to worry that your ancestors are calling you home to glory. Not today.

General location: The north side of Grapevine Lake, near and in the town of Flower Mound, out by Dallas–Fort Worth airport.

Elevation change: The worst climbs may be 50 to 60 feet, but no more. The highest point is around 600 feet above sea level, and the lake is usually 530 to 550 feet.

Season: Year-round, except a day or two after a heavy rain. There's enough clay here that you can ruin it by riding when it's wet.

Services: The trailhead most of my pals use is near Little Pete's restaurant, it's roughly in the middle of the trail and has lots of parking. There's water but no potties or phones. Prepare your equipment and supplies before getting here. The

My pal Marty riding the easy side of the Northshore Trail at Grapevine Lake. You don't need no stinking downhill bike here, but you do need some 'nads. Best trail in north Texas, say many.

restaurant down by the lake has a pay phone. The eastern trailhead is near the dam, in Rockledge Park, and has rest room facilities, but parking can be tough on a busy day.

Hazards: The main thing I am scared of here is oncoming traffic. A lot of spots on the trail have a very little line of sight due to tall weeds. Oncoming traffic is always a threat since this place is heavily used by many fast riders who don't care if they run you over. The technical nature of much of the terrain here is also something to consider. The rocks are hard, the trees have teeth, and the sand will toss you sideways if you hit it fast. Be careful on the paved section, because the old bridge was gone when we started riding here, and it would be a nasty place to crash. This trail crosses several active roads, both paved and gravel. I'd take a real good look before shooting across one of them, if I were you—people drive way too damn fast around here.

Rescue index: Very high. They will find your body here. That day, or the next. Or if you're not hurt so bad that you'll die, someone will come along and find you, and Texans are pretty good about going for help. There are houses near much of the trail, so someone up there might even call the ambulance for you. I'd carry a cell phone. I helped load some guy into a helicopter here once, and he was lucky he had a phone along.

Land status: A National Recreational Trail on anointed U. S. Army Corps of Engineers land. It's here because the lake floods sometimes and covers not only the trail but just about every inch of land between the lake and the homes. Unless someone in Washington goes absolutely nuts, this trail will always be here.

Maps: Check the DORBA website or stop at the Corps Visitor Center just north of TX 121, right before the dam.

Finding the trail: It hasn't moved, but the area around it has grown at a ridiculous rate. I would recommend starting at the Little Pete's trailhead simply because it puts you roughly in the middle of the trail and you'll never be more than five miles from your car.

Little Pete's Trailhead: Get to the intersection of FM 2499 and FM 3040 in Flower Mound. This accomplished with some difficulty by taking IR 635 from Dallas all the way west to where it runs into TX 121. Go north on TX 121 to FM 2499, and head north on FM 2499 to the intersection with FR 3040. Go west on FM 3040 about a quarter of a mile, and turn left onto McKamy Creek Road. Go west on McKamy Creek Road until it ends at Simmons Road. Turn left and go south on Simmons Road until you hit the stop sign in Murrell Park. Turn right and follow the park road until you see the parking area and trailhead just before Little Pete's restaurant. Park and ride. Through the gate to the right the trail takes you to the "easy side," while a left takes you to the "hard side."

Rockledge Park Trailhead: From Dallas take IH 635 all the way west toward Dallas–Fort Worth airport. Take the Bass Pro Drive exit to the north, and then head left (west) on Bass Pro Drive to where it ends at TX 26. Turn left (south) on TX 26 and follow it to the traffic light at Fairway Drive. Turn right (north) onto Fairway Drive. You will pass the Corps Visitor Center and then cross the dam and spillway for Grapevine Lake. Just after the spillway, turn left at the entrance for Rockledge Park. Follow the park road and take the fork to the right when you reach it. At the end of the park road is a circular turnaround and rest rooms. The trail starts just north of the rest rooms, at the corner of the parking area.

Sources of additional information:

Dallas Off-Road Bicycle Association
  (DORBA)
2911 Esters Road
PMB 1414
Irving, Texas 75062
www.dorba.org

United States Army Corps of
  Engineers, Fort Worth District
Grapevine Lake
Reservoir Control Office,
  CESWF-OD-L
P.O. Box 17300
Fort Worth, Texas 76102-0300
(817) 481-4541 office
(817) 481-3576 trail conditions
www1.swf-wc.usace.army.mil

Bicycle Tech
179 S. Watson Road #410
Arlington, TX 76010
(817) 633-4799

Richardson Bike Mart
1451 West Campbell Road
Richardson, TX 75080
(972) 231-3993
or
9040 Garland Road
Dallas, TX 75218
(214) 321-0705

Bluebonnet Bicycles
1204 North Stemmons Freeway
Lewisville, TX 75067
(972) 221-9322

Notes on the trail: This place is a tribute to what a mountain bike club can do when it works inside the system. A former member, long since moved away, hooked up with the park rangers and turned United States Army Corps of Engineers flood right-of-way into one of the finest trails in Texas. Way to go, Tom

Deans, and all the other members through the years who have helped us keep this trail in service. Glance around as you ride here; the trail is practically in the back yards of many homes along the way. And the development shows no sign of slowing. As a result there are lots of recreational riders, hikers, people walking their dogs, and many other trail users who aren't in as big a hurry as we are. Be careful, don't run over anyone, and live to ride another day.

RIDE 12 · Knob Hills Trail—Grapevine Lake

AT A GLANCE

Length/configuration: Just over 5 miles, point-to-point. This is an out-and-back and therefore a two-way trail. The round-trip is about 11 miles.

Aerobic difficulty: There are many nice short climbs, and a few severe ones. I'd say 90% of this is a fairly easy trail for most riders. There are a few places that suck, though—my faves!

Technical difficulty: Some of the loose climbs are challenging; there are one or two I have only cleared maybe once. Most of the trail, however, is pretty straightforward, and this is a fairly easy trail for most of the way.

Scenery: I think it's real pretty here when we're having nice fall colors. I like it in the winter because the prairie sections are very nicely carpeted with native grasses. In the spring there are often tons of flowers. And sometimes you can catch the prickly-pear cactus and yucca plants resplendent with flowers.

Special comments: I have always had a special place in my heart for this trail—I've been riding and hiking here for years. When it's too wet to ride I will often just hike and take along my binoculars. I have met bird watchers participating in the state birding survey several times, looking for that elusive golden warbler (or whatever it is they look for). I just think it's fun to see one of the big trees over by the gravel pit full of buzzards.

I still love to ride out here. You get more different terrain here than in any other ride in the general area of the Metromess. From fine north Texas prairie, covered with native grasses, to sandy bottoms and clay fields, to the black gumbo along Denton Creek. In the fall the colors can be glorious, but in the summer the ragweed can just about choke the life out of this trail. I've often seen it over six feet tall and crowding the trail to the point that it can be a handlebar-banging misery.

This is a pretty good trail for beginners because most of it is fairly easy. There are some short climbs, but nothing major. There are some long flat sections where you can fly, and there are some tight twisty bits where you can use your skills. Not exactly easy; a little more advanced than that.

RIDE 12 · Knob Hills Trails

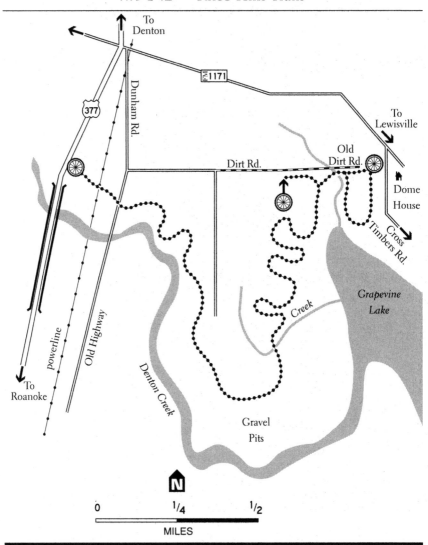

The park here is actually the western end of the same park the famous Northshore Trail lives in. The two trails will never connect for various reasons. Private property extends to some sections that are not rideable, and a lot of the area between the Northshore and here is equestrian trail. You may even see an occasional horse or two on the bike trail. I know I've seen evidence of their passage by the way they chew up the sandy and muddy sections. They're not supposed to ride the parts profiled here, but it happens. I make a point of never being mean to someone on top of a thousand-pound animal; I just stop and let him or her go by.

Parts of this trail are within sight of Grapevine Lake, but there's no access by bike. We used to park over on Pocohontas Road, on the far eastern end of the bike trails, but that trailhead is gone. Now you have three choices for your trailhead: The Dome House trailhead (farthest east), the Dunham Road trailhead (middle east), or the US 377 trailhead (west end). I personally prefer the Dome House trailhead, but the parking is real limited. The Dunham Road trailhead is the one I use here as the start of the ride, because it's the one currently in vogue with DORBA members. Still, a lot of people prefer the US 377 trailhead because of its easy access.

This is a fun ride, not too hard but not too easy, and great at night (but watch out for snakes). Probably not the ideal trail for a hot summer afternoon because so much of it exposes you to the open sky, but I've done it. When it rains this place can become a slippery mess, not fit for man nor beast. In the spring the wildflowers crank up, and in the fall the trees can be beautiful. It depends on yearly weather conditions. I love to listen to the wind blow in the cottonwood trees in the fall, and this place is gorgeous in the winter (when it is dry). Again, it depends on recent weather, so check the DORBA website for conditions.

General location: The far west end of Grapevine Lake, about half to three-quarters of an hour west of Dallas.

Elevation change: Minor, maybe 50 feet total. There are no 50-foot climbs, though; the delta here is gradual most of the way.

Season: Any time it hasn't been raining for a few days. The muddy sections here take over sometimes for months (in the winter), so let it go when it's wet. In the summer the ragweed squeezes in so close to the trail it may not be that much fun for some riders.

Services: Nothing; there's barely parking. Load up before you head out here.

Hazards: I'd be real watchful for oncoming riders and other snakes—or something like that. Since this is a two-way trail around a lake and a creek, you should be careful. Both when blasting through the tall weeds and if you stop for a break. I use a bell to warn oncoming traffic in the sections that warrant it. I would also say a cell phone is probably of some use around here, at least on the open and higher sections of this trail.

Rescue index: Medium-high. This park gets lots of riders, probably every day when it's open, and you're not really that far from civilization. It would be a hike of a couple of miles, but from the most remote sections you could walk out if you had to. Just try to learn the trail so you'll know how far you are from your car or emergency vehicles in case there's trouble.

Land status: This is U.S. Army Corps of Engineers property—more of their flood easement on Grapevine Lake. It ain't going nowhere unless the creeks wash part of it away or something.

Maps: Not available, as far as I know. The one here is the only map I have ever seen besides the topo quad Argyle.

Finding the trail: I am going to direct you to and from the Dunham Road trail-head. From the intersection of US 377 and FM 1171 west of Lewisville (north of Roanoke), you will find Dunham Road branching off to the south, on the southeast corner of the highway intersection. Follow Dunham Road to where it turns east, and continue past where the pavement turns south, onto the dirt, and follow the dirt road all the way east to the barricade at the trailhead. Park and unload, and ride east on the access trail. In a short while it will meet the main trail. Going right from this point it is around four miles to US 377 and the trailhead there. Going left will take you on a mile-and-a-half single-track lollipop. You'll ride up the dirt road to the Dome House trailhead, then turn right and follow the bike signs (stay out of the equestrian area), and you'll loop around to the right and go through some trees and then end up back at the dirt road. Do both ends and you'll end up with around 11 miles on the old clock.

Sources of additional information:

Dallas Off-Road Bicycle Association (DORBA)
2911 Esters Road
PMB 1414
Irving, Texas 75062
www.dorba.org

United States Army Corps of Engineers, Fort Worth District
Grapevine Lake
Reservoir Control Office, CESWF-OD-L
P.O. Box 17300
Fort Worth, Texas 76102-0300
(817) 481-4541 office
(817) 481-3576 trail conditions
www1.swf-wc.usace.army.mil

Bicycle Tech
179 S. Watson Road #410
Arlington, TX 76010
(817)633-4799

Richardson Bike Mart
1451 West Campbell Road
Richardson, TX 75080
(972) 231-3993
or
9040 Garland Road
Dallas, TX 75218
(214) 321-0705

Bluebonnet Bicycles
1204 North Stemmons Freeway
Lewisville, TX 75067
(972) 221-9322

Notes on the trail: This is sort of a lazy trail for the most part, so take your time and just enjoy the woods. There are a few benches in the prairie section. You can stop at these and have a rest break, if you want. Just remember not to punish this place when it's wet. And come out to a workday sometime; I know the trail steward and he's a great guy who always has swag for people who help. Check the DORBA website for current conditions and activities. Get out there and hit the trail!

RIDE 13 · Horseshoe Trail—Grapevine

AT A GLANCE

Length/configuration: This park is a series of single-track loops interconnected by pavement, usually ridden clockwise, about 4 or 5 miles of riding all together.

Aerobic difficulty: Not bad—this is a nice beginner trail. There are some short climbs, but nothing major.

Technical difficulty: There are some tricky bits here, but as I said, this is a good place for beginners. Tight tree passages, roots, and exposed sandstone will help you keep your wits, but this is definitely a 95/95.

Scenery: This park has some places to stop and take in the view, but it's more about being in the trees than it is about looking around.

Special comments: Don't ride here in the rain. I got in trouble for not saying that plainly enough the last time, but this place dries pretty quickly because of the sand. Just respect it and don't trash it, so that we will always have it.

This is a sweet little neighborhood trail that the locals use for everything you might imagine: dog walking, jogging, hiking, biking. It's nestled between a tributary to Grapevine Lake and a housing development, and it gets plenty of traffic. The really weird part is that in spite of the name, they don't allow horses. Not that I have a problem with that, though; I love all animals up to and including expert-class racers. It just seems ironic to me, somehow.

Horseshoe is someplace you can take a kid—or some other beginning life form of mountain biking protoplasm—to learn to love riding. The sand here can be slippery and tricky, but none of the trail is extreme. There are places to practice your skills just the same, in spite of what I just said. This is sort of a little bit of BMX, with some mountain biking poured around the edges for garnish. A single-speed bike, if you're into that, would be right at home here. A cross bike would not be out of the question, but this is definitely a mountain bike trail. I use my gears, but I ride my rigid Breezer here most times. You don't need suspension on this trail.

The one problem I have to mention is that, being right in town, you occasionally get kids who vandalize the trail, like chopping down trees and building bandit trails. It's been happening for years, but I still don't understand why they insist on cutting the tree three or four feet up from the ground. Makes a nice place to hurt yourself if you ask me. What's up with that?

There are few trail markers, but you don't really need them. You can just go out there and ride and have fun and not worry about where the car is. It's only a mile or two away. Get it on, boys and girls. The trail, I mean.

RIDE 13 • Horseshoe Trail

General location: Grapevine, Texas, the south side of Grapevine Lake.

Elevation change: Minimal, maybe 30 feet.

Season: Year-round. One of the few area trails that drains well. It is usually a piece of cake a day or two after heavy rain. That doesn't mean that there are no muddy spots that need to be avoided, and you should not take my words to mean go hit Horseshoe in the rain. Use your judgment and remember that mountain biking is a privilege and not a right. Don't be an idiot. If you're riding in mud, then you're not my friend.

Services: There is nothing at the trailhead but parking. Load up on the way.

Hazards: There might be some poison ivy, and there are plenty of pointy things to give you a flat. My main caution would be to keep your head. This place can be fast, but the sand also makes it slick a lot of times. You can hit a tree, or maybe three, and not see it coming.

Rescue index: High. You are less than a mile from civilization, and I'll bet a cell phone works out here.

Land status: City of Grapevine Parks Department park—mountain bikes welcome.

Maps: Not generally available, check the DORBA website.

Finding the trail: Take IH 635 west out of Dallas, toward the Dallas–Fort Worth airport, until you have to get on TX 114. Follow that west through Grapevine to the traffic light at Kimball Road. Turn right (north) and go to the stop sign at Dove Road. Turn right (east) and go about a mile until you see the pump station on the left (north) side of Dove Road. There you will find the parking lot and trailhead. Ride through the gate and hang a left on the next single-track you see and just wander around until you've had enough. The paved road that bisects the park will carry you back to your car whenever you're ready.

Sources of additional information:

Dallas Off-Road Bicycle Association
(DORBA)
2911 Esters Road
PMB 1414
Irving, Texas 75062
www.dorba.org

Grapevine Parks & Recreation
P. O. Box 95104
Grapevine, TX 76099
(817) 410-3122
www.ci.grapevine.tx.us/depts/parks
rec/default.asp

Bicycle Tech
179 S. Watson Road #410

Arlington, TX 76010
(817) 633-4799

Richardson Bike Mart
1451 West Campbell Road
Richardson, TX 75080
(972) 231-3993
or
9040 Garland Road
Dallas, TX 75218
(214) 321-0705

Bluebonnet Bicycles
1204 North Stemmons Freeway
Lewisville, TX 75067
(972) 221-9322

Notes on the trail: This is one a lot of riders continue to miss. It's short and simple, and sort of hidden across the lake from the Northshore. But your career will never be complete if you don't taste the Cross Timbers–style scrub-oak woods in this park. We used to go out here and drink beer when I lived in Grapevine many years ago, but now it's even better than beer!

RIDE 14 · L. B. Houston Nature Trail—Dallas

AT A GLANCE

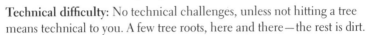

Length/configuration: A loop of tight single-track, about 5 miles. Ride it counterclockwise and you won't make enemies.

Aerobic difficulty: No exhaustive challenges; this trail is table-flat and usually very smooth.

Technical difficulty: No technical challenges, unless not hitting a tree means technical to you. A few tree roots, here and there—the rest is dirt.

Scenery: Trees. Texas Stadium is just across the river if you know where to look. There are some nice bends in the river along the trail, but this is about riding, not looking.

Special comments: Kids, beginners, racers whipped from the hard ride yesterday, all these will find peace here.

This is still my favorite trail. It is an excellent place for a beginner to start finding their dirt-legs. In fact, I probably learned to ride a mountain bike here. I mean really learned about tossing the bike into a turn and finding the edge of that envelope good tires can provide. Someday, if I live long enough, I would like to ride this whole thing without ever touching my brakes. That will take control and confidence. And luck.

What we have here is about five miles of very tight single-track along the Elm Fork of the Trinity River, a stone's throw from famous Texas Stadium, home of the five-time Superbowl Champions, the Dallas Cowboys. Situated in a forgotten corner of woods between Dallas and Irving, the armpit of the Metromess. This ain't exactly the best part of town—not the worst either, but sort of populated by a lot of non–mountain bikers. People come here to fish or drink beer, and just around the corner is another park (with the same name) known as a meeting spot for people who don't necessarily have the same lifestyle as most folks. If you get my drift.

But I still love this place. Dense woods, right on the river in several places, an easy flat trail that is great on a rigid mountain bike or a hybrid. You can bring your kids or pals along who don't have the skills or conditioning to ride the harder trails in the area. I usually don't even carry a patch kit or pump here, because you can easily get back to the trailhead if you have a problem—you're never more than half a mile or so away. As the crow flies, anyway. When you're back there in the woods you'll have no idea where you are, just keep going until you get to the clearing on the west side of the lake. You cross under the railroad tracks twice down by the river, so you can use them as a handy reference point.

This was one of the first trails DORBA brought back to life after I joined the club. Not that I had anything to do with it, but this place was originally used by people to dump trash and old refrigerators and all sorts of crap, until my club

RIDE 14 · L.B. Houston Nature Trail

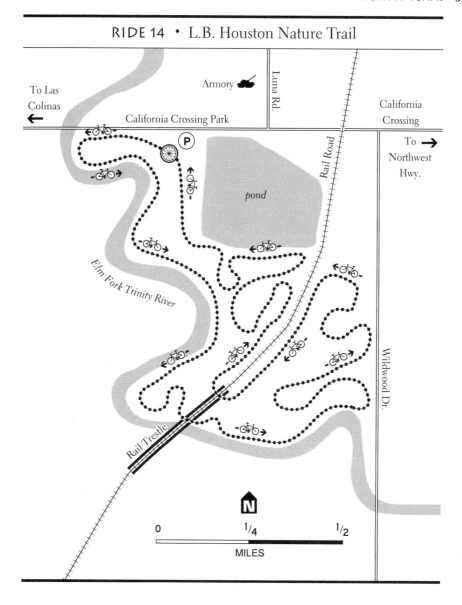

cleaned it up and got the city to let us make it an official mountain bike trail. The name comes from a guy in the Dallas Parks and Recreation Department long ago, who had a reputation for being very straightforward and honest. That's especially fitting, because this trail is both of those things. Just forget about riding here after a rain. Unless you like carrying your bike when it, and your feet, have about 50 pounds of black gumbo mud caked on them. But a few days later, when it's still slightly tacky and has been packed by a few riders, you can't break the tires loose. Lean and learn. It's a blast.

General location: Western central Dallas, a half-mile north of Texas Stadium.

Elevation change: You're kidding me, right? Maybe 5 feet, tops.

Season: Any time it hasn't rained in a few days.

Services: Parking. That's it, boys and girls, so load up before you go. There are convenience stores and restaurants over by the highway.

Hazards: The mosquitoes may be the worst you've ever imagined, unless you're from the swamp. I'd imagine there's some poison ivy too, if you don't know where to look. The mud will make you feel like a fool if it's wet here, so don't even try. Some of the people around the parking lot are kind of scary sometimes. The real danger here is overcooking a turn and hitting a tree or your riding partner (been there, done that, bought the T-shirt).

Rescue index: Very good. You are near many, many people. Carry your cell phone and have no worries.

Land status: Dallas Parks and Recreation Department nature trail. It ain't going anywhere for a long time, unless the river carries part of it away or something.

Maps: Check the DORBA website.

Finding the trail: In Dallas, take the Northwest Highway exit west from Loop-12 and continue west to the first traffic light, by the beer store, at Newkirk Road. Turn left and then right at the stop sign, onto California Crossing. Follow California Crossing west, over the railroad tracks and past the National Guard Armory, and the trailhead parking lot is on the left (south) side just before the river. Head right, into the trees, and just follow the trail until you come back to where you started.

Sources of additional information:

Dallas Off-Road Bicycle Association
   (DORBA)
2911 Esters Road
PMB 1414
Irving, Texas 75062
www.dorba.org

Dallas Parks and Recreation
   Department (DPARD)
Dallas City Hall
1500 Marilla Street, Room 6FN
Dallas, TX 75201
(214) 670-4100
www.ci.dallas.tx.us/html/park_and_
   recreation.html

Bicycle Tech
179 S. Watson Road #410
Arlington, TX 76010
(817) 633-4799

Richardson Bike Mart
1451 West Campbell Road
Richardson, TX 75080
(972) 231-3993
or
9040 Garland Road
Dallas, TX 75218
(214) 321-0705

Notes on the trail: Another fine example of what an awesome mountain bike club can accomplish when it works within the system. DORBA is the reason this place still has a trail, and also the reason this place keeps its trail. A lot of hard work went into this park, so think about that when you ride here. All it takes is a little mowing in the summer and a little corduroy when the muddy areas start to degenerate because of traffic. Maybe you'd like to help us sometime?

RIDE 15 · Arbor Hills Nature Preserve Mountain Bike Trail—Plano

AT A GLANCE

Length/configuration: A clockwise loop of tight winding single-track, just over 2 miles in length.

Aerobic difficulty: Mild; the climbs are short and not steep, so if you want a harder workout just hammer the hills. Or let it fly on the downhills—that always gets my heart rate up.

Technical difficulty: No great technical skills are required here. There are some tree roots and loose conditions, but nothing extreme. The trail is narrow and tight, and keeping your handlebars from clipping trees close to the trail is the biggest challenge.

Scenery: This is not a ride equipped with breathtaking vistas; you'll mostly be in the trees with a few spurts across the prairie areas. Watch the trail, Pilgrim.

Special comments: This trail gets a ton of traffic just about every day, in both directions. The hikers go counterclockwise and the riders go clockwise. The surface varies from light clay to heavy black gumbo. Please let it drain and dry after a rain—don't go out there and punish it when conditions are muddy. Find somewhere else to ride when this trail is wet.

Five minutes from where I live, and then about ten light years to the left of everyday life. This is a delightful place to forget the city grind. You'll forget you're still in a tiny corner of the Metromess as soon as you hit the single-track. Nice single-track is all I need to forget how big and nasty it is getting to be around here. That and some good tires.

If you've got the nerve, feel free to see how well you can follow the trail here as you let the bike find the line. But just remember, everybody I know, myself included, crashes here on a fairly regular basis. I think the trees jump around or something. It can't be all my fault. Don't run over the hikers. I'll stop and let the air out of your tires if I ever see you be rude to another trail user. Got a problem with that?

This trail is squeezed into a couple of corners of a well-planned nature preserve. The city of Plano was wise enough to realize how fast the land around here was being gobbled up by developers, and therefore what an asset saving a few acres for nature could be. This trail is very well thought out, squeezing two miles of fine north Texas single-track into only a few acres of land. It's all about conservation, children—they aren't making any more land.

My friends Allan and Kenley Hetzel were the driving forces behind securing permission to develop this trail, and they did most of the flagging and actual construction, with the help of a lot of other DORBA members. This place is so close

RIDE 15 • Arbor Hills Nature Preserve Trail

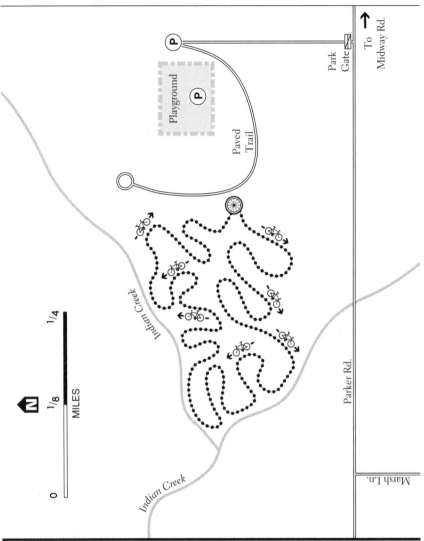

to where a lot of us live that finding someone to help hasn't been the challenge it is farther from the city. And the volunteers have done a fine job, I must say. You can always tell a trail built by someone who learned from Steve and Jeanne Patterson. It will be tight and fast and have a few places where narrow handlebars are not just a good idea, but necessary. Steve always had a thing for building trail between two trees that are just about as wide as the handlebars on my Breezer, give or take a few centimeters.

My pal Marty again, with his son Ryan, enjoying one of the finest urban trails anywhere in the nation, Arbor Hills Nature Preserve.

Too bad Allan and Kenley moved off to Colorado, but they have a trail or two up there to enjoy, apparently. A little more elevation, perhaps, but not as tight and fun as this place. Thanks kids, y'all done good, we're in tall cotton now.

General location: Western Plano, Texas, near Parker Road and the North Dallas Tollway.

Elevation change: Pretty mild, maybe 30 feet of elevation delta from the highest point to the creek bottom.

Season: You can ride here any time it's not muddy. Note that the preserve is gated, and the automatic gates close at 11 p.m. and do not open again until 5 a.m. the next morning.

Services: Water and rest room facilities are available at the picnic pavilion near the parking lot. Plus, you're in the middle of one of the larger suburbs of Dallas. The actual area of the preserve in basically in a residential neighborhood, but there are plenty of restaurants, gas stations, and convenience stores within a few miles, mostly to the east of the preserve, near Parker Road and the North Dallas Tollway. There's also a hospital about a mile to the east, on the southeast corner of the intersection of Parker Road and Midway Road.

Hazards: The main things to watch for here are poison ivy and pedestrian traffic. I promise there are copious amounts of the "plant from hell" here, and lots of people walk their kids and dogs around, and runners are a common sight.

Cyclists are required to do the trail in a clockwise loop, and the peds are generally smart enough to go counterclockwise. But not always. So keep your eyes open and don't run over anybody.

Rescue index: High. Cell phones work here, and there's a fire station immediately to the east, adjacent to the preserve. Since the trail winds around itself in a fairly small slice of land, you can easily return to the parking lot at any time by catching the old road and going uphill. The trail crosses this old road in several places.

Land status: Property of Plano Parks and Recreation Department.

Maps: Check the DORBA website.

Finding the trail: From the intersection of the North Dallas Tollway and Parker Road in Plano, go west past Midway Road. Keep going just past the fire station, where you will see the sign and gates for Arbor Hills Nature Preserve on the right (north). Enter the parking lot and unload the bike. From the parking lot, go west, past the rest rooms and picnic pavilion, onto the paved trail. A kiosk and a bench mark the trailhead. Hang a left onto the single-track and hold on, here you go! You will finish at this same point, and if you need a break before another lap, you can rest on the bench for a few minutes.

Sources of additional information:

Dallas Off-Road Bicycle Association
(DORBA)
2911 Esters Road
PMB 1414
Irving, Texas 75062
www.dorba.org

Plano Parks and Recreation
Department
P.O. Box 860358
Plano, TX 75086-0358
(972) 941-7250
www.planoparks.org

Notes on the trail: This trail is fast, and if you can keep a pace that will see 11- to 13-minute lap times you are going pretty good. Slow the heck down. There's a paved jogging trail that loops around the park, and there's some more single-track on the north side, just off the paved loop. It's got some longer hills and steeper climbs, but I prefer the actual mountain bike trail for a fun ride. Still, the other trail is out there too, so check it out.

RIDE 16 · Boulder Park Trail—Dallas

AT A GLANCE

Length/configuration: A counterclockwise maze of interconnected single-track in a city park, with probably at least 10 miles of trail.

Aerobic difficulty: Medium to hard. There are some fair climbs—not real long, but steep enough that not

RIDE 16 • Boulder Park Trail

everyone will make them. Tree roots and loose gravel make for tougher than average conditions.

Technical difficulty: There is some decent technical stuff here—some of the climbs are challenging because they are loose, and the creek crossings can put anybody down without warning.

Scenery: Not much to see, just lots of trees. The area along the creek could be considered scenic, but that isn't why we ride here.

Special comments: It's easy to get lost here, but since the area of the trails is contained in a fairly small parcel of land you will wander out to a paved road long before you die of starvation. Do not park at the churches south of the trailhead. I have heard stories of people in bike panties wandering into Sunday church services and asking for pay phones or rest rooms. Which is idiotic, as well as rude—so leave the churches alone so that we can keep riding here.

This is still an excellent trail—I have enjoyed every ride I've ever done here. It has more climbs than a lot of local trails, and it's tougher because of the loose limestone surface that predominates, but it is so easy to get lost here. The ride is usually marked with arrows at least once a year, because of races and training rides local clubs and shops sponsor. But it is such a maze that I seldom repeat two laps exactly.

The Dead Dog Turn is gone, but his section of the creek bed is still there, and not many people come here anymore because of the other groovy trails in the Metromess. You still can't find a better intense concentration of fine single-track anywhere in north Texas. This place is only about a mile or so on each side, and there's probably ten miles of trails to peruse. I mean, that is tight. And so are all the sections of Boulder Park.

You get red cedar and limestone and clay for the first bits, then you drop into the trees along the creek where you'll find lots of tree roots, backscratchers, and deadfalls as you try to wind around and not drive off into the creek. Then you'll cross to the north side and wind some more, mostly on dirt, but there's some limestone gravel here. Play in the smaller gullies and head back up by the roads. Again, cross the creek. Then you'll get to the best hills in the place—steep and loose enough to bring most riders out of the saddle. Then you're up on the bluff, by the church, and you'll hit the trailhead.

Again, there's no other collection of trails around here that have so much to offer in such a fairly small squared circle. If you've never been here, check it out! If you're from out of town and Cedar Hill or the Northshore are a little more than you need at the moment, go hit the Boulder.

General location: Southwest Dallas, near Redbird airport and Redbird Mall.

Elevation change: You have around 100 feet, give or take. And you pay the toll a few times around this trail.

Season: Not a good place when muddy. My club has had to cancel a few races here because it just gets too bad. Give it a while to dry. Otherwise, fun year-round.

Services: There isn't even a decent parking lot here. No water, no potties, no pay phone. Everything you need is just south—restaurants, convenience stores, and the like, along Camp Wisdom Road. Or load up before you get here.

Hazards: There is definitely poison ivy here, where you're not looking. The trail surface is loose in many places, and the trees would love to see your bike dump you. Otherwise, this place is basically a confusing loop. I have had flats here—there's plenty of bois d'arc and blackjack.

Rescue index: Bring a cell phone. Someone probably rides through here every day, but if you get hurt you either need a riding partner or some way to contact the medical emergency folks. Getting rescued here should present no great challenges, other than locating your broken, bleeding butt out there on the trail in the middle of the city.

Land status: Dallas Parks and Recreation Department property.

Maps: Not readily available, so check the DORBA website.

Finding the trail: From downtown Dallas, head south on I-35E to the split with US 67, taking US 67 toward Cleburne. Take the westbound exit for Camp Wisdom Road and find a place to park, here among the SUV's in the commercial lots. The first traffic light west of the highway is Boulder Drive. Park at the mall and head north on Boulder Drive until you pass the churches and see a chain-link fence on the east side of Boulder Drive. There's an opening in the fence at the trailhead. Cut right at the gate and follow the trails until you're back where you started.

If you get lost while riding, just remember that the service road for US 67 is to the east (although you will encounter private property before you get there), Redbird Lane is the border on the north, Boulder Drive is the border to the west, and the church property is quite obvious to the south. From the creek, go up the hill to the south until you start seeing light dirt, and then turn west toward the fence. If this sounds too hard, you might want to bring a compass or somebody with a sense of direction along.

Sources of additional information:

Dallas Off-Road Bicycle Association
  (DORBA)
2911 Esters Road
PMB 1414
Irving, Texas 75062
www.dorba.org

Dallas Parks and Recreation
  Department (DPARD)
Dallas City Hall
1500 Marilla Street, Room 6FN
Dallas, TX 75201
(214) 670-4100
www.ci.dallas.tx.us/html/park_and_
  recreation.html

Bicycle Tech
179 S. Watson Road #410
Arlington, TX 76010
(817) 633-4799

Richardson Bike Mart
1451 West Campbell Road
Richardson, TX 75080
(972) 231-3993
or
9040 Garland Road
Dallas, TX 75218
(214) 321-0705

Notes on the trail: The parking situation here is pitiful. I don't know what to tell you—the tiny spot across from the trailhead holds maybe three cars (or two trucks), and you should never park at either of the churches. The mall is just south, as are several commercial lots around the strip malls. Free parking, where you won't get in trouble—so use it or lose this trail.

RIDE 17 · Windmill Hill Nature Preserve Trail —DeSoto

AT A GLANCE

Length/configuration: Looping cloverleaf (roughly) of single-track surrounded by suburbia. Gotta be 4–5 miles of trail back in there.

Aerobic difficulty: Mostly medium, but some is short and steep and touch-and-go. There are a couple of hard parts here.

Technical difficulty: A lot of it is loose, and there's some tricky climbing, but not a real hard trail overall. Some of it is winding and tight and can be loose if it's been dry a while, so be careful until you find the lines.

Scenery: You gotta get a picture or two in the parking area, over by the marker. And down by the bridge. Otherwise, this trail is "head down." Don't be watching airplanes, and don't be playing mental air-guitar. Or you'll run into Mr. Bustyerass de Zaster. Or, more likely, he'll find you.

Special comments: There are two trails in Texas (that I know of) where you can find memorials to north Texas' finest blues guitar player, one Stevie Ray Vaughn of Oak Cliff. This is one of them.

You know, I can't even tell you the story about the windmill, but there must be one. This place has really grown up since I wrote about it before. There are now some serious techie bits around, mostly down by the creek. The creek with the Stevie Ray Vaughn memorial bridge. I'll bet you can't name another trail (if you're sharp you said Town Lake in Austin) with an SRV memorial. I loved that man—too bad he left us so soon.

This park has sort of a cloverleaf-shaped set of single-tracks with the SRV Bridge as their center. You can start from the parking lot and head south into the woods and work your way around and back, or you can go east from the car and do roughly the same. The trails are located between housing developments (to the south and east) and roads (Wintergreen to the north and Duncanville to the west), and employ some of the broken hilly limestone typical of this area. The northern and eastern sections have more dirt, and some steep climbing stuff that is pretty tough in places.

A buddy of mine named Paul Dyer took me out here right after he started flagging it, many years ago. I only rode here a few times and then, years later, I came out here again and freaked out. There is some seriously worthy single-track here. Yeah, it's short, but this is a small place. Just come down here and learn your way around, and then cut a few hot laps. It's nice. Fast and fun, and you'd better be in the right gear or you might die. The little panhandle section is cool—the BMXers can do flips and 360's and all sorts of other tricks I don't know the cool kid names for. They are such a blast to watch. And they wear helmets,

RIDE 17 • Windmill Hill Nature Preserve Trail

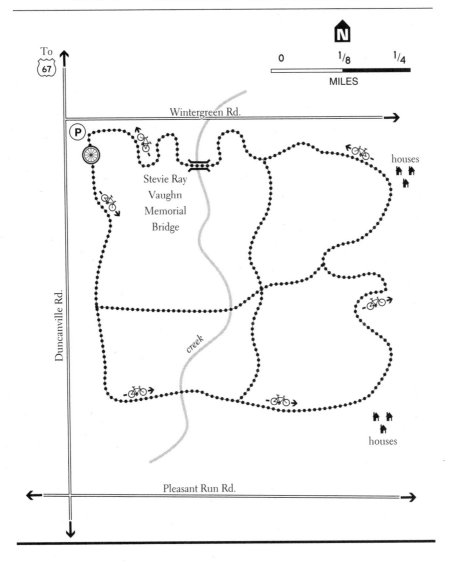

so for the most part they're thinkin'. They just have that green-tipped hair and all that. It ain't my thang, just the same, but they've got as much hand-eye coordination and balance as just about any mountain biker I ever saw.

This is just one more place DORBA helped with, and if you've never been here then you ain't got a full hand yet, Pilgrim. Hell, do it just to remember that boy from Oak Cliff.

I still get chills when I recall the anti-litter ad spot he did for the Texas Department of Transportation before he died. All you could see was the top of the black hat and the guitar strap with SRV on it, with his face leanin' down toward the

We have, and have had, some major musicians here in north Texas. Go on out to Windmill Hill Nature Preserve and pay your respects sometime.

face of that old Stratocaster. Stevie scorched some wicked little riff and raised his head until you could barely see his eyes just under the brim. He drew you in for a second or two, and then growled, "Don't mess with Texas."

'Scuse me, I gotta go get something out of my eye.

General location: Southwest Dallas, between the towns of Duncanville and DeSoto.

Elevation change: You have around 75 feet of delta here. The general area of the SRV Bridge is probably the lowest point, with an area in the southwest loop being the highest.

Season: Anytime it has not rained for two or three days. There is definite potential for mud here, especially near the creek and most of the eastern side.

Services: All you'll find is a parking lot. Load up before you arrive.

Hazards: The trail can be loose in places and the long tempting downhills will beg you to be a fool. Mr. de Zaster is always there, waiting. I didn't see it myself, but I've heard there's poison ivy in the trees.

Rescue index: High. Carry your cell phone (and a buddy) and you'll probably be rescued. Or at least carried out for burial. I have a feeling that more than one or two people circulate here daily, but the immediacy of rescue that a cell phone brings in the middle of town is worthwhile. Just know where in the heck you are on the trail so you can describe your location.

Land status: City of DeSoto park. Hikers and bikers welcome, no motorized vehicles.

Maps: Not readily available, check the DORBA website.

Finding the trail: From downtown Dallas, head south on IH 35E to the split with US 67 and take it toward Cleburne. Take the exit for Duncanville Road/Main Street and head south for a mile or so. You will see where Wintergreen Road hits Duncanville Road from the east; the southeast corner has the parking area.

Sources of additional information:

Dallas Off-Road Bicycle Association
  (DORBA)
2911 Esters Road
PMB 1414
Irving, Texas 75062
www.dorba.org
City of DeSoto Parks and Recreation
  Department
211 East Pleasant Run
(972) 230-9655
www.ci.desoto.tx.us/ParksandRec.
  htm

Bicycle Tech
179 S. Watson Road #410
Arlington, TX 76010
(817) 633-4799

Richardson Bike Mart
1451 West Campbell Road
Richardson, TX 75080
(972) 231-3993
or
9040 Garland Road
Dallas, TX 75218
(214) 321-0705

Notes on the trail: I'm sure this trail will continue to grow as time goes on, even though the amount of land here is very limited. Just be a pal and fight the urge to cut your own pirate trails. Bandits ain't my friends, I tend to respect the system too much. In spite of some of the hard nature of sections of this single-track, lots of the trails here are good for beginners. Someone just starting can get their thrills at Windmill Hill, and not be so far away from the car as to be in a miserable (or dangerous) situation.

RIDE 18 · DORBA Trail—Cedar Hill State Park

AT A GLANCE

Length/configuration: 3 connected loops, the main (outer) loop is about 8 miles, with an additional 3 miles of extended expert loop, if you want. You can pick up another 2 miles by taking a lap on the inside "short" loop. Ride clockwise.

Aerobic difficulty: People from Colorado will laugh, but this is a fairly hard trail because there is significant climbing. You go up and down a bunch and get to savor the elevation delta again and again.

Technical difficulty: Medium. This is not a terribly technical trail, but one to respect. The tree roots are tricky, and the loose stuff will keep you mindful. Be ready for anything.

RIDE 18 • DORBA Trail

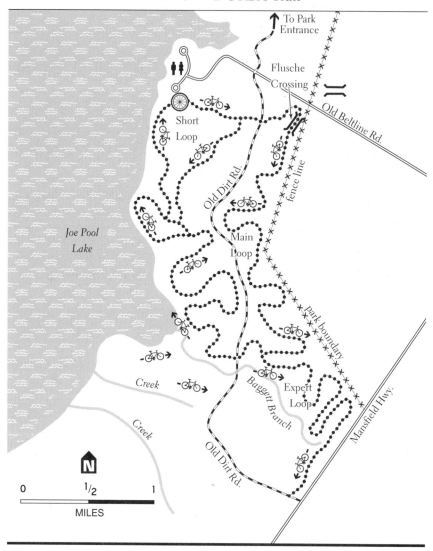

Scenery: Well, this is the prettiest part of Dallas county. You get a few lake views and all that, but that's not why we're here. We are here to ride hard. If you want some nice scenery, then I would encourage you to walk on the hiking trails. They are worthy. Ask the ranger for a map.

Special comments: Don't forget that state parks charge typically $3–$5 per head as an entrance fee. Call ahead and check on trail conditions before you drive all the way out here, since this place closes when it's wet. Also, the park is locked after 10 p.m. at night until 8 a.m. the next morning.

My pal Pam doing a minor drop along the DORBA Trail. That girl can burn the legs off a lot of guys I know.

We started building this trail in 1993. Steve Mayo was the man who laid most of it out, and countless other people helped flag and cut and still help groom it to this day. This place gets a couple of tons of traffic any time it's open. The rangers close it when it's wet, and it can stay that way for months in the winter. The hydraulics of the clay keep some places on the hilltops as muddy as river gumbo for weeks.

This place is a race course and there are usually a few people cranking hot laps around here, somewhere along the trail. Let 'em by so you can ride at your own pace. Lots of climbing and loose dirt make this a ride that your typical beginner might not call a fun day. But if you have the stamina, point your bike and pull the trigger on one of the best Metromess trails.

This is not a good place to forget your patch kit. You name it, Cedar Hill has every type of thorny plant and biting critter: mesquite, bois d'arc, cactus, rattlesnakes. They are all here, along with some monster bluebonnets in the spring. The downhills here are blinding and loose, and Mr. de Zaster is lurking behind every tree, chuckling. He knows you're gonna overcook sooner or later and leave him some skin and blood to remember you by. I have seen many chains broken here, and much puke has been spewed around by people who challenge the heat until it breaks or kills them. Some have actually died here.

I think you will probably find some powder in the summer. Several of the longer climbs can get pretty soft, and climbing those boogers puts most people up on the very edge of the trail. Which furthers the cause of the powder and makes the crumblies rejoice in anticipation of the next rider to come along. Try to take it easy on this trail; it's anything but bulletproof. Locking the brakes is

hard to avoid a lot of the time, but please don't sow the landscape indiscrimi-
nately with skid marks. It chews up the turns and makes it tough for us older guys
to get around without cussing.

The DORBA trail lacks a certain amount of bailout markings and good maps,
but we're working on it. If you can't be patient, then help. Maybe you can help?
Every time I see someone on the web bashing this trail because they got a flat
and didn't know how to get out, I just want to send them one message: Bring yer
stinkin' patch kit next time, and come help us put up signs the time after that.
You can't really cry about trail conditions and expect to get any support from the
people who carry weed eaters and mowing machines around to keep this place
open for other people to ride. Come help us some time, there's always cool swag.

General location: Joe Pool Lake, south of Dallas a few miles.

Elevation change: There's around 100 feet of elevation delta as you ride this
trail. This 100 feet is recycled several times.

Season: Spring, summer, fall. The winter months often find the trail closed for
extended periods due to wet conditions.

Services: In addition to multitudes of convenience stores within a few miles of
the park, the park itself has about everything you will need. There are rest rooms
near the trailhead, and water is available there; there are showers in the camp-
grounds, plus vending machines and a pay phone located at the park entrance
building.

Hazards: Tire-piercing plants, snakes, poison ivy, riding too fast into a tight corner or over some loose terrain. Any of these will bite you if given the opportunity.

Rescue index: High. A cell phone is useful here. The main challenge to being
rescued is locating exactly where you are so you can tell the nice 911 operator
where to find you and your broken collarbone. There's an old dirt road that runs
from the southern border of the property into the heart of the park. As you ride
you will cross it (in a couple of places). Note the locations, and that may help
you figure out where you got stranded.

Land status: Texas Parks and Wildlife Department state park.

Maps: Ask the rangers at the entrance or check the DORBA website.

Finding the trail: The park entrance is located a couple of miles south of I-20
and a couple of miles north of US 67, on the west side of FM 1382 in Cedar
Hill, Texas. From the entrance building, go to the four-way stop sign and turn
left. Follow the park road until it ends, and turn left at the stop sign. There's a circular drive near the rest rooms and a picnic area with lots of parking. At the
southern end of the circular parking lot is the trailhead kiosk. From there, hook
a left onto the trail and proceed clockwise. If you turn left at both of the forks,
you will ride the full 10 miles of the "main" loop. Turning right at the first fork
(less than a mile from the start) takes you to the "short" loop (about 2 miles back
to the start). Turning right at the second fork (way out there on the trail, several
miles) lets you skip the "expert" loop. If you take the expert loop, you will eventually find the southern end of the park and be forced to turn north on the old
dirt road and proceed up to the spot where the "main" loop crosses the road.

Turn left there, into the trees, and follow the trail until you see another fork. A left returns you to the start. You will come from the right while riding the "short" loop.

Sources of additional information:

Dallas Off-Road Bicycle Association (DORBA)
2911 Esters Road
PMB 1414
Irving, Texas 75062
www.dorba.org

Cedar Hill State Park
Box 941
Cedar Hill, TX 75104
(972) 291-3900
www.tpwd.state.tx.us/park/cedarhil/
cedarhil.htm

Texas Parks and Wildlife Department
4200 Smith School Road
Austin, TX 78744-3291

(800) 792-1112 information
(512) 389-8900 reservations
www.tpwd.state.tx.us

Bicycle Tech
179 S. Watson Road #410
Arlington, TX 76010
(817) 633-4799

Richardson Bike Mart
1451 West Campbell Road
Richardson, TX 75080
(972) 231-3993
or
9040 Garland Road
Dallas, TX 75218
(214) 321-0705

Notes on the trail: I helped cut a lot of the trail you will ride around this place, so it's particularly dear to me. There's a particular bridge with a sign—I can tell you the story sometime. When you hit Flusche Crossing, please say hello to Greg—he's around there somewhere, sort of. Greg will help you get up the next hill, if you're nice to him. He's always helped me.

RIDE 19 · Rowlett Creek Nature Preserve Trails —Garland

AT A GLANCE

Length/configuration: About 10 miles of mostly tight single-track. There are about 10 different loops that connect into one big one; ride clockwise.

Aerobic difficulty: A lot of the trail here is flat and fast and pretty easy. The sections along the creek are another matter entirely, packed with assaults on the feeder creeks that are short but steep and very tough in places. You'll be breathing hard, often enough.

Technical difficulty: Again, a lot of this is flat and fast and very easy— anyone could ride it on a single-speed. It's the sections over by Rowlett Creek that you should fear. Tree roots and loose conditions, with sudden elevation and direction changes and camber. Especially nasty when you're

RIDE 19 • Rowlett Creek Nature Preserve Trails

To
190

N

0   ½   1

MILES

Rowlett Creek

N.E. Pkwy.

powerline

Castle Rd.

P

Centerville Rd.

66

Old Rd.

Water
Treatment
Plant

Miller Rd.

Rowlett
Creek

basically hanging onto the bank of the creek. It is expert-level in a few spots. This ride is pretty darned tricky in many, many places.

Scenery: The woods here are really nice, gorgeous in spring or fall, and the areas along the creek are pretty.

Special comments: My buddy Earl Hammond is the man. That guy started building this series of trails right before I finished the last book, so we didn't get it in. This is a great place, where anybody can have fun. Stick to the flats if you can't handle the tough parts, or hammer loops along the creek if you're up to a bunch of challenges.

Oh man, this place is sweet. It's a series of single-track loops right in the middle of a major Metromess suburb. It has something to offer riders of all skill and endurance levels. There's enough easy stuff to ride that you never have to venture over into the technical trails. It also has enough technical trails that you never have to go over to the easy stuff if you don't want to.

You start out on Loop #1 right by the parking lot. The trail here has some tree roots but is mostly fast and flat. Then you get to the fork for Loop #7. This trail wanders under Castle Road and along a creek, right under a big residential neighborhood. There are some pretty tricky places through here—this is no beginner trail. After a loop on #7 you'll cross under the road again and head back into the trees. Hang a left at the fork for Loop #8, cross the creek, and follow the trail north until you cross under Northeast Parkway. There are a few sneaky places on #8, but it's not that bad. Loops #9 and #10 are out across the flood plain and are flat and smooth. At the far north end of #10 you cut under the power lines to the east and into the trees. The trail gets very tricky through here; you're hitting quick drops into the creek and climbs back up the other side and having to negotiate tree roots and tight conditions, all along Rowlett Creek. Be careful and don't miss any of the turns, or you'll end up at the bottom of the creek. Pretty soon you'll go under Northeast Parkway again and back toward the west of the power lines.

At this point, you'll ride the back sides of the earlier loops until you pass within sight of the parking lot. Keep heading steadily south and you will again go under the power lines and into the woods on Loop #3. More tight technical bits, some more ups and downs, deadfalls, and poison ivy. The trails down here can get soft and loose sometimes, and the weeds high. Keep going and you'll cross under TX 66 and, soon after that, a very low railroad trestle. Keep riding along the creek until you find yourself heading west, just before Miller Road. You will ride by the water treatment plant and be in and out of the trees for a while. Then the railroad again, more in and out, and then you'll hit an old road. Hang a right, and right before the power lines the trail will go north and back into the trees. Before you know it, you're back at the car. From the southern end, these are Loops #6, #5,#4, and #2. This stuff was named as it was constructed, as I recall, and obviously not in the order you'll ride them.

General location: Eastern Garland, Texas.

Elevation change: There's about 50 feet of elevation delta if you ride this whole thing, but most of it is fairly flat.

Season: Any time it hasn't rained in a while. It gets real slimy in the rainy season, and you can just forget it at that time. Check the DORBA forum for current conditions.

Services: Picnic facilities, portable toilets, and drinking water. Anything else you need is probably available around the corner down on TX 66 somewhere.

Hazards: Poison ivy. Poison ivy. And more poison ivy. Maybe the occasional water moccasin. The real dangers here are crash related. There are several places along the creek where you might make a blind climb or turn and find that an immediate course correction is required to avoid riding off into the creek. It has happened before. Be very careful in the technical sections.

Rescue index: Medium to high. There are a lot of people who ride here, and you're in the middle of town. Bring your cell phone and a map and somebody will come along eventually. Plus, you're never really that far from the car, a mile or two tops. If you can get out of the trees and find the open stretch along the power lines, you can easily get back to the car if you're lost.

Land status: City of Garland park.

Maps: Check the DORBA website, they have a good one.

Finding the trail: 2525 Castle Road, just north of TX 66 on Centerville Road in eastern Garland. The trailhead parking area is on the east side of Castle Road, plainly marked from the street with a big sign. Pull into the lot and you'll see the beginning of Loop #1, marked with a kiosk. The trail is not marked really well in places, and if you don't know your way around you should carry a map. There are presently 10 different loops here, and it's easy to get confused about which is which. If you ride the whole thing, you will bounce back into the lot from the south.

Sources of additional information:

City of Garland Parks and Recreation
  Department
P.O. Box 469002
Garland, TX 75046-9002
(972) 205-2000
www.ci.garland.tx.us/PARKS/
  cogmain.htm

Dallas Off-Road Bicycle Association
  (DORBA)
2911 Esters Road
PMB 1414
Irving, Texas 75062
www.dorba.org

Notes on the trail: An excellent place for a night ride, once you know and understand the lay of the land. But it's a place to forget about when it's wet— you'll have to drag your bike out because it won't be rideable. Hearty thanks to all the volunteers who have put so much hard work into making this one of the best trails in the DORBA arsenal.

RIDE 20 · Sister Grove Park Trail—Lake Lavon

AT A GLANCE

Length/configuration: Two connected clockwise loops of single-track, about 6 miles total. Some of it is open, and some of it is tight in the trees.

Aerobic difficulty: This trail always seems harder than it really is. There's some gradual climbing, nothing really tough, but you always feel the ride here for a day or two.

Technical difficulty: There are some tree roots and a lot of loose

RIDE 20 • Sister Grove Park Trail

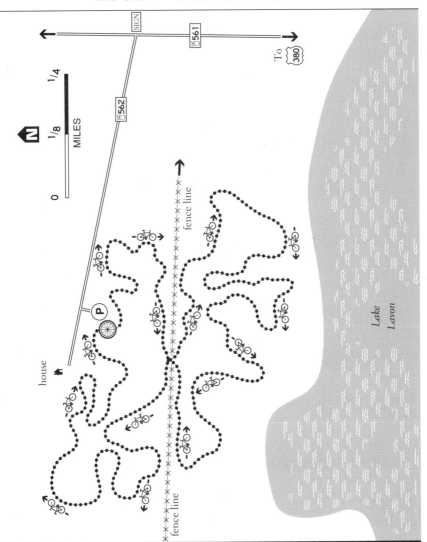

conditions, but this is a 95/95 trail. Nothing is really hard, so this is often called a beginner trail.

Scenery: You can see Lake Lavon from a couple of places, and I really like the prairies of Texas in the winter and spring. The grasses just take on a glow in the setting sun. Since a lot of this trail is exposed, you'll get to see some nice stuff.

Special comments: I am very fond of this place; I've been riding here since it opened. It is not a good ride when it's muddy or in dead summer

My pal David Lingle burning down the Grove. He moved away a few years ago. We miss ya Dave.

when it's crumbly and full of gigantic cracks in the clay. I still love it—it's quiet and far from the river of noise.

I have ridden and hiked here many times; this is a nice quiet trail tucked away on the north side of Lake Lavon. It may get a little noisier during duck season, though, since hunters have access rights both along the shore and on the main trail to get to the shore hunting areas. That's OK—this trail is often so wet during duck season that it's not rideable anyway.

This trail always seems a little harder than it actually is because the surface is often so rough and bumpy that it's hard to get any really fast clean lines through many sections. Otherwise, I would generally call this a suitable beginner trail, fine for just about anyone with a mountain bike. The climbing is very gradual, for the most part, and the only really hard sections would look pretty mild on just about any other area trail.

The first part of the trail carries you across the prairie and down into some tight sections of single-track in the trees. You'll pop back out and find the cutoff for the lakeside sections, which brings you to more prairie. The trail is well marked and certain sections bear signs telling the names of those areas. You'll ramble along until you've returned to the main trail, and after that you'll have pretty much left the lake behind. You'll hit some very tight single-track down around the ponds and along the creek, and then you ease back up toward the highest point, the parking lot.

General location: On the northwestern finger of Lake Lavon, about an hour from Dallas.

Elevation change: You'll probably range around 50 to 60 feet of delta as you make the loops, and you repeat much of that several times.

Season: Open 5 a.m. to 8 p.m. daily. This place can be ridden any time except after substantial rain (the surface turns to goo). On dry winter days the prairie can be quite stunning, especially around sunrise and sunset.

Services: Nothing except a chemical toilet. Load up on the way. You pass through McKinney and Princeton on the way, and each has numerous places to get stuff.

Hazards: You should bring a patch kit and pump—there are lots of things here to give you a flat. The surface is often broken and loose, sometimes even powdery, and in the summer the clay shrinks to develop large cracks as big as a bike wheel. I reckon there's a fair amount of poison ivy around, and perhaps a snake or two. This trail is one-way, clockwise, but you might find a rider or two out there who don't know this.

Rescue index: Medium. You are probably beyond any consistent cell phone connection, and not a lot of people ride here. The redeeming factor is that you're never more than a mile or so from the parking area, but it is several miles from any sort of aid or assistance. This is a fairly remote spot, for this region.

Land status: Collin County park, not likely to ever be developed unless the county gets in a bad way for money and has to let it go some day. I saw an interesting website supporting the park that you might want to check out; see below.

Maps: Check the DORBA website.

Finding the trail: From US 75 in McKinney, exit onto US 380 eastbound and follow US 380 for about 14 miles until you're on the bridge across Lake Lavon, where CR 559 connects. Turn left and follow CR 559 north as it winds for a mile or so, and then turn left onto CR 561, at the sign for Sister Grove Park. Go west a short ways until you see the next Sister Grove Park sign and turn left (south) into the parking area. The trail starts on the west side of the parking lot, by the gate and sign.

Sources of additional information:

Dallas Off-Road Bicycle Association
  (DORBA)
2911 Esters Road
PMB 1414
Irving, Texas 75062
www.dorba.org

Collin Country Open Spaces
  Commission
Sister Grove Park
County Road 561 at
  County Road 562
Lavon, TX 75070
(972)424-1460 ext. 4141

Citizen's group "Save Sister Grove"
www.pro-web.net/templates/save_
  sister/home.html#

Bicycle Tech
179 S. Watson Road #410
Arlington, TX 76010
(817) 633-4799

Richardson Bike Mart
1451 West Campbell Road
Richardson, TX 75080
(972) 231-3993
or
9040 Garland Road
Dallas, TX 75218
(214) 321-0705

A.J. Barnes Bicycle Emporium
4900 Eldorado Parkway
McKinney, TX 75070
(972) 547-6767

Notes on the trail: Go left (south) and follow the trail as it arcs back around and into the trees to the east of the parking lot. You will wind up and down and around for little over a mile, and then you'll find the split and a sign pointing you to the left onto the lakeside sections. This will loop around for a couple of miles and bring you back to this same location. Take a left out of the lakeside section and you will enter the creekside sections. Follow the single-track as it winds around in the trees and gradually carries you back up to the parking area, a total ride of nearly six miles.

The folks in DORBA have poured a ton of sweat and tears into this facility. It is fairly remote and we are always anxious to find people in the area who might be inclined to pitch in and help with trail maintenance. Trail workdays are listed on the DORBA home page as they are scheduled, so check it out. While you are in the McKinney area, you might want to check out the Heard Museum or the other mountain bike trail, Erwin Park.

RIDE 21 · Erwin Park Trail—McKinney

AT A GLANCE

Length/configuration: An 8-mile clockwise loop of single-track.

Aerobic difficulty: Not real radical; some output is required, but it's mostly a moderate trail.

Technical difficulty: Some tricky bits are found out here. The tree roots and tight conditions make it a technical trail. If you're scared, get off and walk, and live to ride another day. Otherwise you are free to push the envelope.

Scenery: Not why we are here. Let's watch our front tires and where they're going.

Special comments: Another fabulous facility brought to you by the local mountain bike club, DORBA. Another new place, since the last edition of this guidebook anyway. My home club has put a ton of work into making this a trail to be savored, a trail to enjoy and have fun with for many years to come. It is a place most people can enjoy, use to hone their skills, and just groove on wasting time in the woods.

This was going to be our Olympics trail, but we lost out on our bid for 2012. Probably just as well—I wouldn't want all those people out there walking around and throwing PowerBar wrappers and Bud cans on the ground. Oh wait, we already have that. I see more wrappers and flat tubes and crap here than anywhere, I think. Even worse than Cedar Hill. What are you morons thinking?

But I'm descending into pessimism by going there. This is a sweet collection of sneaky single-track, and it's one I love. This is a good place to do laps for con-

RIDE 21 • Erwin Park Trail

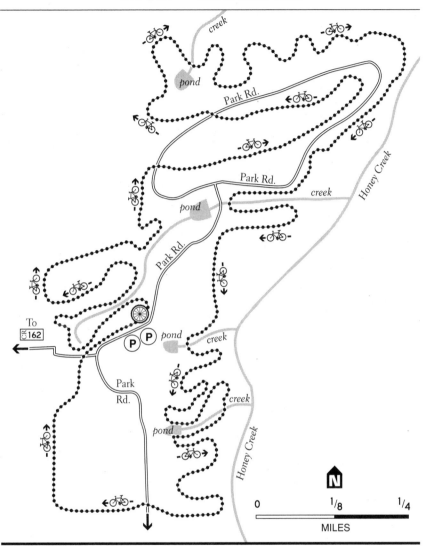

ditioning, both mental and physiological. It's not so hard or so far that you can't have fun for several hours, but never push yourself over the edge. It's tight, and it's tricky, and it was designed by evil people who want you to learn how to ride your bike. Imagine that. If you can master the stuff here then you can call yourself my brother. And you can ride any trail in this book.

The trail here is something nearly anyone can find the legs for. A lot of it is out across the prairie, fairly flat and in the blistering sun during summer afternoons. Then you get the trees, and the skeeters. The drops and climbs have

My pal Marty, again, at Erwin this time. The temperature is about a hundred degrees at this point, a nice summer afternoon in north Texas, and we are having so much fun we can hardly stand ourselves.

quick steep approaches, and maybe an odd tree root or rock garden, but they're short. If you have to walk a few, then hope maybe nobody's looking, eh? I've been there, here. Many sections almost seem aimed at convincing foolish riders they have it going on; then "lagniappe" takes over. That little something extra that makes the whole experience a new and worthy one, rich in adrenaline. A tree root that's polished like glass, a quick gear-and-weight shift that you have to know is there, and sometimes a blind drop into the unknown. Pretty darned cool, if I do say so myself. And I didn't build any of this one. I was on mountain biking sabbatical when it happened, nowhere near the crime scene, Officer.

Learn this place before you think you're some cross-country champ. We like to play tricks on yer head at DORBA. We hide things, and we make 'em clever. That's the fun part of building trails with people who know how. If you have the stones, you might join us sometimes. This trail takes a fair amount of mainte-nance, and there's always another bridge to be built, a bridge into the center of your mind, perhaps. Come on out sometime, check the Internet for current workdays and races and conditions and all that. My bud Paul Sollenberger is the main mountain bike man around here, and the Sollo Crew has done mighty well with this trail and made me proud.

Let's ride. I'd love to take a picture of you with my pal Mr. de Zaster some time. He has such nice knees. But leave him alone, he has enough knees, just taken off my pals and me lately. He don't necessarily need no new knees from you.

General location: A few miles northwest of McKinney, Texas.

Elevation change: Moderate, not over 100 feet from anywhere to anywhere, and it's pretty gradual for the most part.

Season: Year-round if dry. Please do not try to ride this in the mud—you aren't doing any of us a favor if you trash this place. I have helped fix a place or two that idiots trashed. I definitely do not support that sort of adolescent behavior.

Services: There are potties and water available in the summer, but I'd bring everything I need, if you were me.

Hazards: Poison ivy, possible snake activity, flat tires. The usual for this area of the Lone Star state. The trail can get loose, and there are plenty of techie bits around to offer knee-on-dirt interface opportunities. People have been carried out of here in choppers before, so be careful.

Rescue index: Medium to high. This trail sees a lot of riders, and you're fairly close to help, since McKinney is only a few miles away. Your cell phone will probably not waste space on this trip.

Land status: McKinney city park.

Maps: The DORBA website has a good one—I recommend it.

Finding the trail: From US 75 North in McKinney, take Exit 41 for US 380 and go west toward Denton for a couple of miles. Just past the airport turn right (north) on CR 1461 and drive about two miles until you see the signs for the park, at CR 162. Turn right. Almost immediately you will turn right again at the stop sign, go east for about a mile, and then turn left (north). Follow the signs and make a right turn (east) into the park. Follow the pavement to the T and then turn left. Parking for mountain bikers is immediately ahead, and the trail goes by just to the north on the east end of the parking area. The actual trailhead is northeast, up the pavement, but whatever. Either way, when you hit the single-track hang a right onto the trail and follow it until you're back to the car. And then again if you got the energy.

Sources of additional information:

McKinney Parks and Recreation
  Department
1550 South College Street
McKinney, TX 75069
(972) 547-7699
www.mckinneytx.com

Dallas Off-Road Bicycle Association
  (DORBA)
2911 Esters Road
PMB 1414
Irving, Texas 75062
www.dorba.org

Notes on the trail: Are we having fun yet? I've shown y'all some of our best. If you don't like Texas then that means you don't like Texans, and that ain't very healthy around here, Pilgrim. If you think this trail would have been a ridiculous site for the Olympics, then I agree. But for my personal pleasure and self-gratitude, it is right up there with the best.

RIDE 22 · Johnson Branch Trail
— Ray Roberts Lake State Park

AT A GLANCE

Length/configuration: A clockwise loop ride of about 7 miles, mostly single-track with some old jeep roads connecting to the parking area.

Aerobic difficulty: This trail is a pretty good workout. It is not a beginner trail because of some of the technical stuff, but it's not terribly hard either.

Technical difficulty: Plenty of tricky bits. There are rock gardens and lots of tree roots from one end of this trail to the other. This is no beginner trail — it could probably be called an intermediate difficulty route.

Scenery: Not really much to look at except the woods. I'd watch my line if I were you, and not let the old brain go to sleep.

Special comments: State Park entrance fee of $5 required, unless you have a Conservation Passport.

The trails on Ray Bob started out kind of weak. The state drove a bulldozer through the trees at Isle du Bois Park and called it a mountain bike trail. Then they built the Greenbelt Corridor trails between Ray Roberts Lake and Lake Lewisville. I've still not ridden down there. I'm sure it's nice; those trails run along the Trinity River's Elm Fork Branch. Then the state let the mad dog mountain bikers loose, and we put in some of the best single-track in north Texas. This trail is far enough from the city that it's not real well known, and you may not see another soul while you're riding here. I just love stuff like that.

The whole area of the park where the mountain bike trails live is laced with old jeep trails and primitive campsites. The trail is not really well marked yet, but it is established well enough that a few simple directions will be all you need to have a nice afternoon blasting through the trees and over the rocks. I have ridden my Breezer here, but this is a trail well suited to some squish on at least the front of your bike. And if you like to shred, you will probably enjoy this place; it begs you to see what kind of speed you can lay down. Then it will smack you down, suck some skin off your knee, and drag that fancy bike across rocks with surfaces like large grit sandpaper (for the most part). Hello Mr. Scratched Bike, and hello to you too Mr. de Zaster. He knows where you live.

Most people can ride most of this thing — there might be some hike-and-bike involved for less gutsy riders or newbies, but that always puts things in perspective for me. I like walking. But I've been able to ride everything here, on at least the second try, anyway. The approaches to some of the short hills are very tricky, having been designed by evil mountain bikers to keep you from feeling too studly. The trees are tight, and there are some tough places with roots. Still, this is a very rideable trail and most people can have some fun with it.

RIDE 22 • Johnson Branch Trail

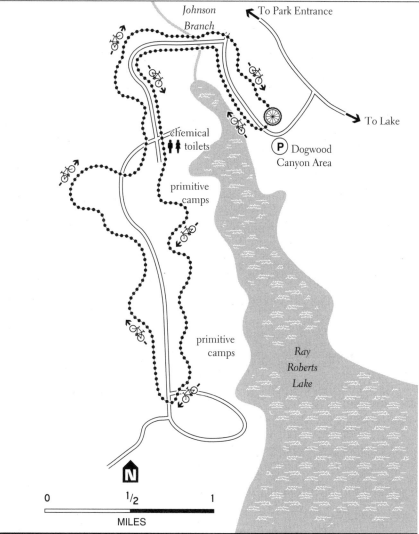

This is one of the few places locally that might be useable within a day or two of rain. It drains well and has enough sand in the soil that the next day there's often no evidence of a slight rain the night before. That doesn't mean you can go nuts out here if the trail is muddy. Don't be a dope—use your noodle and don't be destructive. And don't be disrespectful to any other trail users you might encounter, even if they forgot their bikes. And even if they're on horseback. You might see a few of those, so obey trail rules and don't act like a jerk.

General location: Northeast of Denton, Texas, half an hour or so. Right on the north shore of Ray Roberts Lake.

Elevation change: I'd say there may be 100 feet of delta on this trail; at least the potential is there. The lake is usually around 620 feet, and there are several pieces of property around here over 700 feet.

Season: Year-round, unless there's a race or something, or if the weather gods have been evil the previous week. You might want to call ahead and check conditions. Or hit the DORBA forum—you can usually get reliable trail reports there.

Services: This is a full-up state park. There are rest rooms (chemical) at the parking area and a pay phone at the ranger station, but you should probably bring in any specialized materials you might desire, like food or drink.

Hazards: This place looks like prime copperhead domain, if you want my opinion. I'd be real careful where you step when you stop. The surface can be loose and bordering on powder in places, and many of the turns are very tight or off-camber; ride like you mean it. With all the rock sticking out of the ground, your knees will suffer if you go down, even just barely down. Take your patch kit and tools—it'll be a long miserable walk back to the car if you break something or have a flat.

Rescue index: Low to medium. There are not a lot of people out here riding every day, and your cell phone might be useless in places. You are on state park property and the rangers will get you out if they know where you are. It's a good idea to have a buddy who can go get them—if you ride alone you might die alone.

Land status: Texas state park.

Maps: The DORBA website has a pretty good one, and the rangers are supposed to make some new ones very soon, so just ask 'em.

Finding the trail: From IH 35 north of Denton, take Exit 483, Lone Oak Road/FM 3002, and go east. Soon you will cross a bridge over part of the lake, and just a few miles beyond that you will see the signs for the park entrance on the south side of the road. Pay your fee, grab a map, and head into the park. Drive a short way and take the right turn for Dogwood Canyon. Park in the lot near the chemical toilets. Drinking water can be had from spigots in the area. Head off northwest, passing the chemical potty, and onto the old jeep road. This is where giving directions gets trickier. There are carsonite signs with bikes showing you where to turn left (west) onto the next road. Follow the jeep road back to the chemical toilet for the Dogwood Canyon primitive camping area. The single-track starts just south of the potty; look for the sign. Follow the single-track as it loops around and returns you to the area near the chemical potty again, and then jump on another lap if you want. DORBA is currently laying in more single-track to carry you back near the parking area, but for now you will probably be riding the roads back the way you came. The last right turn up to the parking area is easy to miss; it's not well marked at this time. Just there, at the turn, is where the new trail will come through and head up into the trees; in fact, some of it is already in place. Check it out.

Sources of additional information:

Ray Roberts Lake State Park
Johnson Branch Unit
100 PW 4153
Valley View, TX 76272-7411
(940) 637-2294
www.tpwd.state.tx.us/park/rayrob/
 rayrob.htm

Dallas Off-Road Bicycle Association
 (DORBA)
2911 Esters Road
PMB 1414

Irving, Texas 75062
www.dorba.org

Bluebonnet Bicycles
1204 North Stemmons Freeway
Lewisville, TX 75067
(972) 221-9322

Notes on the trail: This is a new trail. It is still under development, and by the time you read this there will probably be a few more miles of fine single-track. This is a well-designed series of obstacles, very durable, and a lot of fun. I am so proud to be connected with DORBA, and I just can't say enough good things about all the hardworking individuals who help build and maintain places like this. Thank you all a million times.

Ride 23 • "The Breaks" at Bar-H Ranch—Saint Jo

AT A GLANCE

Length/configuration: There are over 20 miles of well-marked trails open at the moment. Various loops of any kind of riding you can stand are possible, so consult trail maps or other riders for advice on which parts are hard and which are easy.

Aerobic difficulty: I would have to say that there are parts of the terrain here that are very difficult and others are just real hard. There are parts that are sort of medium, and some that are even beginner level. Truly something for everyone.

Technical difficulty: Everything from impossible to easy; it depends on where you wander. Most of the climbing is steep and loose, and there are sections that you just about have to walk. At least I do.

Scenery: Very, very nice. Up on the ridge you can sit on a bench and look out across the entire property—the view is quite handsome. You're practically on the Red River; it's only a few miles from here, this is sort of in the valley. These hills are probably the prettiest in north Texas.

Special comments: This is a private ranch; a fee of $6 per person is required. And it's well worth the price of admission, to be sure. This is

RIDE 23 • "The Breaks" at Bar-H Ranch

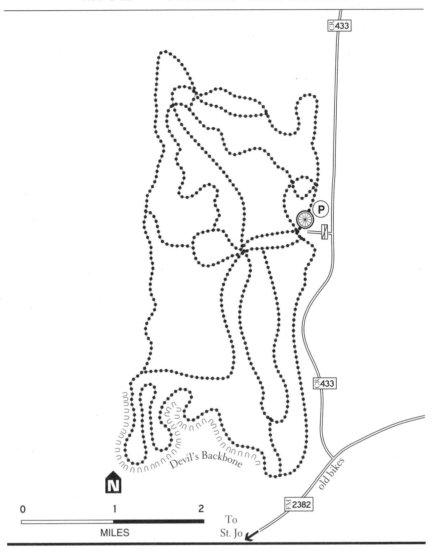

some of the best riding anywhere in Texas or Oklahoma, and the people who live here are strictly top shelf. Thanks, Uncle Billy and Tia. Y'all are swell.

Well, just go ahead and dig me a hole up on the 'bone, you can bury me right there when I go on to mountain bike heaven. This place is almost too good to be true. Many miles of superior trails, friendly people who love for us to go ride there, and just generally a great place to go on a riding escape for the day or the weekend.

My pal Geoffrey at the approach to the 'Bone. A lot of steep and loose Bar-H Ranch terrain is just past this sign. It deserves the moniker.

Some pals took me up here one hot summer morning and made me sweat about a bucket. If you're smart, you will hit the steeper stuff first and then wander down into the valley and ramble around the pastures and creek. The terrain up on the ridge is mostly chopped up limestone strewn up and down on some fast, off-camber, scary single-track that will never seem the same two times around. The climbs are tough, and the downhills are enough to make you think you will probably die here. You will find the areas down in the valley are often sandy, or even muddy, down in the creek. There's a ton of great single-track all over down there. And then there's the Devil's Backbone. An honest thousand feet of climbing in about four miles. This is where they should have the Olympics, someday. This is a place those pro riders won't be able to laugh at.

I can't even begin to tell you about every piece of trail here; some of it I haven't seen yet, some of it the builders haven't seen yet. By the way, a lot of trail here was apparently built by some professional mountain bike trail builders. They are called Arrowhead Trails, Inc. I've never met any of them but they do good trail. This place is growing, they want another twenty miles of trail some day. My club has races here a lot, and a lot of the Okies will even drive down to ride here. It is massive and everybody loves it.

Check out their website; they have full maps and descriptions of each area with honest difficulty ratings to help you decide what you have the gonads to try. Remember this, though—this place is not indestructible, you can't just go play like you're from British Columbia or something. Don't go laying down any more skid than you have to, and don't ride if it's muddy. If you're inclined to jump off of things, go ahead, there's ample stuff to get air from around this ranch. But don't get hurt, and don't be abusive to animals or the people who live here. If you drove two hours just to get sent home because it rained a toad-floater the night before and the trails are slush, don't be mad. That just means you're foolish for not calling ahead or checking the weather or whatever. I'm sorry, but this place is a treasure and I don't want to ever lose it.

General location: About an hour-and-a-half northwest of Dallas, Texas, near the tiny town of Saint Jo.

Elevation change: There are 300 no-BS feet from one extreme to the other on this property. You'll get as much of it as you can stand—the trails seem like they're half climbing and half more climbing, with a third half of nuts-in-your-throat downhills.

Season: Year-round if the weather's been nice. Just call and ask.

Services: They'll give you a drink of water and a place to put your tent, but this is the country, so bring just about anything else you might need.

Hazards: Don't be ashamed to get off and walk the scary parts, because they are legion. There's just about everything you can imagine in the technical realm, and the trail is pretty loose and marbled most days. Some of the tightest stuff is right on the side of the ridge, and a lot of it has camber. There are tree roots sprinkled throughout, and several demonic switchbacks and climbing turns. Tools and patch kits are definitely the order of the day, because at times you will be far from camp.

Rescue index: Medium to high. They're gonna know if you're out there and don't come back, plus this place gets quite a few riders. I don't know if a cell phone is any use here, but it's easy to get back to the area of the main house if you can get down to one of the dirt roads. Pack in a pal and you'll be fine.

Land status: Private property.

Maps: Great ones are available on the ranch's website; see below. Often they're stocked at the fee box as well.

Finding the trail: From Dallas, take IH 35 North to Gainesville, and then go west on US 82 to the town of Saint Jo (about 20 miles). Turn right (northeast) on FM 2382 (at the Dairy Queen) for about 4.5 miles until you think you've found it because you see bikes on the fence. Lots of bikes. Turn left (north) onto the dirt road (CR 433) and go about a mile north until you see the sign on the left. The sign with the 1942 bicycle, by the gate. Pretty cool, huh? Pay the nice people and get a map. From here you're on your own. There are trails in several directions; choose wisely based on your skills and experience level.

Sources of additional information:

The Breaks at Bar-H Mountain
Bike Ranch
943 CR-433
St. Jo, TX 76265
(940) 995-2309
www.barhbreaks.com

Dallas Off-Road Bicycle Association
(DORBA)
2911 Esters Road
PMB 1414
Irving, Texas 75062
www.dorba.org

Notes on the trail: I am honored by some of the people I meet along the way, and by the places I ride. While researching this book I saw a lot of trail and I met a lot of people. Probably the ones who amaze me the most are the private parties who have either taken it on themselves or made friends with others to put marvelous trail on their ranches and farms. These people love us. Like we love their trails. Let's honor them by obeying the rules and being good cycling citizens. It beats a poke in the eye with a sharp stick, and I know where I can get you one of those if you need it.

CENTRAL TEXAS

The beautiful heart of Texas. Most of what I describe here may also be called the Texas Hill Country. It's got the friendliest people and the prettiest swimming holes you've ever seen. And some of the best riding in the state.

A lot of the trails here have substantial elevation changes (delta) and technical situations galore. When Davy Crockett said, "Texas is the most beautiful place I ever saw," he was talking about central Texas. The only place to be. You can get the best Tex-Mex and BBQ anywhere right around the corner from many of these trails.

You can also experience some of the history of Texas, and of Texas mountain biking, right around the next corner. I'm going to take you to a bunch of places that drip with local flavor and substance. We will start in the north and sort of wander south, and hit the best of it. We'll miss a few, but that's what being involved does for you. It helps you find the places I didn't report on.

Get out there and ride your bikes—trails don't get much better than these. Have fun; eat, drink, and be merry; and ride like it matters. It matters for your survival. And your respect of these places matters for the survival of our sport.

RIDE 24 · Fossil Rim Wildlife Center—Glen Rose

AT A GLANCE

Length/configuration: You can ride 5 miles or you can ride 15, it all depends on which tour you go for.

Aerobic difficulty: Most of it is not that bad; they've got lots of beginner-level stuff, but there are also a few places that will kick your butt. There's this old dirt road up over a hill that I have only made once. I think you still get a Fossil Rim water bottle if you get all the way to the top without a dab. Hit it after a rain; that's the best advice I can give you.

Technical difficulty: As described above, most of it is 95/95, but there are

RIDE 24 • Fossil Rim Wildlife Center

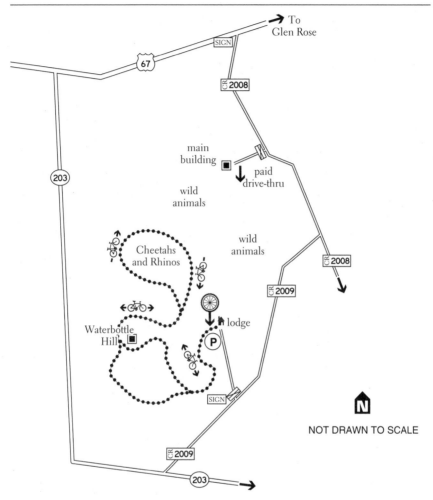

a few places to hold on tight and grunt. Lots of the trail here is loose, chipped limestone. Always good for a few laughs, or scabs.

Scenery: Fossil Rim is located in a nice little valley on the north end of the Texas Hill Country. Lots of live oak trees and prairie grasses.

Special comments: Guided tours, only, at $30 a head. Sure, this ride is expensive, but you should do it sometime in your life. It's a special experience like none other I have had. Wild animals (the kind with two legs and four), real-life behind-the-scenes dramatic conservation efforts, and a bunch of fine employees.

I had to dip into the archives for this one. The shot is from long ago, but the trails of Fossil Rim Wildlife Center are still there for you to have a flat tire on. That's Adam Eyres (left) and Steve Patterson (with a flatted Curtlo, as I recall). Steve was eaten by a rhino right after this was taken (just kidding).

I have ridden here in the dead of winter, and I have hit the trails here when it was so hot you could suck a PowerBar right out of the wrapper. I had fun both times. There isn't another place around quite like this exotic game preserve. Not because of its technical impact or scenic beauty—the trails here actually fall somewhere in the middle of the road for the Texas Hill Country. I just love it 'cause I know the people here, the guys who lead the rides, and you never know what you'll see. You get to do stuff here that none of the hoards in their minivans ever dream of.

There are over ten miles of single-track, rocky and somewhat technical, that you get to ride if you take a mountain bike tour. The guides will show you things the average tourist never gets a sniff of. All sorts of schmoozy behind-the-scenes stuff. You might see a pregnant rhino, or a baby cheetah. You might make it up the big hill and get a water bottle, or you might crash in the creek. You'll get to see where the wolves and jaguarundi are kept (they've got several endangered species here). This isn't quite like a zoo, unless you ride with me, but it is definitely Animal City. The opportunity to get up close and personal with at least two types of rhinoceros will come your way. They scare me, so I don't like to get real close. To make a long story short, this place is really special, and so are the people who work here, care for these animals, and lead the rides.

If you take the automobile tour you will freak. There are thousands of critters running free, everywhere. Ostriches, giraffes, monster deer. They just sort of roam around at will. You hunters won't believe your eyes. Some of these things have huge racks. They are docile enough when you're in your car with the windows up, but an addax or scimitar-horned oryx could give you a whole new respect for the continent of Africa, if you were goofy enough to try to bike the car tour. Man, those horns are wicked.

Take a ride on the wild side, by spending a morning or afternoon relaxing and learning about animals whose natural habitats are being consumed by ever-expanding humanity. The rhinos are some of the only ones Zimbabwe and Australia have exported to the world, released to be raised in captivity. Their brothers and sisters now live in places like this because they aren't safe from poachers in their home country. There's no place else like Fossil Rim. Well worth the price of admission.

General location: Near Glen Rose, Texas.

Elevation change: There's probably a total of 200+ feet of elevation delta that can be enjoyed, but the easier rides will take you around most of the severe terrain.

Season: Pretty much year-round; they close on some of the major holidays and stuff, but as long as it isn't raining like mad you can usually ride. Call ahead for conditions.

Services: They can feed you, or even put you up for the night if you like. They have nice cabins in the group area. You will be given some munchies and drinks for the ride, and a neato T-shirt. Phones, potties, a restaurant, a gift shop—they've got all that stuff here.

Hazards: I have seen poisonous snakes here. There's plenty of mesquite and cactus to puncture your tires (right by a big old copperhead, probably). The trails can be loose and tricky, so be careful. And don't forget all those wild animals with weapons growing out of their heads (you don't ride through that part—I'm only kidding).

Rescue index: High. You can only ride here as part of a guided tour, and the leaders are well equipped to get you out of a bind in case you have a boo-boo. This is one of the safest rides around.

Land status: Private wildlife refuge.

Maps: Not generally available; the rides are guided and you won't need one.

Finding the trail: From Glen Rose, go west on US 67 to County Road 2008 and turn left (south) until you see the signs for the park, not far, maybe a mile or so. Drive through the gate and park by the visitor center. Tell 'em you're there for the ride and some PowerBars.

Sources of additional information:

Fossil Rim Wildlife Center
P.O. Box 2189
Glen Rose, TX 76043
(254) 897-2960
www.fossilrim.com

Rhino Ridge Outfitters
P.O. Box 2027

Glen Rose, TX 76043
(254) 897-3866
www.rhinoridge.com

The Bike Rack
1352 East Highway 377
Granbury, TX 76048
(817) 573-5033

Notes on the trail: All of the mountain bike tours are customized and you may ride at any technical level you can handle. You will not be allowed to roam at will, since there are a higher than average number of ways to get hurt, maimed, eaten, or killed here. The guides are pals of mine, so treat 'em right; they're good people and they really love these animals. Make sure they show you all the cool stuff—the rhino barns and the goat cave—see everything! Thirty bucks is a lot of money to ride your bike, I know, but you'll be exchanging your money for something so much cooler: experiences.

My friends will not let you leave unsatisfied. Ride and then go do the auto tour and feed the goofy ostriches. I warn you, they will stick their heads in your window. And they want to be fed, so don't argue with 'em.

RIDE 25 · Cedar Brake Trail— Dinousaur Valley State Park

AT A GLANCE

Length/configuration: Various looping single-tracks and old roads, pretty much ridden any direction as far as I can tell, totaling about 10 miles.

Aerobic difficulty: There's some decent climbing here but nothing extreme—I'd say this trail rates medium for aerobicness.

Technical difficulty: Another medium rating. This is pretty much a moderate trail—most of us can ride most of it. There are some loose conditions, usually, and some ledges and tricky bits, but this isn't a real hard trail.

Scenery: The area around the river is quite nice, and I personally like these woods, but this is no Old Ore Road. But they do have dinosaur tracks. Top that, Colorado.

Special comments: Generally an accessible and enjoyable series of trails; usually the weather is not as hard on this place as it can be elsewhere. Call the rangers and check with them if it's been wet because you cannot get across the river to the trails if it's up too high. Don't come up here and ride like a moron—I've seen way too many 25-foot-long skid marks around this place. This is another Texas Parks and Wildlife Department state park that extracts the typical $3 to $5 entrance fee.

This a place that you really oughtta go check out sometime. It's pretty typical Texas Hill Country—broken limestone and rolling hills—but this is the only place I know about with real dinosaur tracks. Right over there, close to where you get on the trails. Be sure and ask the rangers for all the great maps they've got that

RIDE 25 • Cedar Brake Trail

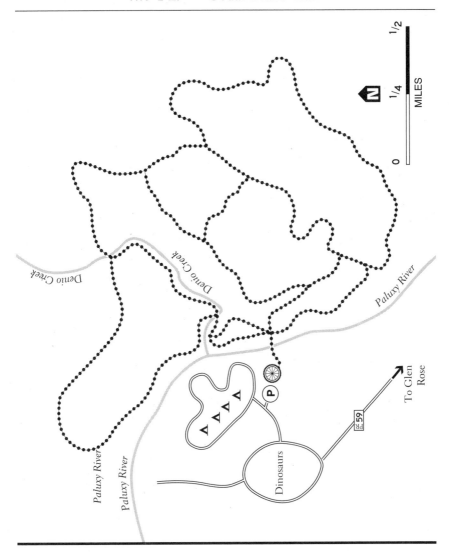

show you where the cool stuff is, and go take a photo or two by the "real" dinosaurs.

You can take the family out here and camp and take the kids for a ride, then take your pals for a ride, then eat some burgers, and then ride some more. All the trails are in a reasonable proximity to the main camping area, right across the river. Be sure and take a map, although you'll probably get lost anyway. It's easy to get turned around here because of the maze of various loops that wind around the hills. With all the trees it's hard to see any familiar landmarks, but you will occasionally find a spot with a nice overlook.

The Paluxy River bisects the park, separating the main area from the land where the trails hang out. Some of the riding here is really easy, but some of it is more advanced. The areas south of Denio Creek are broken limestone and have some elevation delta, primarily in the trees. You can basically just wind around, hitting all the loops, and then if you've had enough you can easily return to the trailhead. Or you can cross Denio Creek and find some other nice climbs on the trail that loops to the north and then brings you back to the creek. A lot of this is right along the fence that is the border of the park, and it's out in the open.

You could get a flat here; there's plenty of cactus. You could also leave a knee (or two) on one of the turns. Plenty of marbles and babyheads to get the old tires to drifting. A lot of riders get lost here, but the trails are fairly well marked. If you carry a map, you'll be able to find your way around just fine. Still, be alert; there are several interconnected loops, and I've seen more than one rider walking down Denio Creek looking for the trailhead. The creek itself offers some pretty interesting riding, and the areas adjacent to it are laced with mucho single-tracko.

The whole area here around Glen Rose is one of the nicest places to do a lazy road trip. It's only an hour or so from Fort Worth, and there are a bunch of cool places to check out in the general area. You can tube or canoe on the Brazos River, eat some mondo BBQ, or take in a bunch of wild animals over at Fossil Rim Wildlife Center.

General location: About an hour southwest of Fort Worth, Texas, near the town of Glen Rose.

Elevation change: The Paluxy River appears to be around 650 feet, and the highest point along the trail is about 850 feet, so you've got a pretty easy 200 feet of delta to ride.

Season: Any time the Paluxy River is not too high to cross. If, however, you decide to ride here when it is raining or has rained, you might find misery. The limestone will be so slick it'll make you think you've died and gone to Hell. And you might find some mud...or yer ol' bud Mr. Bustyerass de Zaster.

Services: The park has water and showers, basic vending machines, and a pay phone. The nearby town of Glen Rose has convenience stores and restaurants.

Hazards: The cactus here will easily take you out, so don't touch it or get any closer to it than necessary. This is kind of a silly thing to say, because the trail winds through several places where prickly pear is all along the trail. I swear I can pick up needles by just looking at the little monsters. You can easily build more speed than you can handle in a few places along the way, so discovering Mr. de Zaster is quite easily done anywhere along these trails. This is his winter home.

Rescue index: Medium-high. You are not all that far from civilization, and there are probably riders on these trails any day the trail is open. I don't know if a cell phone will always work here, but it would be worthwhile as a fashion accessory. Know where you are by referencing the maps you have, and take a partner along just in case.

Land status: Texas Parks and Wildlife Department state park.

Maps: The park has some decent ones; they don't show the elevations but they show about 80% of the trails you might find.

Finding the trail: From I-35W, south of Fort Worth, go west on US 67 toward Cleburne and Glen Rose. Stay on US 67 and go west, past Glen Rose, to FM 205. Stay on this road for about four miles until you see the signs for the park and PR 59. Go north about a mile to the entrance to the park. Pay the nice rangers the entrance fee, and turn right at the first road in the park, over by the Tyrannosaurus Rex and the Brontosaurus. Turn right into the first parking area you see, over by the portable toilet and trash dumpster. This is the trailhead. Grab the bike and your stuff and head off east on the single-track you'll see right there. Follow this down to the river and cross where you can. The trails start just south of where Denio Creek runs into the river. From here follow the map.

Sources of additional information:

Dinosaur Valley State Park
P.O. Box 396
Glen Rose TX 76043
(254) 897-4588
www.tpwd.state.tx.us/park/dinosaur/
    dinosaur.htm

Texas Parks and Wildlife Department
4200 Smith School Road
Austin, TX 78744-3291

(800) 792-1112 information
(512) 389-8900 reservations
www.tpwd.state.tx.us

The Bike Rack
1352 East Highway 377
Granbury, TX 76048
(817) 573-5033

Notes on the trail: The area south and east of Denio Creek is a web of interconnected loops that will wind you around and take you north, to the park boundary. Follow the trail northwest from there and you will find Denio Creek. You can either hang a left and go along the creek until you find the river again, or you can cross over and follow the single-track loop that leads west and around to north of the main bend in the river. This very same single-track will then wind around and return you to Denio Creek. When you cross the creek from the end of this loop you will once again be near the river and where you started. Ride some more, or cross over and return to the car on single-track and find somewhere to get a cold drink.

This is not a bad place to pack in your compass and map, especially if you don't know the area well and it's a cloudy day. This place is a favorite of a lot of north Texas mountain bikers; if you go ride it, you'll see why. And the dinosaurs are pretty darn scary. I'd say that that alone ought to be enough of a recommendation to get you out here. Have fun—come and enjoy the Texas Hill Country.

RIDE 26 · The Seven Mile Loop—Cleburne State Park

AT A GLANCE

Length/configuration: Guesses, anyone? A 7-mile loop of single-track. Counterclockwise would be the choice for direction.

Aerobic difficulty: Damn hard in spots. There are a lot of grueling climbs, none real long, but each is loose and steep and pretty tough.

Technical difficulty: There are plenty of tricky technical challenges along this trail. Loose limestone, steep climbs—it's a lot harder than it looks on paper.

Scenery: You have a pretty nice view of the lake area as you take to the hills on the east side, but this place is more about riding and paying attention to the trail than about sightseeing.

Special comments: Pretty fair trail in most weather. There are some spots that might get soft, but the limestone normally drains sufficiently well to be rideable a day or two after a rain. Another state park; they all have a $3–$5 entrance fee, per head.

Somebody told me about this place recently. I had been to the park before but had no idea they've got such a monster mountain bike trail. This is probably some of the hardest riding for a hundred miles or so. Challenging, but with a nice limestone and cedar scent.

This is sort of an out-of-the-way park; the locals around Cleburne and the mountain bikers of north Texas are about the only people who ever come here. Maybe the occasional bird watcher or hiker, but this is normally a nice quiet place. There's a small lake, shady picnic areas, and a lot of campsites. The Civilian Conservation Corps constructed the dam for the lake and several of the park facilities shortly after the land was turned over to the state of Texas in 1934. This is one of the oldest Texas State Parks.

The first section of the trail winds around in the trees as it approaches the creek below the lake spillway. I noticed several reflective trail markers on the trees in this area; it might be a nice ride after dark. Soon you'll reach the fork where the markers carry you left and onto the shorter loop, if you want. You and I are going right, across the creek and into the trees. Almost immediately, the climbing begins to the left. You spend the next several miles going up and down the hills, following a buried cable cut for a ways, and then through the trees and onto some of the more expert-level sections. There are a couple of scary downhills here, where you better have good brakes and confidence in your ability.

You essentially skirt the park boundaries as you ride this trail, with a few excursions into the woods. Now, I'm never into promoting abusing a trail, but a lot of people come here and ride when everything else in the area is too muddy. Most of this trail is hard surfaces, but still, there are some places that could be

RIDE 26 • The Seven Mile Loop

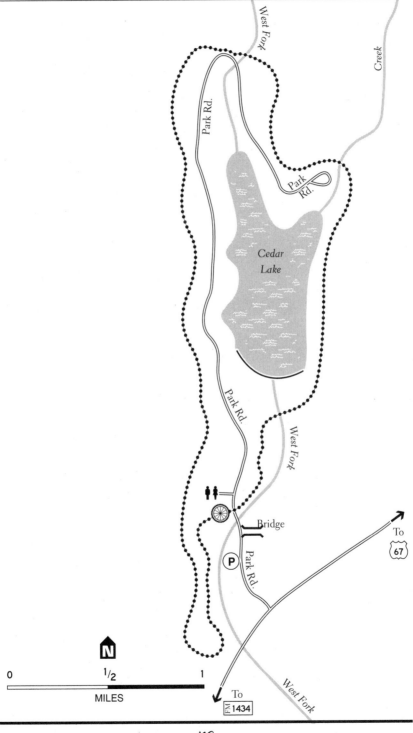

West Fork

Creek

Park Rd.

Park Rd.

Cedar Lake

West Fork

Park Rd.

Bridge

To 67

P

Park Rd

West Fork

N

0   1/2   1

MILES

To FM 1434

West Fork

OK, it looks easy here, but this is one tough ride. It is hilly and loose, and Cleburne State Park may be your only hope for a ride during the rainy season here in Texas.

muddy. If in doubt, please call the rangers and ask if the trail is open before you drive all the way out here. Still, this may be your only hope for riding in the winter, depending on where you live.

Most of the trail is near park roads or camping areas, but you'll only see these a few times due to the dense foliage. There aren't a lot of markings out in the woods, but the trail is so well established that you would have to try pretty hard to get lost—just follow the single-track. I found a couple of spots where side trails go a short ways into the woods, but you always have to turn around and retrace back to the main trail and make a directional decision there.

General location: About half an hour south of Fort Worth, Texas.

Elevation change: The extremes here are from around 700 feet on the southern parts of the trail, near the end, up to nearly 850 feet on the high places north of the lake. An honest 130 to 150 feet of cyclic delta.

Season: Just about year-round; call the rangers and ask in case bad weather might have the trails shut down.

Services: The park has the normal compliment of full camping facilities with showers. There is a pay phone and swimming area near the park store, but don't count on the store to be open every day. Load up with what you need before you head out.

Hazards: I'd reckon there's likely to be quite a bit of poison ivy in the area, and maybe a snake or two. Some of the trail is very tight in the trees and can be tricky.

The most dangerous aspects relate to the loose conditions and steep inclines. It's pretty easy to get up to 25 mph on one of the downhills here, until you crash and burn. Just be careful and you'll do fine.

Rescue index: Medium-high. You're never far from the road and help, but it might be worthwhile to carry your cell phone. Bring a trail map along, and a partner if possible, and a rescue could happen.

Land status: Texas Parks and Wildlife Department state park.

Maps: The park rangers have decent ones—just ask for them.

Finding the trail: Take US 67 west from Cleburne until you see the exit for PR-21. Take PR-21 south a few miles until you see the entrance for the park on the right (west) side of the highway. Enter the park, pay the fee, and proceed past the first picnic area you see and keep going until you come to a rest room on the left. The rest rooms here were closed when I was down, but you can park in the lot there. Between the rest room building and the bridge over the creek you'll see where the trail crosses the pavement. Go left onto the single-track and follow it until you reach the creek. The trail forks here—left takes you on the short loop, while going right (east, across the creek) leads you to the longer, outer loop. Follow the single-track until you reach the far north end of the park. There's a camping area here, and you're forced to go west on the pavement for a hundred yards or so and then cut back to the right and onto the single-track again. Follow the trail up and down the hills until you can go no farther south, and the trail will curve left (east) back into the trees and wind around some more until you pop out on the road, by the rest room, where you started.

Sources of additional information:

Cleburne State Park
5800 Park Road 21
Cleburne TX 76031
(817) 645-4215
www.tpwd.state.tx.us/park/cleburne/

Texas Parks and Wildlife Department
4200 Smith School Road
Austin, TX 78744-3291
(800) 792-1112 information

(512) 389-8900 reservations
www.tpwd.state.tx.us

Johnson County Bicycle Association
Southwest Golf & Sport
701 West Henderson
Cleburne, TX 76031
(817) 641-7858

Notes on the trail: This land was run by the Comanche Indians before the Civil War. They used to hide out around here while they were out doing raids on the settlers. Doesn't that sort of make you want to paint your face and tie some feathers on your bike when you ride here? Ummm, maybe that's not such a good idea after all—the rangers might get the wrong idea. Especially if you mentioned my name in the process.

RIDE 27 · Cameron Park Trails—Waco

AT A GLANCE

Length/configuration: A maze of interconnected single-track all along and around the bluffs above the confluence of the Brazos and Bosque Rivers. There is probably at least 10 miles of trails in here, each signed with some clever name.

Aerobic difficulty: Brutal in places, not so bad in others. Parts of this could be called 95/95, along the river, maybe, but the stuff up in the bluffs is hard and steep and has many long climbs.

Technical difficulty: As above, there are some easy sections—the trail along the river is a piece of cake. But when you head up into the woods you're entering a different world. A world of steep, loose single-track, tough climbing turns and switchbacks, and plenty of tight tricky bits.

Scenery: It is beautiful here; you have a nice quiet section along the river that is lined with trees, and then you have some spectacular views from up on the bluffs. The bulk of the ride, however, is hidden in the trees, and I'd be paying attention to the bike and not the birds if I were you.

Special comments: Years ago I met the city park guys who were responsible for this property. They promised to mark it and map it and make it a lot more user-friendly than it once was. And they've done a mighty fine job of making that happen. The trails here are well marked, each has a fun name, and there's a ton of fun stuff to ride. Thank you to all the volunteers who have helped with the trails here—y'all are some of the best.

I raced here in the rain once, long ago. It was evil and grueling, slow and slippery, and I had no fun. On the other hand, I've had some great times riding these trails with my friends, when the conditions were right. This is for sure one of the best trail systems in either state, and I am honored to see that the local volunteers have poured so much of their hearts and souls into sustaining these superb trails.

There was a time when I knew my way around here pretty well, but it has changed a lot. I always used to get lost anyway, except for the few times I found the trail marked for the races, but I have never stopped enjoying just wandering through the trees and challenging the terrain. And it is challenging. There are some climbs here that will take you to the edge of your oxygen intake and heart rate capabilities. If you rode this thing every day you would be in awesome condition, your skills would be top-shelf, and your legs would be ready to ride anything in Texas or Oklahoma.

I love it here—the woods are gorgeous and the trails are outrageously evil. Sneaky, clever, well thought out, expertly designed; there's everything you can

RIDE 27 · Cameron Park Trails

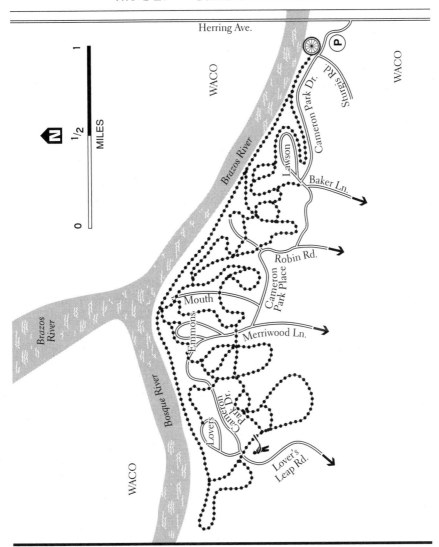

handle out in this park, and then some. If you ride along the bluff from the start, until you're way out on the western end (by the ball fields), and then work your way back, you'll see all the good stuff. Some winding around and testing your navigational skills will give you a good full day of riding. Bailouts on the pavement are always possible—just look at the map.

On the other hand, I often get to the trailhead and then catch a left on the first trail I see—I guess that's California 56 (a ferocious series of hard climbs). I can always use that easy ride back along the river as my return. I'm usually cooked at the end of a ride in this park, anyway. You can wander around, up and down the hills; find cool little places like Hale-Bopp, Lock-M-Ups, Act of Faith, or Lover's Leap, and get a belly full of mountain biking. All you can stand. Right here on one of the sweetest pieces of property known to mountain biking–kind, anywhere in the good old U.S. of A.

General location: Western Waco, Texas.

Elevation change: Substantial; a lot more than you would think from just driving through Waco on I-35. You have 150 feet of delta, easily.

Season: The park is open year-round, but please respect the trail and don't come out here when it's wet. Aside from the fact that a muddy tire on wet limestone is a recipe for disaster, you'll just be hurting the trails. I don't care much about your shins.

Services: Parking, potties, water. Bring anything else you will need.

Hazards: The terrain here is severe once you work your way into the heart of the woods. There are technical hazards galore, so please ride with extreme care. It wouldn't surprise me to see a copperhead around here sometime, so be careful and look around before stepping off your bike. I'm fairly sure this place is laced with poison ivy, too, by the way. This park has just about every hazard you can imagine, aside from being a remote location. Any paved roads you cross should be examined for oncoming traffic; they are all active.

Rescue index: Medium. You're in the middle of town, essentially, but it's easy to wander into sections of the park that may not get ridden every day. A cell phone would in no way be a waste of silicon here. Bring a buddy and a map, and you will probably get rescued.

Land status: City of Waco park.

Maps: The trailhead kiosk has a nice one posted, and you can download the same thing from the City of Waco website. It is one of the best trail maps I've ever seen—everything is marked. It's practically an inventory of the trail pieces.

Finding the trail: I can get you to the trailhead, but from there you're on your own. There is so much trail back in here that I'm not sure there is an easy way to turn it into a consistent loop unless you know your way around really well. From I-35 in Waco, go west on University Parks Drive, following signs for Cameron Park and the zoo. Continue west until you enter the park, and then you will go under the overpass for Herring Avenue. There on the left is a picnic pavilion, where I normally like to park (in the lot right in front). You may, however, choose to park under the bridge; there are lots of spaces to choose from. Start from here on your bike, and get on the trail headed west, between the road and the river. Shortly you will find the trailhead, marked with a kiosk showing you a map of the area trails. Ride whatever you think you can handle, and you'll eventually return to this spot and can then retrace your steps back to the parking areas.

Sources of additional information:

City of Waco
P.O. Box 2570
Waco, Texas 76702-2570
(254) 750-5638 general
(254) 750-8057/8647 park rangers
www.waco-texas.com/city_depts/
    parks/parks.htm

Waco Bicycle Club
P.O. Box 21441
Waco, TX 76702
www.wacobicycleclub.org

Bicycles Outback
4707 West Waco Drive
Waco, TX 76710
(254) 772-2453

Tailwind Cycling Center
1005 South University Parks Drive
Waco, TX 76706
(254) 751-1301

Notes on the trail: I have to gripe a little about skidding. This is a place you will lock your brakes occasionally, but there's no sport in doing it just for fun. It just chews the crap out of the trail surface and is unforgivable. As you ride here you will see places where some trail sections have been closed. This place almost got out of control at one point, when people were just riding anywhere they wanted. I strongly urge you to respect the wishes of the land managers—don't build new trails and don't cut the existing ones. If we behave, we will have this place to ride forever, and it's one of the best trails in the state.

RIDE 28 · Barton Creek Greenbelt—Austin

AT A GLANCE

Length/configuration: An out-and-back single-track trail, about 8 miles long, 16 miles round-trip.

Aerobic difficulty: This is hard to report in any unbiased sense. Most of the trails here are just about flat, but the horsepower output that's involved with crossing the creek and staying alive is pretty substantial. A lot of this trail is really easy; just blow along. If you're not tired when you get to the western end, then climb the Hill of Life. This is not considered a beginner trail mostly because of the techie bits.

Technical difficulty: A bitch. I don't even like riding some of this all that much. It is tough—a series of rock gardens and creek crossings that will scrape some part of you to bits. Or your bike. Or both of you. This is not a beginner trail.

Scenery: Beautiful. Probably the single most gorgeous part of a very scenic area, Austin. You cannot say you've seen it all until you've been here at least three times. The bluffs along the creek are enough to make you forget the urban sprawl just over the hill, and being up in the trees and along the pools creates a very special feeling.

RIDE 28 • Barton Creek Greenbelt

Special comments: A premier Texas mountain bike trail. Considering all the traffic this place has seen, it is in remarkable condition. But I have to get up on my soapbox; don't ride out here when it's wet, don't abuse the trail surface and the rights of the rest of us. As I did in the first edition of this book, I will warn you, we will not always be allowed to ride here. Someday the hikers will get us kicked off. And that will be because of the fools who ignore the rules. If it's been raining and you have to ride your mountain bike, go to Emma Long, if you've got the nerve. Don't ride Barton Creek when it's muddy.

This is the Big Dawg, the Granddaddy, the Numero Uno and A-Number One, of all Texas mountain bike rides. As far as I know—and I think history will bear me out on this—this is the original. An escape from the crushing throng of the city, a place to be quiet and swift in the trees, to sneak around, and forget about the world. A mighty fine place to do any or all of the above, and then some, in my humble opinion. If you've never been here, then you can't die yet; you've still got something to see, and this is it.

This is a hard ride in places, easy in some, impossible in others. I guarantee I will be walking a lot of this trail. It is several pieces of single-track on each side of Barton Creek, some easier than others, and you might find a place to scrape a shin or break a collarbone. Others have done both, I promise. In many places the trail is a series of large outcroppings of rock, harder than any shin. There's ledges, loose gravel, and some dirt when you think you deserve it. I always find myself wandering back and forth across the creek, trying to find something consistently rideable. Some of the trail is right against the bluffs, tall weeds and deadfalls the whole way. Some of it is fast and swoopy, and all of a sudden it will go off-camber on you. And Mr. de Zaster laughs because he likes to see nice boys and girls kiss the dirt. This is his summer home.

I have to warn you that there are all manner of trail users here. Mountain biking sharks that will run over your head if you fall in front of them, some joggers and rock climbers, and some more gentle types walking their dogs. Don't be disrespectful to any of them, please—we ride because of their good graces. Now don't get me wrong; you can ride here as hard as you can stand to, just don't run over anybody. There will be other people out there in the woods sharing this special place with you.

Ramble roughly southwest from Zilker, riding when you can and pushing when you have to, and the creek will eventually carry you under MoPac and TX 360. You will note the bridges for these as you pass, because they are fairly close to one another. Then you'll be in the western sections and headed more northwest. As far as I can tell, you're allowed to ride all of the trails here, but stay away from anything signed otherwise. Near the western terminus you can head north and climb the Hill of Life. That thing sucks—I just love it! You ride up an old jeep trail, loose with one ledge after another, until you have climbed this monster. Three hundred feet in about a quarter of a mile. If you feel a need to shred, then try shredding that thing, it will taunt you.

Extremely worthy woods. A sincere thank you to the Austin Ridge Riders for keeping this trail open to those of us who are not worthy. Keep up the good work, you trail monsters.

General location: Near Zilker Park, western Austin, Texas.

Elevation change: The trails are not bad, maybe 20 to 30 feet; it's the hill at the end of the first leg that's just incredible. Let's just call it the Hill of Life—300 feet of climb in a quarter of a mile. Laugh if you want, but I've got the maps that confirm this. You don't have to ride it, unless you've been bad. Most of this ride is fairly flat.

Season: Not in or after rain. Otherwise it's a year-round jewel of Texas mountain biking.

Services: You start from Zilker Park, dead in the middle of some of Austin's finest food. Tex-Mex, BBQ, or anything else you can imagine may be enjoyed right up there on Barton Springs Road. The park has potties and parking, but not much else.

Hazards: Rocky technical conditions are the biggest threat. There might be some poison ivy around. There is mesquite, for sure, so take along your patch kit and tools.

Rescue index: High. This trail has a ton of riders—it's an everyday thing for some lucky people. Your cell phone will work. Take along a map so you'll know where to tell the rescuers to find you.

Land status: City of Austin park.

Maps: Several good ones may be had from the Internet; check below.

Finding the trail: We will start from Zilker Park, just east of Mopac (TX 1), south of Barton Springs Road. Pull into one of the parking lots for Zilker Park. Get ready, and then ride south to the creek. You will find the pool there, and a bunch of park buildings; turn right and head west to the end of the parking lot. At the end of the park developments the trail will begin, plainly marked with signs. Right now (2002) it's all torn up with construction, so I don't know what the final trailhead will end up looking like. Ride past the construction, southwest and then northwest, until you've had enough, and then ride back. Simple. Yeah, right. Just try to stay upright and unhurt.

Sources of additional information:

Austin Parks and Recreation
  Department
P.O. Box 1088
Austin, TX 78701
(512) 974-6700
www.ci.austin.tx.us/parks/parks.htm

Austin Ridge Riders
P.O. Box 300014
Austin, TX 78703-0014
www.io.com/austinridgeriders

Bicycle Sport Shop
1426 Toomey Road

Austin, TX 78704
(512) 477-3472
or
10947 Research Boulevard
Austin, TX 78759
(512) 345-7460

Barton Creek Greenbelt maps from
the web:
www.texasoutside.com/bartongreen
  belt.htm
www.runtex.com/images/barton
  creek.pdf

Notes on the trail: This is one of the finest rides to be found anywhere in urban America. It will work you, and if you're smart you will plan on a recovery period afterwards at one of the fine culinary establishments to be found nearby. One of the best bike shops in town is also right over there, behind all the restaurants. Tell my pal, Hill Abell, that I said "hey," and spend some money there. Is that a great name for a cyclist, or what?

RIDE 29 · Emma Long Motorcycle Park—Austin

AT A GLANCE

Length/configuration: A 6-mile loop of treacherous single-track; ride it counterclockwise (unless otherwise advised).

Aerobic difficulty: Major. This is no beginner trail—there are a ton of tough climbs and difficult conditions. This place is a miseryfest.

Technical difficulty: About as hard as it gets in Texas. The trails here are loose and steep, the approaches and braking zones are short, and the terrain is very sudden. There are ledges that a motorcycle would probably have no trouble with, or a DH bike with six inches in the rear, but normal riders will have to get off and walk.

Scenery: Rocks. A bunch of trees. Don't let your mind wander when riding here; watch the trail ahead of you. And hold on tight and hope you know how to wheelie-drop.

Special comments: Because of idiots riding like they own the place, the city has closed some parts of this park. I have no problem with that. I'd like for my friends' grandkids to be able to ride here. So don't abuse this land.

This place is terrifying when it's completely dry, and don't try it in the rain. I would never consider wearing body armor, but if I did, this would be the place for it. This old motocross loop is one big drop after another, and if you like to shred this may be your place. You'll be a human missile for about two seconds as you fly off the ledges. Then you'll be impaled on one the cedar trees, and give the rest of us something to talk about for years. The braking zones are way too short to give you much leeway—you'll die if you get stupid.

If you have a new full suspension bike and you just can't seem to find the right place to use it all, well, do I have the ride for you! There are many drops here that exceed three feet, and there are monster downhill screamers that will let you squeeze every inch out of your bike and wrists and spine. If you're goofy enough to try to fly, you can do it here. Go ahead, get some air; just make sure that you paid your insurance premiums first. This place is deadly serious, and riding it with a carefree attitude might get you hurt. No bull.

You start from the parking area and hit the main loop just north of there, up a slight hill. Look for the signs—this trail is very well marked—and hold on for dear life. Now you might get the impression that I don't like this trail. WRONG! I love riding here, but I'm a slowpoke and I don't like air. I get off and walk some, and still have a blast. This is a trail worthy of the best of your technical skills (and gonads); a place with a thrill for the boldest of riders. Get out there and rip.

RIDE 29 · Emma Long Motorcycle Park

Follow the trail around as it winds over the broken limestone, watch the signs, and don't ride into the areas that have been closed. The city has taken part of this away from us for ten years because it was abused. People cut their own bandit trails and were stupid jerks, and now the rest if us don't get to use that part any more. What a shame. Be a responsible trail user—ride what's open (hell, it's more than you can handle anyway) and then go home without broken bones or bad karma. Life is better that way.

General location: Northwest Austin, Texas.

A photograph just does not do this place justice. Emma Long is a series of hard loose climbs and daring drops. Fun with several inches of suspension, just use good judgment because it will bite you if you get too foolish.

Elevation change: Apparently there's only about 100 feet of elevation here, but it sure seems like more when you ride it.

Season: Year-round, but not when it's wet. Unless you've got a boatload of cajones and no sense at all.

Services: Parking, maybe a porta-potty, nothing else. Bring what you need.

Hazards: The terrain is deadly. There are three-foot drops and a bunch of loose limestone, so you can bet Mr. de Zaster and all his cousins were raised here. It's a very dangerous trail, even for an experienced rider with a suitable machine.

Rescue index: Medium. You will be found, because people ride here. And your cell phone will probably work. I strongly urge you to bring a pal along so when you screw the pooch someone can go get help.

Land status: City of Austin motorcycle park.

Maps: There are usually some available at the trailhead; check the kiosk.

Finding the trail: From northbound MoPac (TX 1) or TX 360 (the "Capitol of Texas Highway") in far northwest Austin, hang a left (northwest) onto FM 2222 and go to the first traffic light. Hang a left (roughly southwest) on City Park Road. Follow this for a few miles, winding around up and down, until you see signs for Emma Long Metropolitan Park. Turn left at the intersection with Oak Shore Drive and follow the pavement another mile or so until you see the signs for the motocross park. Turn left and drive in to the parking area. Check the trail maps for the current orientation of the trails (they change every few years). Park and ride. The trail starts to the north, up on the slight hill, and returns from the west.

Sources of additional information:

Austin Parks and Recreation
Department
P.O. Box 1088
Austin, TX 78701
(512) 974-6700
www.ci.austin.tx.us/parks/parks.htm

Austin Ridge Riders
P.O. Box 300014
Austin, TX 78703-0014
www.io.com/austinridgeriders

Bicycle Sport Shop
1426 Toomey Road
Austin, TX 78704
(512) 477-3472
or
10947 Research Boulevard
Austin, TX 78759
(512) 345-7460

Notes on the trail: This park is full of places where the trail used to be three feet wide but has grown to twenty. You get these morons who can't ride the middle, so they try to go around the outside. Pretty soon the trail is out of control, and it has sprawled enough that it's a twenty-foot-wide piece of unrideable terrain. If you can't ride it, walk it. Get off and push. Don't keep going around on the edges and tearing up that much more delicate terrain. I know this is a motorcycle trail, but I have never seen a motorcycle out here. All I've ever seen is evidence of mountain bikers who are too arrogant to just get off and walk where the trail is really hard. You babies. Stop making the trail wider, and walk what you are too weak to ride. I do it all the time; it's no big deal.

RIDE 30 · Walnut Creek Park Trails—Austin

AT A GLANCE

Length/configuration: This park offers a multitude of trails, some are simple 1-mile loops and some are a maze of single-track in the trees, not connected in any easily discernible pattern. I'd say there must be at least 10 miles of trail here, but I'm not sure I found it all.

Aerobic difficulty: There are some pretty decent short climbs here, but most of the trails here seem reasonable, not too extreme. Most of this is 95/95, but there are some sections that will make you breathe hard.

Technical difficulty: Again, most of this seems to be 95/95, especially the front loops, but there's some stuff on the back side of the property that has been designed to provide respectable challenges. If you have to, just walk the toughies.

RIDE 30 · Walnut Creek Park Trails

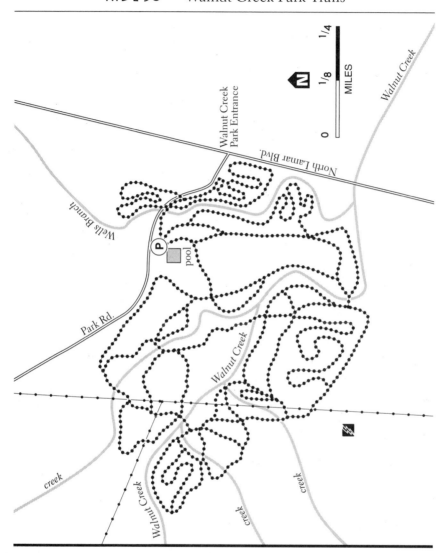

Scenery: You're in the trees here, and the woods are lovely, but this is not a trail for long views or vistas. Watch that front wheel.

Special comments: I'm told there is a guy from the Austin Ridge Riders who has built and maintained most of this. Thank you to Mark Henneke, and the Austin Ridge Riders, for all their hard work making this one of the most enjoyable and rideable trail systems in the entire city of Austin.

Walnut Creek has an excellent array of fun terrain for your fat-tire perusal. Just watch that limestone down there in the creek. This guy came flying out of the creek and promptly pointed the rubber-side at the moon (and I failed to get a photo of it).

This place is marvelous. Fine, tight single-track, with creek crossings and jumps, that swoops up and down and around and through Walnut Creek. You have to either know your way around or be led by someone who knows their way, because the back side of the park is a web of fine single-track. Or just get brave and go ride. You can only get so lost—the property's not so big, but it is packed with trail after trail after trail.

There are two or three short loops near the road and the park entrance that are fairly flat (I only found two of them), with no monster climbs. These have lots of tight curves, whoop-de-dos, and quick assaults on short hills. The front loops are called #1, #2, and #3, and are pretty much beginner-level single-track. Each is roughly a mile in length and will return you to the area of the parking lot via the paved road. Look for signs that will indicate the correct direction of travel. Loop #2 seems to be generally ridden clockwise, with #3 ridden counterclockwise. Watch for the arrows. I don't think I ever found #1, so I can't say what the orientation is there.

The areas along and across the creek are harder riding. You have more elevation to play with, and a bunch more miles of tight, tricky single-track. If you exit the parking area to the southwest and follow the old dirt road down toward the creek, you'll find places where trails run off on either side. Feel free to explore these; most seem to wander in the trees and eventually lead you down to the creek crossing. Ride around and enjoy yourself—the boundaries of the park will keep you from getting too lost or too far from the car.

Across the creek is where the real trail miles are. Once you cross and climb the exit on the south side, you can follow the dirt road some more and soon find the power lines. The main power lines run north and south; use them as a reference point on your location. There are little single-track excursions into the trees in just about every direction. Explore, learn the area, and try to see it all. I am told there are soccer fields back in there somewhere to the southeast, but I never found them. There's a power substation on the far southwest corner of the property. The trails here are not well marked, and it's easy to get turned around and fumble looking for the way out. Go toward the creek and look for the main dirt road that cuts this place in two. Follow the road across the creek and up to the parking area.

General location: Northern Austin, Texas.

Elevation change: As far as I can tell there's about 60 to 80 feet of delta along these trails. Not severe, but you will feel it.

Season: This is a year-round park; I probably wouldn't recommend getting out here when it's wet, however. The surface of this trail is likely to dissolve to a certain extent when it rains.

Services: Parking, potties, water. I'd bring my own refreshments.

Hazards: The trails here are fast and the turns can get loose, so crashing has to be at the top of my list for dangers. Don't launch into any blind turns or drops without doing some reconnaissance, so you'll know what's coming at you.

Rescue index: Medium-high. There are a lot of riders here, and you're in the middle of the city. So take your cell phone and a pal, and you'll be rescued if Mr. de Zaster should make an appearance.

Land status: City of Austin park.

Maps: Check the Austin Ridge Riders website.

Finding the trail: The park is just south of Parmer Lane, on the west side of Lamar Boulevard. This is roughly halfway between I-35 and MoPac (TX 1). Enter the park and follow the road west until you see the parking area on the left (south), by the pool. There are three "front" loops; two just east of the parking area on the south side of the parking, and one across the road on the north side. These are just the tip of the Walnut Creek iceberg; the bulk of the trails are south of the parking area, along and across Walnut Creek. Head out past the picnic tables and follow the old road down to the creek, riding whatever you find along the way.

Sources of additional information:

Austin Parks and Recreation
   Department
P.O. Box 1088
Austin, TX 78701
(512) 974-6700
www.ci.austin.tx.us/parks/parks.htm

Austin Ridge Riders
P.O. Box 300014
Austin, TX 78703-0014
www.io.com/austinridgeriders

Bicycle Sport Shop
1426 Toomey Road
Austin, TX 78704
(512) 477-3472
or
10947 Research Boulevard
Austin, TX 78759
(512) 345-7460

Notes on the trail: The Austin Ridge Riders are another monster mountain bike club, with a long list of accomplishments. I cannot thank them enough for all the hard work and dedication they have poured into the dirt in Austin to give us so many wonderful places to escape the crowds. Get involved, and bask in the glory of being part of a highly respected gang of mountain biking superstars.

RIDE 31 · Muleshoe Bend Trail—Bee Caves

AT A GLANCE

Length/configuration: A clockwise loop of single-track about 7 miles long.

Aerobic difficulty: Not too bad; there are some short climbs, but it's mostly doable. This is a 95/95 trail, in my opinion.

Technical difficulty: Again, this is 95/95; if you're a newbie you should probably walk in places, but most of it is doable. By the hardheads and other experienced riders, anyway.

Scenery: This place is nice, the woods are pretty. As with some other trails, however, this is a watcher (of your front wheel), not a looker (at the scenery).

Special comments: This is a fee area, so don't cheat—put your $5 in the honor box and ride with good karma. If you're lucky there will be maps, and it won't rain on your head.

What a sweet piece of Hill Country single-track. I love this trail; it's not too hard and it is in a nice quiet woods. We're out in the boonies here, boys and girls. A good place to relax, or to take your newbie friends, maybe. You will see signs of people blowing around laying down some serious skids, but I don't see Muleshoe as that kind of place. I passed several hikers along this trail, and I wouldn't want them to get the wrong idea. There are other places, back in the city, to rip. Leave this one in good shape when you go. Please?

RIDE 31 • Muleshoe Bend Trail

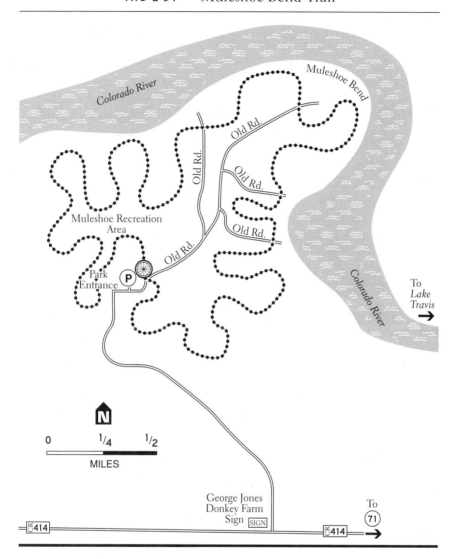

The name Muleshoe Bend comes from a bend in the Colorado River that you will ride near. The trail is on the finger of land that's stuck into the bend. Weird—I lived in a place called Muleshoe, Texas, once. It's much prettier here than there—in fact, it's downright "tall cotton." The park is actually called the Muleshoe Recreation Area by the Lower Colorado River Authority (LCRA), the land managers. The Texas Hill Country is one of those places where everyone wants to live. It's the beautiful heart of Texas. Trails like this one are only a small reason for that, but a substantial one. Trails like Muleshoe are few and far between and should be savored and cherished. Good mountain bike trails don't grow on cedar trees, they only come into existence a few at a time. Don't ride here when it's wet, and don't punish the trail surface unnecessarily with your brakes. I saw a ton of places with long skid marks and chewed-up downhills — there just ain't no reason for that, you dorks. This is not a race trail. Go do that crap somewhere else.

If I seem negative, it's only because I want trails like Muleshoe to be available to riders for years to come; I don't want them to get chewed and widened and destroyed. There's no future in that. And that ain't what real mountain biking's all about, in my opinion. Which is worth exactly what you paid for it, coincidentally.

General location: West of Austin, Texas, about an hour or so.

Elevation change: There is probably the best part of 100 feet of elevation here, but there are no 100-foot climbs or anything like that; it's pretty mellow.

Season: Not in the rain, or even shortly after. Otherwise this is a year-round trail.

Services: Parking, maybe a porta-potty. Nothing else. Bring what you will need.

Hazards: This is a fast trail, loose in a lot of places. I'd be very careful and not impale myself on any trees, if I were you. I could probably find a copperhead, if I looked hard enough, so don't go there. You will cross roads that are open, so look both ways and don't get squashed.

Rescue index: Lower medium. The terrain here is fairly remote, and your cell phone may be useless, but lots of people ride this trail on a weekend. During the week it's pretty lonely. Take a pal, someone who can find his or her way to the road, and bring your cell phone just in case it might work.

Land status: Lower Colorado River Authority recreation area.

Maps: The kiosk by the trailhead has a nice one posted, very accurate, but there may or may not be copies available from the box.

Finding the trail: Take TX 71 west from Austin, past Bee Caves, and continue on and over the Pedernales River. About two miles past the river you will find Paleface Road; turn right (north). Follow Paleface Road for a few miles until you reach CR 414, and turn right by the Kountry Kitchen and George Jones' "Country Music" Miniature Donkey Farm (this alone is worth the drive out here). In a couple of miles you will enter the park. Pull into the parking area just past the entrance, and you'll find the trail just beyond, to the east, right along the parking area. Hang a left and ride until you come back here. Stay on the single-track unless you need to bail on one of the dirt roads. Go uphill on any of these until something looks familiar.

Sources of additional information:

Lower Colorado River Authority
  (LCRA)
P.O. Box 220
Austin, TX 78767
(800) 776-5272 ext. 3366
www.lcra.org

Austin Ridge Riders
P.O. Box 300014
Austin, TX 78703-0014
www.io.com/austinridgeriders

Bicycle Sport Shop
1426 Toomey Road
Austin, TX 78704
(512) 477-3472

or

10947 Research Boulevard
Austin, TX 78759
(512) 345-7460

Notes on the trail: Thank you to the Austin Ridge Riders for keeping this place useable—they're good folks and provide the locals with some mighty fine trails to enjoy.

RIDE 32 · Bluff Creek Ranch—Warda

AT A GLANCE

Length/configuration: A loop of single-track, about 10 miles in length. Some awesome riding.

Aerobic difficulty: Places here will work you hard and places here will let you breathe. This trail has the whole range. I would call parts of it beginner, and other parts expert. The climbing is not extreme, so I give this one a medium rating.

Technical difficulty: There are plenty of technical challenges as you ride here. Tree roots and loose conditions, and Gas Pass is just nuts. Respect this place and live to ride again.

Scenery: It's really nice here on the ranch. You have some pretty single-track and a glassy pond or two, and then there are Texas Longhorns, real ones. Back in the pines you'll want to forget that you have to go to work tomorrow, it's so quiet and still.

Special comments: This is another pay-per-use facility; the cost is currently $5.50 a head per day, and well worth it. This is the only trail I know that has a built-in bike shop. Dr. Nolan has his own little shop—he calls it the "Bike ER." If you break down or need a tube, you've come to a good place.

I'll tell this story again. I met Paul Nolan out on Maverick Road in the Big Bend one afternoon. He and a friend were rolling through the sand on their bikes, headed over to Santa Elena canyon, and I was oozing up the road in my truck, headed over to Lajitas for the big race. It was so cool to see something out there on the horizon, and then to realize that it was a pair of cyclists. I stopped to yack at them for a minute or two, and then I went on over to a shower in Lajitas. I ran into Paul again later that weekend, and then I raced this course and met him again a couple of months later. The pesky guy just keeps turning up.

That might be because he has an awesome trail on his property. I wish I could see him and Susan every day, and I would if I lived anywhere near here. This

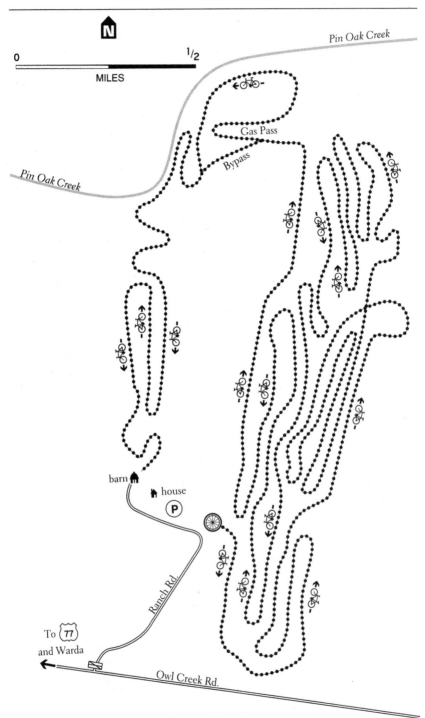

The trails at Bluff Creek Ranch are so well marked you will know whether to sit or wind your watch.

trail is a great place to ride—you can push the limits and find out what you've got or you can just do an ooze-along and shoot some film along the way. Bring a bunch of pals and make a day of it.

One of the wild things about riding here is that there are cattle scattered all around. You have to ride over special bike gates to get from one section to another, so be careful on those. I've crashed on stuff that was a lot less scary. This place has all kinds of cool features. Lots of challenging trails, all extremely well marked and established; and this is another one that has held up extremely well over the years. People have been racing here for a long time, and there are a lot of folks who come here often to enjoy the ride.

If you forget something, or break something, Dr. Nolan is The Bike Doc. Drag your machine up there to the house and ask him to please get you on the trail again. He has a fully equipped bike shop right here, at the ranch. Oh yeah, and hang out back there around the shop for a while and check out the purple martins, or whatever they are. They have feeders back there, and those silly birds are a hoot to watch, the way they swoop around in these tight loops along the back of the house and the trees.

Gas Pass, the Sidewinder, Billy Pond, the Roller Coasters, Oh S-it, and all the other spots I can't remember the names of—this place is memorable just the same. There are mile markers along the way to keep you oriented. This is a trail where you're going to have fun—heck, just laughing at the names of the spots along the trail will keep you in stitches. You will want to come back as often as you can. Get out there and pass some gas.

I cracked up when I met this trio along the Bluff Creek Ranch Trail. The silly dogs were sailing along and having as much fun, or more, than the gal on the bike. She stopped for a few seconds to yack and the dogs were gone up the trail.

General location: About an hour-and-a-half east of Austin, Texas, or roughly the same distance south of Waco.

Elevation change: There is only about 60 feet of delta here, altogether, but it will seem like more.

Season: Year-round. This place holds up well in wet weather, but the Nolans will keep you off the trails until it is dry enough to use. Call ahead and see what the current trail conditions are, or check the Internet.

Services: You can camp here or picnic here or just enjoy excellent single-track. Over by the barn is the bike wash, and up at the house are the showers. Anything else you need you should bring into the ranch with you.

Hazards: This trail is fast and it's easy to let the bike get away from you. Be careful of getting in over your head. Mr. de Zaster was born here, I think. There might be some poison ivy somewhere (I don't really notice it), and snakes are always a possibility. Be careful around the cattle and the electric fences, and respect the downhills. Walk Gas Pass if you're scared. It is a steep descent made of concrete, slick in dry conditions sometimes, and there's a drop-off and sharp turn at the bottom. The gates between pastures scare me, but they're actually pretty lame. There's cactus and other "flattering" flora, so take your patch kit.

Rescue index: High. This guy is a real doctor. And he is going to notice if your car has been sitting there, in front of his house, all day. I don't know how much use a cell phone is, so take a bud so one of you can go get help in an emergency.

Land status: Private property, an active cattle ranch.

Maps: They have a good one you can get when you pay up. The trail is extremely well marked, but carry a map so you know where you are in relation to the start.

Finding the trail: From US 77 on the north edge of Warda, go east on Owl Creek Road for a mile or so, until you see the signs for Bluff Creek Ranch. Turn left into the property and go through the electrified gates (just drive through them, that's what they are made for) and up to the house and barn. Announce your presence, pay your fee, get a map, and ride. The trails start south of the house, by a corral. Get on the single-track and ride, following the map and signs. The trails here are extremely well marked and established, so it's practically impossible to get lost. As you ride you will occasionally come back up to the high pasture and be in sight of the house and barn. If you need to bail, you will find several good spots. Ride until you can't any more, and then call it a day. Whew.

Sources of additional information:

Bluff Creek Ranch
537 Owl Creek Road
P.O. Box 110
Warda, TX 78960
(979) 242-5894
www.bcrwarda.com

Austin Ridge Riders
P.O. Box 300014
Austin, TX 78703-0014
www.io.com/austinridgeriders

Notes on the trail: Obey the rules. This is not hard to do because they all make good sense. Be careful, carry your patch kit, and just generally enjoy one of the neatest places to ride in Texas. Race it sometime if you think you're bad; it may change your opinion of yourself.

RIDE 33 · Rocky Hill Ranch—Smithville

AT A GLANCE

Length/configuration: A roughly counterclockwise loop of single-track sections connected by old dirt roads. The whole enchilada is about 16 miles long. That's a big enchilada, even by Texas standards.

Aerobic difficulty: Some sections on this trail system are pretty hard. There are some sections that aren't real bad, but overall riding here is a workout and you will leave some carbon dioxide along the way. You may also pick up some lactic acid in one or three spots.

RIDE 33 • Rocky Hill Ranch

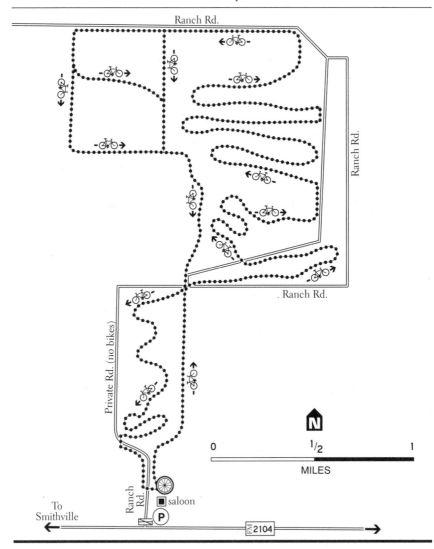

Technical difficulty: This place has a high level of technical riding. Loose conditions, tricky climbs, steep ups and downs, tight single-track. You will either use or lose all your skills here.

Scenery: Don't be letting your eyes wander; keep 'em on the dirt ahead of you. This is not a place to be staring at the sky trying to spot UFO's.

Special comments: This is a pay-per-use facility, and the cost of riding here was $6 when I wrote this. It is well worth the price of admission. If you haven't ridden here yet, well get down to Smithville and take it in,

Grasshopper. Also, this is an active ranch with livestock in residence. If you have to open any gates to get around, be sure you close them behind you.

I'm sitting here at home writing up the passage for Rocky Hill Ranch and there is a Godzillathon on the tube. All day I have had my fingers stuck to this keyboard while downstairs the monster destroys Tokyo, over and over and over. I don't know how he does it and he still keeps such a cute figure. This is fitting, actually—the trail described here is sort of the Godzilla of Texas mountain bike rides. And it cuts such a cute figure.

This place has held up very well over the years, considering all the traffic it gets. There are markings all along the ride to keep you pointed in the correct direction, and there are signs to show you the names of the cool sections. This is a very well marked facility for good reason. They have races here every year, including one that is a 24-hour event. That's an interesting proposition, eh? Can you imagine blowing up and down these trails at night? You had better bring a good headlight. The normal people will prefer to do this in the daylight because your eyes need to be functioning. There are water coolers in a couple of locations in case you need a drink, and most have a bench or something in case you need to sit down. And you will, probably right after Fat Chuck's Demise. I'm not Fat Chuck, by the way. I was nowhere near the crime scene.

The Drop Zone is a lot of fun, and so is Grey's Way (Grey is the guy who owns this place, but he is in Aransas, Texas, or somewhere now). Fat Chuck's Demise is always good for a laugh—check out the fake grave marker and bones, and the bike in the tree. The best sections—at least my favorites—are probably Off The Lip, Tris Cross, and Omar's Hollow. These run you up and down through creeks and into some tight single-track. There ain't a bad section on the whole place—it is all excellent single-track. The Tunnel of Pines is lined with some amazing big pine trees, so look around as you ride along this part. The Longhorn Loop is fun, and the Black Track really is expert-level. Be ready to find something inside you that you might not have known about before. Skills, I mean.

Don't freak out about some of the things you will see along this trail, or up in the trees. The people here are loads of fun and have a mountain biking sense of humor. They swear they don't know where the bikes up in the trees came from.

The rest stops have water and some really nice tables and stuff made from old tree snags, all in keeping with the generally easygoing atmosphere around the Rocky Hill Ranch. What other trail do you know of that has a saloon at the trailhead? My kind of place. Buy me a Shiner?

General location: About an hour east of Austin, Texas.

Elevation change: The best I can tell, this place ranges from about 300 feet down by the saloon to around 500 feet up on the highest sections. You have 150 to 200 feet of delta to contend with, no doubt.

Season: Just about any time of year. They have races here pretty often and the trail may be closed sometimes. Be sure and call ahead, or get on the Internet, and make sure everything is cool before you drive all the way out here.

Services: A bar. Uhhh, and a shower and potties. They will feed you down at the saloon, so have a burger. There are primitive camping facilities, several good ones, so ask about what's available when you pay your fee at the saloon.

Hazards: The deadfalls are tricky, and there are many. The trail is loose in most places, the approaches and exits to the creeks are short and steep, and many experienced riders have crashed on these before you. You know, I think I could probably find a big old rattlesnake if I looked hard enough. And I guarantee anyone who is allergic to poison ivy could find some here if they didn't try.

Rescue index: High. If you go off for a ride and don't come back they are going to notice your car sitting there. I'm not sure how much use a cell phone would be on a lot of this trail, but it is well marked and well managed by the people at the saloon. Bring a buddy, carry a map, and you can probably get saved here if you need it. There are lots of riders that use this place, so someone will wander by, sooner or later. Try to crash and burn within earshot of the trail if you can, and then you can flag down a passing rider for help if you need it.

Land status: A mountain bike haven on private property.

Maps: The ranch has some really good ones; ask at the saloon.

Finding the trail: From Smithville, Texas, go east on TX 71 for a couple of miles and then turn left (north) on FM 153. Go about two miles and the entrance to the ranch will be on your left (west), with signs. Put on your Stetson and saunter over to the saloon to inquire about trail conditions, get a map, and then do what they tell you. If you follow the signs and the map you will have no problem finding all the trails, and when you're through riding you can find your way back to where you left the car. Cool setup, huh?

Sources of additional information:

Bike Ranch at Rocky Hill
P.O. Box 984
Smithville, TX 78957
(512) 237-3112
www.rockyhillranch.com

Austin Ridge Riders
P.O. Box 300014
Austin, TX 78703-0014
www.io.com/austinridgeriders

Bicycle Sport Shop
1426 Toomey Road
Austin, TX 78704
(512) 477-3472
or
10947 Research Boulevard
Austin, TX 78759
(512) 345-7460

Notes on the trail: If you have to pass through a gate, be sure and close it behind you, please. And be sure and stop by the saloon for a burger and a brew. These hamburgers are legendary, and they have cold Shiner Bock on tap. Need any more reason to ride here? I know I don't. Tell Paul and Diane I said, "hey."

RIDE 34 · Wolf Mountain Trail — Pedernales Falls State Park

AT A GLANCE

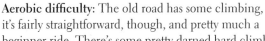

Length/configuration: Old dirt roads that lead up to a nice loop of single-track; the total ride is around 7 miles.

Aerobic difficulty: The old road has some climbing, it's fairly straightforward, though, and pretty much a beginner ride. There's some pretty darned hard climbing on the single-track. No, it is not the Canadian Rockies, but it is quite invigorating in places.

Technical difficulty: There are some real technical challenges here. The dirt roads aren't that bad; you could call them beginner-level. But the single-track out there has some little gnarlies.

Scenery: This is a nice ride with lots of stuff to see. There are ruins and historical spots along the trails, and the views from up on the high section are worth the climb.

Special comments: There is the typical $3–$5 entry fee here. I used to come here to backpack when I was in college in Austin. Sometimes I look back and realize I did more cycling and backpacking than going to school. I was more a student of fun than anything academic, back then. Still am. This part of Texas is good for having fun; there's a lot to do.

It is always such a homecoming for me to return to the banks of the Pedernales River. I have always had a real special place in my heart for this park. While I was going to school here we set records for the numbers of people to drown in the falls. It was sort of a big party place. Nowadays, the gnarliest sections are closed to swimming and all that, but there are still some real nice places to take a dip in the beautiful Pedernales River. On a hot day it would be foolish to drive all the way out here and not go fall into the river for a while. I do it every time.

The trail here is mostly an old dirt road that runs out of the south side of the main park area and winds back to a couple of springs. The kind with water, not the bouncy ones. Great places to take a break and snap a few shots of your bike. Or girlfriend, or whatever. Take your shoes off and dip them in the water when you can. Admire the scenery. Don't be in a hurry; this is a place for relaxing, smelling the prickly pears and all that.

After the road, you can connect with a couple of miles of fairly serious single-track and go up on the ridge (they call it Wolf Mountain). The climbing is substantial and tricky because most of the trail surface is loose rock or exposed rock, and there's a place or two that just might be scary to an old guy like me.

RIDE 34 • Wolf Mountain Trail

And don't mess with any of the ruins you may run across, that stuff has been there for a long time and should remain for a lot longer unless vandals tear it up. The state takes a real dim view of people who molest archeological stuff.

General location: Southwest of Austin, Texas, about an hour's drive.

Elevation change: If you just did an out-and-back on the old dirt road you would have several miles of mostly beginner-level stuff. There are some nice climbs, but they're all short; you don't trade more than 60 or 80 feet of delta. If you ride up on the mountain you give and take another 100 feet or so in addition to that. The delta is no more than 200 feet between the extremes.

Season: This place drains pretty well, but if it's been raining there'll be some nasty mud and the limestone will be slippery, very slippery, especially on the single-track.

Services: The park has some real nice camping facilities—showers and potties and all that. There is a pay phone at the entrance. In addition to that, there's some great BBQ in the area, so stop on the way out here, wherever you see the signs. Haul anything else you need in from town.

Hazards: The water crossings can be as slick as you know what sometimes, so be careful as you ride over them. Much of the surface here is very loose, and taking a spill is always a possibility. I have reached 20 mph coming down from Wolf Mountain, and I wasn't really trying, so be very careful. This is Texas, so there might be a snake or two in this county.

Rescue index: Medium to high. The trails here get a lot of traffic, so your body will be discovered shortly after you pass on. Maybe before. I don't know if your cell phone will work here, probably not unless you're up high. Take a pal so one of you can get out to rescue the other in the event of disaster.

Land status: A Texas Parks and Wildlife Department state park.

Maps: The rangers have a pretty nice one; ask at the entrance.

Finding the trail: From US 290 about 30 miles southwest of Austin, you will find FM 3232 heading north. Follow this for a few miles until it ends. The entrance to the park is here; drive in and pay your money. Ask the ranger for a map. Turn right at the next opportunity, there's a sign, and park in the lot near the trailhead kiosk. Go through the gate and onto the old dirt road. You will cross Bee Creek, then Mescal Creek, and then you will find where the road forks. Go left and follow this until it ends, near Jones Spring. Bear right at Jones Spring and soon you will see a sign directing you onto the single-track. Follow this as it climbs Wolf Mountain and you will find a fork at a primitive camp. Go right; to the left leads to CR 201 across the pipelines. Near the top there will be another fork. You may go either way; both parts loop around the top of the mountain and meet on the other side. From there it is more road, steep and loose, back down to the main dirt road. Hang a left there and in a couple of miles you're back to the car.

Sources of additional information:

Pedernales Falls State Park
2585 Park Road 6026
Johnson City TX 78636
(830) 868-7304
www.tpwd.state.tx.us/park/pedernal/
    pedernal.htm

Texas Parks and Wildlife Department
4200 Smith School Road
Austin, TX 78744-3291
(800) 792-1112 information
(512) 389-8900 reservations
www.tpwd.state.tx.us

Austin Ridge Riders
P.O. Box 300014
Austin, TX 78703-0014
www.io.com/austinridgeriders

Bicycle Sport Shop
1426 Toomey Road
Austin, TX 78704
(512) 477-3472
or
10947 Research Boulevard
Austin, TX 78759
(512) 345-7460

Notes on the trail: The rangers will tell you about, and the maps will show you, more riding than just Wolf Mountain, over there across the river. I've been over there, but I never found anything but some real nasty old roads that didn't look worth the sweat. I could be wrong, and I certainly don't know everything, so go over there and look for yourselves. Buena suerta.

RIDE 35 · McAllister Park Trails—San Antonio

AT A GLANCE

Length/configuration: The local club, South Texas Off-Road Mountain Bikers (STORM), says there is probably 20 miles of trail in here, and I don't doubt it. I rode about half that.

Aerobic difficulty: There are some spots requiring an output of serious horsepower, but this is mostly a 95/95 trail, just about anybody can get around here. Even if they don't ride all the hard stuff.

Technical difficulty: You can find yourself ability-challenged here; there are tricky creek crossings and tree roots and loose conditions. Still, this is a 95/95 trail.

Scenery: It is kind of nice back here in the woods, but this is a riders trail, not a lookers trail.

Special comments: The local mountain bike club, STORM, has done well to sustain this park, considering all the traffic it must support. They've got some big plans to get some newer trails into the market, places they call 700 Acres, Government Canyon, and Leon Creek Greenway. Look for some great new trails in San Antonio in the near future. Thanks, mountain bikers.

There is some pretty cool trail in here. Not the hardest in the state, or the prettiest, but worthy woods just the same. There are trails and trails and trails out here—you may wonder if you know where you are from time to time; I know I did. The loop I rode was fairly well marked, as if for a race, and I think a local bike shop may have been involved. I'd spend some money there if I were y'all.

The trails wander all through the trees along the creeks in the park, and you will find a challenge or two in the technical vein, but mostly this is a relatively easy trail. You can crash off into some creeks if you want, test the rear suspension and all that, but just don't run over anybody. There are a lot of people out here on a nice afternoon. Or, if you're like I am, you can just do an ooze-along and forget some stress.

The trail has several offshoots that will carry you into some sweet little pieces of these woods, but mostly you will be herded around and kept in the core by the power lines for a while, then by a residential neighborhood, and then some ponds. I thought it was a nicely designed setup, with lots of fast and loose stuff to keep you on your toes. I did a lap, shot some film, managed to miss most of the trees, and then drove up to Austin for the weekend, dreading the elevation delta the future would bring. I don't think I really did McAllister Park justice. I'd like to ride here again, with people who know it, and not be on a deadline. I'll bet it would be a blast.

At first I was disappointed in this place; I had heard so much about it, and I had a hard time finding where to park and all that. Once I hit the dirt my attitude

RIDE 35 • McAllister Park Trails

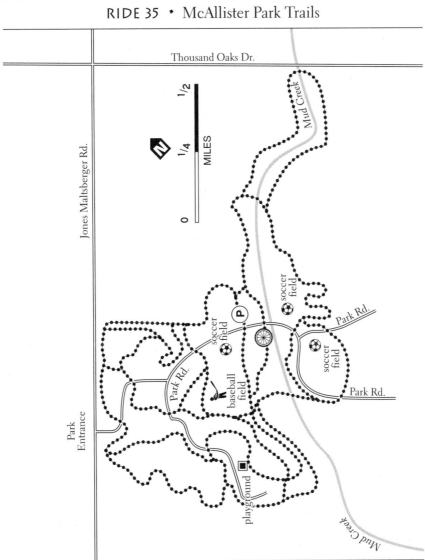

changed, and I was ready to roll. I found some sections that reminded me of other trails close to my heart, and I found some new stuff I haven't seen the likes of before. I think this is a really good trail to learn on, and then you can do some of the San Antonio stuff I missed. They have some fine terrain down here in Alamo-town.

Earlier I had tried to tap into a couple of other local trails, but I kept finding "No Trespassing" and "Danger" signs. I didn't think it wise to send the masses into land marked like that, so I settled on McAllister Park. The trails here are fun and fast, and if you're smart enough to hook up with the locals, they can show you some other stuff that's even better than this. I know I shortchanged San Antonio on coverage; there is definitely a bunch of other good stuff you can ride here.

General location: Right on the northeast side of the big airport in San Antonio, Texas.

Elevation change: Pretty minimal, about 50 feet, maybe, from top to bottom.

Season: Open year-round. I wouldn't try to ride this when it was muddy, though. I'd say it's useable if it's not wet.

Services: Potties and parking, that's it. Come prepared.

Hazards: Mesquite, loose rock, tight trees and associated roots. Mosquitoes for sure, and maybe some poison ivy in places. The terrain is not extremely severe but should be respected just the same. I'd be careful of automoron traffic when crossing paved roads, and oncoming trail users when in the trees. This place has hikers, joggers, and cyclists, all circulating in various directions.

Rescue index: High. There are just about always other riders around, and you're in the middle of a big city. Bring your cell phone and be careful, and you should be OK.

Land status: City of San Antonio Parks and Recreation Department land.

Maps: The STORM website has a nice one; take a look.

Finding the trail: The entrance to the park is about half-way between the airport and Thousand Oaks Road, on the southeast side of Jones-Maltsberger Road. You can take the Bitters Road exit from US 281, roughly east, and follow Bitters Road until it splits, and then follow Starcrest Road left. Hang a left onto Jones-Maltsberger Road at the light, and watch for the park entrance on the right. Turn into the park and then take a left at the intersection with the other park road. Follow the signs back to the athletic fields. Park somewhere around the fields or picnic area. The trail runs by, just east of the athletic fields and the Harmony Hill Optimist Club Family Park. Jump on, preferably going left, for a clockwise lap. Follow the single-track until you're back where you started.

Sources of additional information:

San Antonio Parks and Recreation
    Department
950 East Hildebrand Avenue
San Antonio, TX 78212
(210) 207-3000
www.sanantonio.gov/sapar/index.asp

South Texas Off Road Mountain-
    Bikers (STORM)
P.O. Box 12371

San Antonio, TX 78212-0371
www.storm-web.org

Cycle Logic Bike Shop
12319 Wetmore Road
San Antonio, TX 78247
(210) 490-8251

Notes on the trail: There is another great mountain bike club behind the scenes here. I'd strongly recommend you get hooked up with them and find out how to bring many more marvelous trails to life in San Antonio—y'all got some fine terrain down here. Thanks to STORM for all their hard work on the trails here and in other parts of Texas. Another interesting note is that the bike shop I mention above is basically backed up to the trails here, so look 'em up, they're good folks. Go spend some money.

RIDE 36 · Flat Rock Ranch—Comfort

AT A GLANCE

Length/configuration: Two loops of the finest Texas Hill Country single-track you and I will ever behold. The first loop is about 11 miles, and the other is nearly 8. That's 18 miles total if you ride the big loop.

Aerobic difficulty: The climbs here are tough. In the heat they can be grueling since many are 10- to 15-minute ordeals. This is no beginner ride.

Technical difficulty: Tough; tricky bits abound. This place will make you use just about everything you've learned during your career as a mountain bike stud/studette. Again, this is not a beginner trail.

Scenery: This is the beautiful heart of Texas, one of those gorgeous little valleys you find around the Texas Hill Country. Now, I have to admit I am pretty much partial to Texas, but this place is superb.

Special comments: A monster race course or a great fun ride if you're ready, but a miserable death march if you aren't prepared. This ride is right up there with any excellent trail in Texas or Oklahoma as far as being a cool place to ride. This is a ride you all should do some day. Please note: This is a pay-per-use facility, and at the time of this writing the fee was $5. Oh, it's worth it!

This is one of the finest rides anywhere. There are long, serious climbs and screaming, blistering downhills, all connected by some expertly designed and maintained single-track. The folks who own this ranch are super-nice, and the club who maintains it (STORM) is one of the finest in the state. I ran into a couple of the members when I was here and they really helped me out by giving me expert advice and directions for my attack the next day. Thanks, you guys, y'all are swell.

This place is an active ranch with livestock scattered about. When you come to a gate you need to open for passage, remember to close it behind you so the cows don't come home. Use this property with respect—treat it like it belonged to your best uncle or something. Be careful flying down the trail and into the trees; one of those big old 800-pound steers wouldn't be fun to run into. You might knock him over (crushig you and your bike in the process), but then he'll probably jump up and stomp a hole through you as he tries to run away.

The western side of the property is where you will find the older loop. Here are many monster climbs and some cruel terrain. The trail markings are excellent—

RIDE 36 • Flat Rock Ranch

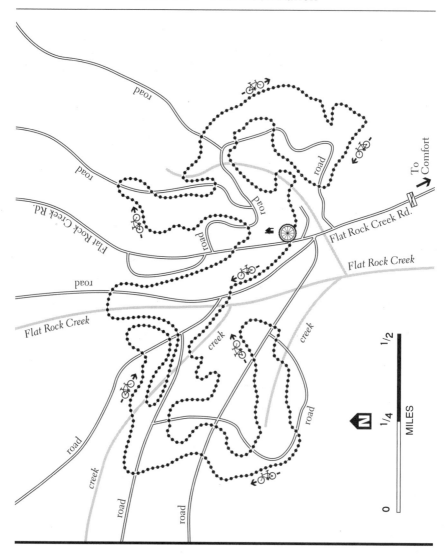

they are consistent and have mileage indicators so you have sort of a clue where you are. From several spots along the trail you get views of the Flat Rock Creek Valley, great vistas where you can see the entire property. Other places are on the far side of the western ridge, and you'll have no idea where you are. There are some evil switchbacks, some nasty off-camber stuff, lots of marbles, and some rock gardens and exposed limestone. An expert rider will blow through these, but you and I may have to walk occasionally. You will find several deer stands along the trail, and when I was here the spoor was thick on the trail in several places.

The bike stops here. The rider, however, found a way to have a meaningful interface between my favorite forearm and the dirt. Watch your line at Flat Rock Ranch.

The eastern loop isn't any gentler. I found some fire ants over here — I tried to get them to eat my leg but they found something better to eat (the PowerBar I left on the bike for a second). Then I found some cows that looked at me like they'd never seen a mountain bike before. I also found one really scary looking switchbacks that tore me up. I sort of chickened out and had to bail off the bike. I wanted to go high-side, but things did not work out. There's some tough riding over on the new loop; it may be worse than the old one. Some gnarl that might make you fall over, too. This might be the scarier loop, in fact, or maybe I was just tired by then. Or the climbing had cooked all the oxygen out of my brain. If left to my own devices, I would probably call this the expert loop. It ain't no downstream trail. This here is Texas at its best.

A great ride? Yepperee. A monster trail? Absolutely. A worthy use of leisure time? No doubt, bro. I'd pack myself a lunch next time. I might even drag along a 20-ounce cola or two.

General location: Near Comfort, Texas, about an hour or so west of San Antonio.

Elevation change: As best I can tell, the start area is around 1,600 feet above the Gulf of Mexico, and the highest points reach up to over 1,900 feet. I think most of the trails here cover about a 300-foot elevation range. I hope you like climbing, because you will discover every foot of delta about six or eight times.

Season: The deer stands make me think the fall is not such a good time. The summer sun will cook you. The best advice I can give you is to call and ask Jimmy if it's OK to ride next weekend. If he likes you, he won't lie.

Services: Water. A place to park. Portable potties. They have an outdoor shower for the riders and a bike wash for the steeds.

Hazards: Several overhanging tree limbs, backscratchers deluxe. Lots of difficult and technical sections, lots of off-camber turns, rock gardens, loose and exposed rock. Watch out for the cattle—you may come flying down a hill and find about half a dozen of them standing in the trail. The spiders here can be fun, especially if you're on point early in the morning, when they like to spin a web across the trail and then sit right in the fat middle of it. The speeds you can attain on the downhills are enough to put hair on your chest, so keep a couple of fingers on your brakes. Be ready for some deadfalls, they seem to scatter themselves around this trail where you least expect 'em.

Rescue index: Low, unless you bring a buddy who knows his way around. As a general rule, go down the hill to the east from the old loop and to the west from the new. At the bottom of the hill is a creek; just hope that you went down the hill that leads you to Flat Rock Creek. From there you're near the trailhead. The good part is there are several dirt roads back in the woods here, and most of the ones heading down are possible return routes. Choose carefully and you will find your way back. I don't know if a cell phone is any good here, but how much can one weigh? Carry it just in case.

Land status: This is private property, and an active cattle ranch. Be super nice and remember the magic words "please" and "thank you."

Maps: The ranch has an excellent one on their website; check it out.

Finding the trail: Well, finding Comfort is probably gonna be a road trip all by itself. It is east of Kerrville, west of San Antonio an hour or so. Get to Comfort, and then go east of town on FM 473 about a mile. You will find a road called Flat Rock Creek Road going north; take this for about four miles. The pavement ends at the front gate for the ranch. Let yourself in and be sure to close the gate after you. Follow the dirt road up to the trailhead kiosk, near the house. Pay your $5 at the box—don't cheat! Markers are visible on the trail right behind the kiosk. Park in the shade and backtrack until you're at the gate into the pastures. The trail is extremely well marked, so if you can't find your way around here you're not really trying. Catch the start just inside the pasture gate and follow the markings.

Sources of additional information:

Jimmy Dreiss
Flat Rock Ranch
Comfort, TX 78013
(830) 995-2858 after 7:00 p.m.
(210) 213-3006 after 5:00 p.m.
www.flatrockranch.net/serv01.htm

South Texas Off Road Mountain-
Bikers (STORM)

P.O. Box 12371
San Antonio, TX 78212-0371
www.storm-web.org

Hill Country Bicycle Works
1412 Broadway
Kerrville, TX 78028
(830) 896-6864

Notes on the trail: Your mileage into the ride is constantly posted as you ride. The trail often crosses some dirt roads; nearly all these lead back to the trailhead area and pastures, if you go downhill to the east. You also cross the downhill course a few times as you roam the ranch; there are warning signs. Follow the old loop until you have gone about 11 miles and pop out of the woods behind the house where you started. Quit if you're cooked, or continue following the signs and do the new loop. If you just pay attention to mileage and the map, you will probably survive. Go up and down some bad hills. And then some more, meaner hills. When you've finally left all the brutal climbs behind, you will wind around a little on gentler terrain and finally end up back on the dirt road that carries you up to the trailhead.

Thank you, Jimmy, and all the folks in STORM—you've made yourselves a mighty fine trail around this ranch. I'd pack that extra bottle of water and something to eat. It's gonna be a long day, Grasshopper.

EAST TEXAS AND
THE GULF COAST

It rains here. A lot. And most of the land is OK with that as far as riding goes. Not always, but mostly.

I have ridden and written about some stuff you may not want to love. It can be steamy here, with the humidity and mosquitoes, and the mud can make you hate both me and your bike. I'm always surprised that so many good rides have grown down here, grown like fungus. They pop up like little mushrooms, where you'd least expect it, and then they disappear. Only to show up again after the next flood, just like you left them, ready to be rediscovered.

The last time I rode at the Anthills I had such a blast. I thought I was in heaven—it was so quiet and all the cars on I-610 sort of ceased to matter. I oozed along and took some pictures and fell in love with a new trail. About two weeks later Houston had some of the worst flooding in its history, and Buffalo Bayou was a hundred-foot-wide rushing mess. But the trail came back, in a bigger way, and it is still one of the sweetest on the coast.

Padre is special; even with all the garbage, I just swoon every time I see a peregrine falcon. I love that beach. If you think Texas Gulf Coast water is ugly, that's because you've only seen Galveston.

I give you the piney woods as well, and I will always think of old Sam Houston every time I smell a pine tree. For the rest of my life. At least we don't get the ticks and chiggers as bad as they do in Oklahoma. Thank God.

I won't make any Aggie jokes, even though I know some good ones. Those cadets down there have themselves a mighty fine place to ride. And Tyler, man, what a monster trail that is, even to this day.

RIDE 37 · Bonham State Park Trail—Bonham

AT A GLANCE

Length/configuration: Counterclockwise 7-mile loop of single-track running around the perimeter of the park lake. There are short connecting sections of park road, but most of the ride is in the trees.

Aerobic difficulty: Medium; this is not a really hard trail. There are some sections with short climbs, but overall this trail is a 95/95—most people can ride most of the trail.

Technical difficulty: There are some interesting bits but nothing extreme or severe. This place can be called a good beginner trail.

Scenery: Most of your time is spent in the trees and there aren't a lot of opportunities for sightseeing. If you slow down and look around you might see some wildlife—other than your friends, that is.

Special comments: This trail often hosts clinics for beginner-level riders and racers and is a good place to break a newbie into mountain biking without taking them somewhere too scary. Like all Texas state parks, there's an entrance fee of $3–$5 per head.

This is a pretty neat place to ride—it's far enough east of the Metromess that you're going to get in a little bit of a road trip, but it's worth the drive.

The bulk of the Bonham State Park trail is in the trees, hidden away from sight, but a few short jaunts on the park road will be necessary to complete the entire loop. There are many places to park and connect to the trail, but I will describe the loop the way I ride it; start at the park entrance fee station and ride all the way around until you return to the same spot.

Some of the trail surface here is loose broken rock, but a lot of it is dirt, especially the areas under the dense woods. The trees are the typical mix of oaks, bois d'arc, and red cedar that graces much of this part of Texas. Several sections are covered with native bluestem grasses, and the wildflowers can be very nice here in the springtime. As far as critters go, you might see a raccoon or the occasional armadillo.

This is a nice place to camp for the weekend or picnic for the day. You can wander over to the swimming beach and fall into the lake after your ride, if you like. There are a couple of interesting ruins out along the trail, nice places to take a break or a photograph.

General location: Bonham, Texas, about an hour and a half northeast of Dallas.

Elevation change: You've probably got 50 feet of delta here, but most of it is gradual climbing that won't work you too awful hard.

Season: Any time except during or shortly after severe weather. Probably at its nicest in the winter and spring.

RIDE 37 • Bonham State Park Trail

Services: The park has rest room and shower facilities, as well as clean water to drink. There are vending machines and a pay phone at the park headquarters. Anything else you need will have to come from town somewhere, so load up on the way.

Hazards: I suspect there might be poison ivy in more than a few areas, and it's easy to get a flat here. I'd be real careful crossing paved roads, because they are all active. Some of the trail is very loose, and interesting bike handling may occur when you least expect it. One or two of the descents are fast and lead into the aforementioned loose spots. And did I mention snakes? Yeah, there's probably a snake or ten in the vicinity.

Rescue index: High. You are just about always within earshot of the park camping and picnic areas. A cell phone might be a waste of time, but probably worth carrying just the same. If you have your map along you can get to the road and flag down help if you need it.

Land status: Texas Parks and Wildlife Department state park.

Maps: The park rangers have a nice one, for free.

Finding the trail: From Bonham, take TX 78 south to FM 271, go east a couple of miles to PR 24, and turn east into the park. The start is right by the entrance fee station, a short ways back toward the main gate. If you have parked elsewhere, the spot where you hit the pavement can determine which way is the shortest return route to your vehicle. Carry a map and you'll be fine.

Sources of additional information:

Bonham State Park
RR 1 Box 337
Bonham TX 75418
(903) 583-5022
www.tpwd.state.tx.us/park/bonham/
    bonham.htm

Texas Parks and Wildlife Department
4200 Smith School Road
Austin, TX 78744-3291
(800) 792-1112 information

(512) 389-8900 reservations
www.tpwd.state.tx.us

Dallas Off-Road Bicycle Association
    (DORBA)
2911 Esters Road
PMB 1414
Irving, Texas 75062
www.dorba.org

Notes on the trail: As described here, the trail heads south from the park road and winds around out to the boundary fence and then gradually east and eventually back north to the park road. When you reach the pavement you will be a short distance from where you originally entered the woods. Turn right on the pavement and follow it a few hundred yards to where you see trail signs on your right, and jump back into the trees. This section is sort of part bike trail and part hiking trail; follow the bike signs. You'll amble around for a while longer in the trees and then find yourself popping out of the trees by the group camp area. Head west, following the trail, until you reenter the trees on the single-track. Soon you will cross another paved road, twice, and be into the trees again on what is probably the most fun part of the trail. Hold on, and soon you'll be at the fork that goes by the spillway; there is a sign, but we will be jumping on the pavement here and following the park road back to the guard shack at the entrance.

The trails are fairly well marked and close to park facilities, so getting lost or too far from your car is not a problem. This is sort of a secret place; lots of area mountain bikers have never been here. Go check it out sometime and try to drag a few of your pals along. This trail is a lot of fun with a group—things get racy real fast.

RIDE 38 · Tyler State Park Trail—Tyler

AT A GLANCE

Length/configuration: Four loops, run 'em clockwise and you'll find 10 miles of the finest single-track there is anywhere in east Texas.

Aerobic difficulty: Aerobic. Difficult. Yes, we have that here. It is a workout—one lap will cook most of us.

Technical difficulty: Short steep climbs, trees (with roots), soft sand, rock

RIDE 38 • Tyler State Park Trail

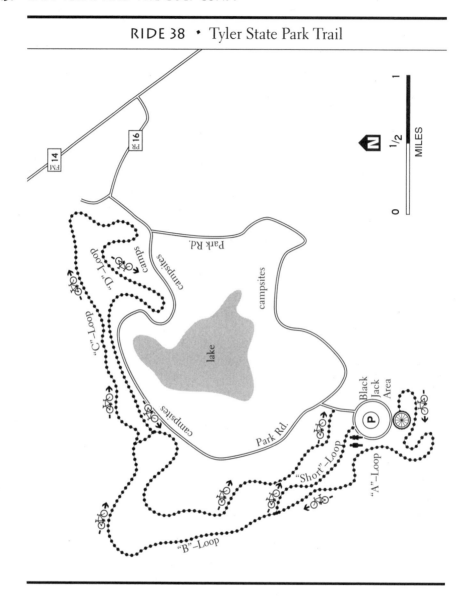

gardens, switchbacks, rock gardens, soft sand, roots (with trees), longer steep climbs. Technical—yeah, definitely.

Scenery: Keep your eyes on the dirt in front of you—this is not a place to be looking around for UFOs.

Special comments: I have ridden here the day after a monster rain. Now, that doesn't mean we should go tear this place up when it's delicate, but it drains well and most of it is sandy, loamy, pine-needley dirt that looks amazingly intact despite many years of hard riding. If the ranger says the trail is closed, leave it alone. Otherwise, this trail will get you breathing hard when almost nothing else can. This is a fee area, so pay the nice rangers and have fun.

Oh, any time you're ready, you little girlie mountain bikers! This is one of the finest trails in Oklahoma and Texas. A prime racecourse from way back, you can get it on here like almost nowhere else.

Start on the good old "A" loop and do a couple of miles of sandy warm-up. If you're feeling babyish then take the connector back up to the parking lot when you hit the "B" trail. If you're not feeling babyish enough, then follow Mr. "B" until you are. Wander the creeks and stuff that looks like parts of Oklahoma. Still not tired? Catch the "C" and a switchback or ten. If you fall over because you can't get out of the pedals on a switchback, then try to aim for the pine needles (they are fairly soft). When the "D" pops out, ride it too and climb a few loose hills. Punish yourself—you've been bad.

The Tyler Bicycle Club has been doing a splendid job of keeping people like you and me riding this runaway freight train for many a moon. They built the trails here and they keep them open and very sexy. The markings are pure Texas–state park magnificent and you won't get lost, especially if you listen to an old guy like me and bring along the excellent map the rangers will give you for the reasonable fee they charge to ride here. The map they gave me shows all the trails, all the roads, and all the medical emergency bailout points. This last piece of info might be handy if anyone gets crashed or bonked trying to prove how manly or womanly they are while riding here. I've seen stronger riders than me, both male and female, puke their ever-living guts out on this trail. It can be tough in the heat. I've never booted here, not yet anyway.

I, me, Chuck Cypert, the muddy trail-nazi, have ridden here when the trail was wet. I wouldn't do it in the rain, but I would head here the next day. Of course, I am a smart guy, and I would call the rangers and ask their opinion of my lofty plans before I drove all the way over here. My point is that this part of Texas is generally more insensitive to rain than a lot of places. That does not mean you can do any stupid thing you want to in this park. That does not mean you can do any stupid thing at all in this park. But if you're jonesin', this might be a place you can do when the evil black gumbo quagmire takes over the trails in the city. Call up Mr. Ranger and say, "mother, may I?".

There are lots of things to do here. You can let the kids fish, swimming is not out of the question, and picnics are never a waste of leisure time at Tyler State Park. Bodacious BBQ up by the highway should send me ribs once a week for all the times I've eaten there. Grab one of the screened shelters some time, bring some firewood, and give the family a camping trip to remember. And then sneak off with the bike. Hahahahaha…we aren't evil people, we just have a problem with mountain biking. They haven't come up with a 12-step program for that yet.

General location: Near Tyler, Texas, off I-20 in the east. About an hour and a half from Dallas.

Elevation change: Some. Repeated. Maybe 100 feet on a good day.

Season: Year-round. Any time the ranger says so is good with me.

Services: Food and all that along the highway; check out the BBQ store down there. The park has pay phones, showers, camping, parking, potties, and all that non–mountain biking stuff. They have an awesome trail here. Oh yeah, that's why I'm telling you this story.

Hazards: Getting cooked from overcooking. This trail is fast and will tempt you to do things you cannot. The deep sand can be a misery sometimes, the trees can smash you into a bruised mess with no effort on your part, and the rocky parts love the bottoms of your pedals. You can get hurt here. Don't. Pretend you did.

Rescue index: High. A cell phone might not help, but a partner and a map sure will. You are in a place with lots of well-trained employees, and they will help you if they can. Don't get yourself in a situation where you need to be rescued, but if you do, this is the place. The trail has several medical emergency bailout spots and the general mood is, "we're from Texas, how can we help?"

Land status: Texas Parks and Wildlife Department facility, here until the sun goes supernova.

Maps: Ask a ranger; they're so nice. The maps, too.

Finding the trail: Tyler State Park is slightly east of the US 259 cutoff to Tyler "proper" from I-20. Take the exit for FM 14 and go north, past Bodacious BBQ. A couple of miles later there's a flashing yellow light, and the entrance to the park is to the left. On the right is the last convenience store on your route. Enter the park and ask the nice rangers for directions (and a trail map) to the Blackjack Campground. Find that, then park and potty and hit the trails.

Sources of additional information:

Tyler State Park
789 Park Road 16
Tyler TX 75706-9141
(903) 597-5338
www.tpwd.state.tx.us/park/tyler/
    tyler.htm

Texas Parks and Wildlife Department
4200 Smith School Road

Austin, TX 78744-3291
(800) 792-1112 information
(512) 389-8900 reservations
www.tpwd.state.tx.us

Tyler Bicycle Club
P.O. Box 6734
Tyler, TX 75711
www.tylerbicycleclub.com

Notes on the trail: On the western side of the parking/camping area called Blackjack is the trailhead for the "A" loop. By the potty on the north side of the parking area is the end of the "A" loop. You'll find this if you bail down there in the woods where the "B" loop connects. There's a little paved loop that winds around back in there, by the way. But, if you're out on the "A" loop doing the ride, in about three miles you'll hit the split with "B". You follow "B" until you hit the dirt road (which is a mile or so later). Turn right on the road and go until you see the sign. Go left into the woods, or continue south on the road if you are dying. In another mile or so you hit another trail split. Take the "C" to the left and continue, or the "B" to the right and return to the dirt road. The "C" is going to carry you into the tougher, or "expert" section, where the big trees and switchbacks are. It looks like the Womble Trail in Arkansas (that is major flattery, but fitting). You get through the switchbacks and some serious riding, and in another mile or so you hit the split for the "D" loop. Take "C" and shorten the ride, or take "D" and see some more fine single-track, some climbing, and some grunting. Ride on—you're getting into the really fun stuff now. Ride the power lines and see what your legs have left on them. Ride a ravine or two, wind around, spend some more of your legs, and after about nine miles you're back at the car. What a fun trail. What a piece of work.

Still a mother, this is one of the finest trails anywhere, in any state or on any planet. You will see signs here that say "No Pedestrians." I don't really know why, 'cause I don't have a problem if peds want to come here. There's lots of room. Mountain bikers can share.

RIDE 39 · Lake Bryan Trails—Bryan

AT A GLANCE

Length/configuration: Counterclockwise loop of single-track about 8 miles long.

Aerobic difficulty: Not real bad—this place is 95/95. There are some short climbs, but nothing grueling or severe.

Technical difficulty: There are some tricky places, but this is almost a beginner trail for the most part. The surface is loose and the trail is tight in the trees, but there is nothing the 95/95 crowd will not enjoy.

Scenery: Ahhh, it's nice, but this is a trail for riding and paying attention to the conditions and not looking around for UFOs.

Special comments: A fee is required to enter this park, $5 per carload. An annual pass is available for $50; ask at the gate. This is one of the coolest trail systems I have seen; well marked and sustainable. I really have to hand it to the Brazos Valley Mountain Biking Association (BVMBA) for putting so much into this place. Thank you, I really enjoyed this one.

Though not the last chapter in the book, this was the last trail I rode while doing research. It was a long hard year—I got rained on half my days in the field, and it sucked a lot of times. I would try to hit two or three hard trails on some days, make notes and take photographs, and I was pretty tired by September. I came out here not really sure what to expect, and found one of the nicest areas of trail development anywhere. It is fairly easy for us tired old guys, but it is sufficiently tricky that you can't not love it. And it appears to me to be fully sustainable. Somebody has been putting a ton of work into the dirt here and has created something to be proud of. Thank you.

RIDE 39 • Lake Bryan Trails

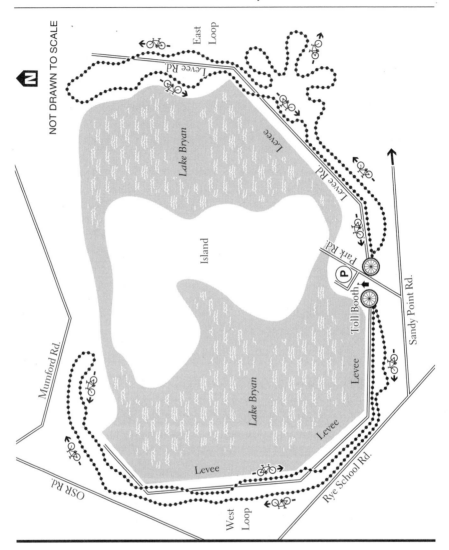

There are actually two networks of trails here, the "east loop" and the "west loop." I rode on the east side because the west had been bulldozed, because the city is building something down there. I learned from the BVMBA website that they plan to get back in there and rebuild all the trails, and that the stuff on the west is the hardest. I found the "east loop" to be full of tight turns, sneaky approach/exit patterns in the curves, and a lot of bouncing up and down through some creeks. I thought the Godzilla's Tail was a nice touch, a sort of elevated bridge over what must be a muddy spot in the wet season, and the Route of All Evil was fun. I dug the Munnerlyn Loop, too, apparently named for the guy who built a lot of this.

There are lots of deadfalls that you might want to walk, and maybe a few other tricky places that require thought, but this trail is very fast and rideable. I am enthused by how well marked the trails here are—you're shown how to bail and find an escape if you need it, and you're informed of the name of each section as you enter it. These folks have packed several miles of fine single-track into not that much land by wrapping it around and around and shooting you back out by the levee to approach the next section. The Blair Witch Woods were really fun, and I like the Skinny Dip Loop section for obvious reasons. If at any point you are too cooked to continue, you can just hop up on the levee and go west to the start area.

After a lap on the east I headed across the park road to the west. It truly was destroyed—I am so sorry. I would like to have ridden it before they 'dozed the land. I know these guys will put trail back in there when they can, and I did manage to ride some short sections of what remained. I don't think they get so much traffic over here—the trails were not nearly as well marked or established, but the BVMBA website alleges another 8 miles or so of single-track will be available again, soon, over there.

General location: Just northwest of Bryan/College Station, Texas.

Elevation change: Minimal, from the top of the levee down to the bottom of the trail is probably 50 feet, and it is spread around pretty evenly. The levee itself is the biggest hill.

Season: Pretty much year-round; I think it should drain well and be useable within a couple of days after mild rains. Don't go out here when it's wet; the sand will suck your tires down until your axles are tasting dirt.

Services: Parking, potties, water. Bring everything else you require.

Hazards: A snake or some poison ivy might not be a stretch. The trails can be loose and sandy, and crashing while leaning the wrong way into a turn is a distinct possibility.

Rescue index: Medium-high. This place gets a fair amount of traffic, and you're not far from town. Take a map and your cell phone, and if you have a pal along you will probably get rescued.

Land status: City of Bryan park.

Maps: The local mountain bike club, BVMBA, has an excellent one on their website.

Finding the trail: From TX 21 just west of Bryan, go north on FM 2818 to the blinking yellow light and turn left (west) on Sandy Point Road (FM 1687). In a few miles you will see the entrance to the park on your right (north); turn in and pay the fee. Continue past the front gate and turn left into the boat ramp area. Park somewhere in the shade and grab your bike. The trail crosses the park road right before the tollbooth, on the south between the gate and the highway. Hang a left (east) at the trailhead gate, by the sign saying Lake Bryan Mountain Bike Trail East Loop, and ride onto the levee. The first section, Rockgarden, will enter the woods to your right. Ride as much as you can and you will return along the levee from the east. The trailhead for the west loop is just on the west side of the road, near this same spot, and has a large kiosk.

Sources of additional information:

Brazos Valley Mountain Biking
 Association (BVMBA)
3802 Carter Creek Parkway
Bryan, TX 77802
http://bvmba.txcyber.com/index.htm

City of Bryan Parks
300 South Texas Avenue
Bryan, TX 77803
(979) 361-3600
www.ipt.com/city/bryan/bparks.htm

Notes on the trail: These trails are fairly near Texas A&M University, and I know there are some mountain bikers going to school down there. I strongly urge y'all to get involved with the local club and let's get that "west loop" back in shape. I gotta see some more of this place—it has a lot of potential and a lot of substance. Cheers, let's ride.

RIDE 40 · Double Lake Park Mountain Bike Trail—Coldspring

AT A GLANCE

Length/configuration: Marvelous 8-mile loop of tight sandy single-track.

Aerobic difficulty: Not bad, to the point of being minimal. A good beginner trail.

Technical difficulty: There are some tree roots and loose conditions, but this is not a real hard trail. Again, this is a nice beginner facility.

Scenery: This trail is all in a beautiful pine forest that surrounds a quiet little lake in the woods.

Special comments: This park charges a $5 entrance fee. In the summer when you ride you get the strong smell of pine trees, rich and thick and pungent. From now on that will always remind me of old Sam Houston and the national forest that bears his name.

This is a fine trail, a fun place to ooze along or to ride hard. Your choice. You can bring your kids or your beginner-level significant other and they won't hate you. This is a trail that anyone should be able to enjoy, and it's here year-round. I have ridden here the day after moderate rains, and there was no standing water anywhere and only a very slight amount of mud.

I think this trail would probably be a blast at night, and it would be great on a single-speed mountain bike. Most of it is fairly flat, the climbing is gentle and spread out well, and the technical output is minimal. You can fly through the trees here and really test your cornering skills. Though some of it is very sandy, this is not a real slippery place to ride; you can hang it out some and not get yourself into too much danger.

RIDE 40 • Double Lake Park Mountain Bike Trail

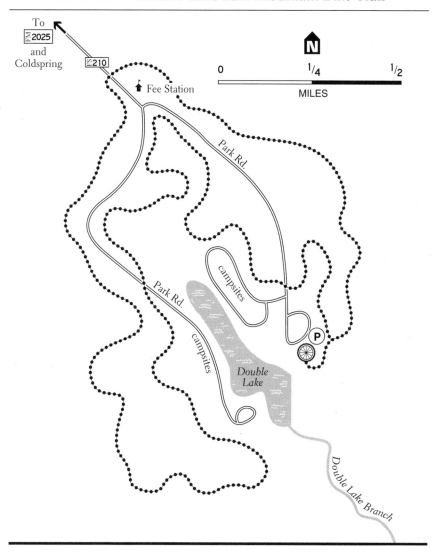

The trail is shaped sort of like a horseshoe that wraps around the lake on the west, north, and east. I always start at the main trailhead and do my lap counterclockwise. Be aware that you cross the main park roads in three places, and you must look both ways for traffic. You're gonna look pretty dumb sticking out of the front of an RV if you ignore this warning. The Double Lake Mountain Bike Trail is well established and easy to follow; don't mess around and you can't get lost. Be careful, my friend, there is a surprise around every corner, so don't be stupid. Ride hard and have fun.

Double Good, Double Fun, Double Lake Trail! Think of that old Virginia and Tennessee gentleman we stole the name of this forest from. Old Sam was quite a character. And he was also the first President of the Republic of Texas. Yeehaw. Long may the Lone Star wave in glory. Remember the Alamo and Goliad.

General location: Northeast of Houston, Texas, about an hour's drive.

Elevation change: Not bad, maybe 30 to 40 feet, spread around pretty evenly.

Season: I have ridden here a couple of times on the day after a rain and I can tell you it holds up very well. This might be a really nice winter ride; there wouldn't be any bugs and the air wouldn't be thick as steam the way it can be in the summer.

Services: The camping here is quite nice, with the typical water and electric tent and RV sites. There are rest rooms with showers, and a concession stand with a pay phone. When the little store is open you can get fed and get cold drinks. Otherwise, drag what you need in with you.

Hazards: Mosquitoes, snakes, and poison ivy. The trail is loose in places and has deadfalls and tree roots crossing it in many spots.

Rescue index: Medium. This park is fairly remote and I doubt your cell phone will work here. I equally doubt that it will take more than a day or two before they find your body—this trail gets few users. If you carry a map and keep your wits so you know where you are, the park road will be a reasonable bailout to return to the car if you need to.

Land status: A Sam Houston National Forest recreation area.

Maps: The rangers at the park will give you a nice one.

Finding the trail: The entrance to Double Lake Recreation Area is about 17 miles north of US 59 at Cleveland. Go north on FM 2025 until you are about a mile south of Cold Spring. On the eastern side of the road you will see the park entrance. Pay the ranger his money and get a map and head into the park. When the road forks, go left and follow the pavement to the end. The mountain bike trailhead is plainly marked, located near a rest room building. Park here, near the kiosk, and head onto the single-track. When it forks, you have to decide whether you're going clockwise or counterclockwise, not that it really matters. If you go left, you do the loop clockwise; if you go right the route is counterclockwise. Ride this beautiful single-track until you're back to where the trail forked and then back to your vehicle.

Sources of additional information:

Double Lake Recreation Area
301 FM 2025
Coldspring, TX 77331
(936) 653-3448
www.r8web.com/texas/Recreation/
Sam%20Houston/double_lake.htm

Sam Houston National Forest
Ranger District
394 FM 1375 West

New Waverly, TX 77358
(936) 344-6205
www.r8web.com/texas/Default.htm

Greater Houston Off Road Biking
Association (GHORBA)
3614 Mapleglen Drive
Houston, TX 77345
www.ghorba.org

Notes on the trail: I think the old Houston area club, HAMBRA, used to take care of this place. The same club is now called GHORBA and is apparently still doing quite good work here. Somebody is taking good care of this place. Thanks, whoever you are.

RIDE 41 · Memorial Park Trails—Houston

AT A GLANCE

Length/configuration: Several loops, roughly connected by a perimeter of dirt road. There isn't a ton of mileage, maybe 5–6 miles. There are many ways to ride this park—I recommend wandering the main area south of the trailhead and then hitting the "Green" trail.

Aerobic difficulty: You can definitely get some exercise here if you take to the mid-level trails (Blue and Orange), or the expert loops (Yellow, Red, and Green). Short and fast and steep and sandy. The perimeter (Purple) trail is much easier, beginner-level.

Technical difficulty: You can hone your skills on these trails, there are some tricky bits. You have to really learn your way around to hit the best spots, but if you just go on an ooze-along, you'll find all you need.

Scenery: Mosquitoes and trees and sand. And poison ivy.

Special comments: I must commend the local mountain bike club, GHORBA, and the city parks folks, for keeping this place alive. The last time I was here it was nuts. Now the righteous have established control and these trails will be with us for a while.

This is all a lot of Houston mountain bikers know. And this is still the quintessential Houston-area mountain bike trail. The older maze of ridiculousness and general foolish riding has become a thing of the past. You will see barricades where bad places have been closed off; hopefully this will result in some healing over the years. This is now a nice park, probably not all beginner, but there are plenty of 95/95 parts. There's some mid-level stuff to tease you into thinking you're "da man," and there are some respectable expert-level assault zones, if you know where to look. The Purple and Blue trails are not real severe, the Yellow and Orange offer more challenging riding, and the Green and Red are downright expert in places.

Memorial Park is a place you can just go do laps of each little bit that appeals to you. Mix in a lap over here, one over there, a loop of this part, a loop of that, ad nauseam. Watch for other trail users; there appears to be no set approach to how riders and hikers use these trails, people seem to just wander. And I mean you are right in the belly of the beast here. This is Houston—you are a bike toss from downtown and some of the major monster freeway interchanges.

RIDE 41 • Memorial Park Trails

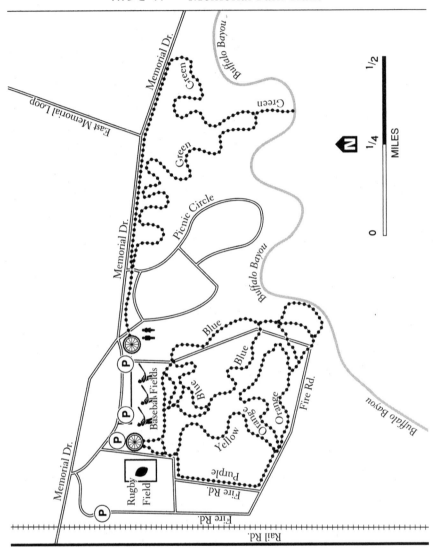

I rode here for the first time when I was working on this guidebook's first edition. I rode here for the second time when I was working on the second edition. What a difference a few years can make! This place was seriously in danger of becoming extinct because it was overrun with bandit trails and abusive riding. Since my first visit the local club and the city have found common ground, an arrangement that will be sustainable, in this observer's humble opinion. You will now find a well-established and well-maintained series of nice loops of enjoyable single-track. Several places have been closed where the trails were just too extreme for the land here, and the rest has become an admirable network of fun rides, right in the middle of the city. Amen, and job well done, Houstonians. Old Sam would be proud of you. This what the old Ho Chi Minh should have been all along.

General location: Practically in the middle of Houston, Texas.

Elevation change: Minimal, maybe 20 feet in the extremes.

Season: Not during or after any rain, for sure. Check the GHORBA website for conditions and use good judgment.

Services: Potties, water to drink, and parking.

Hazards: Other riders, mosquitoes, poison ivy, and deep sand. And abusing this place to the point that we'll lose it—don't do it!

Rescue index: High. There are just about always people out here in the daytime. A cell phone is a sure thing. They will do what they can to save you if you find yourself in need of emergency response. Oh yeah, and bring a partner to go get you rescued if you get stranded.

Land status: Houston Parks and Recreation Department park.

Maps: Check the HPARD website, they have one just like what's posted at the trailhead kiosks.

Finding the trail: Memorial Park is located along Memorial Drive, southeast of the intersection of I-610 and I-10. Take Memorial Drive or Woodway Drive and go east of I-610 to where these two streets merge, near the railroad tracks. Just past the railroad tracks is where the athletic fields are. Park around here somewhere. The Purple trail is the perimeter of the area containing the mountain bike trails, and it is accessible by going south from either trailhead kiosk, the one by the rest rooms on the east end of the baseball fields or the one on the west end between the football and baseball fields. Ride the Purple until you see signs that direct you into the woods on any of the various other loops, the Blue, Orange, Yellow, or Red. Ride around in there for a while and then go back to the trailhead by the rest rooms, east of the baseball fields. Cross South Picnic Lane and you will see where the Green trail goes into the woods between South Picnic Lane and Memorial Drive. Follow the green trail for a couple of miles until you pop out by Memorial Drive again, and then ride the dirt next to Memorial Drive to the west, back to your car.

Sources of additional information:

Greater Houston Off Road Biking
 Association (GHORBA)
3614 Mapleglen Drive
Houston, TX 77345
www.ghorba.org

Houston Parks and Recreation
Department (HPARD)
2999 S. Wayside Drive

Houston, TX 77023
(713)845-1000
www.houstonparks.org

Cyclone Cycles
2528 Sheridan Street
Houston, TX 77030
(713) 668-2104

Notes on the trail: This is a heavily used park. There are facilities for just about any sport you find in the city—mountain biking, road biking, jogging, baseball, tennis, and soccer. The upshot of all this is that you may dart over here for a few laps, a time or two a week, and expect to continue to enjoy the trails for a long time. Just as long as we continue to respect this land.

RIDE 42 · The Anthills/Terry Hershey Park—Houston

AT A GLANCE

Length/configuration: Point-to-point single-track about 8 miles long, 16 miles round-trip.

Aerobic difficulty: There are some short, steep hills here that will work your legs, but not a long bad one anywhere in sight. The sand can be interesting, though…

Technical difficulty: Plenty of basic techie bits. There are tree roots, deep sand and loose surfaces, tight trails in the trees, deadfalls, and the rest. Most of this is probably not too far beyond beginner level, though—I think it's a good 95/95 trail.

Scenery: It is so beautiful down here along the Bayou, I completely forgot I was in the middle of town. You ride along the south bank of Buffalo Bayou, down in the trees. Prettiest ride in Houston, no doubt.

Special comments: This is a mighty fine trail, but you would never think it was here if you didn't stumble onto it. I rode here the day after a rain and the trails were fine, no moisture anywhere in sight (that means it is OK to ride when there is mud elsewhere). There's paved jogging trail along part of this ride, making bailouts easy, if needed.

I had been dragging around Houston for a couple of days, riding a bunch of stuff that I had seen before, and I fell into this place. Terry Hershey Park has some of the nicest trails in Texas. Not the hardest, not the longest, but some of the most relaxing. In one afternoon, I completely fell in love with this place.

All you are going to do is wander Buffalo Bayou from around Eldridge Parkway east to just beyond Wilcrest Drive and back. It is all single-track carved out of the banks of the bayou. There can be considerable sand, and there are always lots of tree roots, but you won't find any long climbs. What you will find is some easy, wide riding on white sand, and then some more energetic stuff with lots of up and down, tight in the trees on redder sand. The eastern end of this trail is definitely the most fun for most riders. You can practice some gnarly maneuvers, catch some air, and even break a sweat on the longer hills. On the western sections you can just do an ooze-along, riding along peacefully and enjoying the ambience.

RIDE 42 • The Anthills/Terry Hershey Park

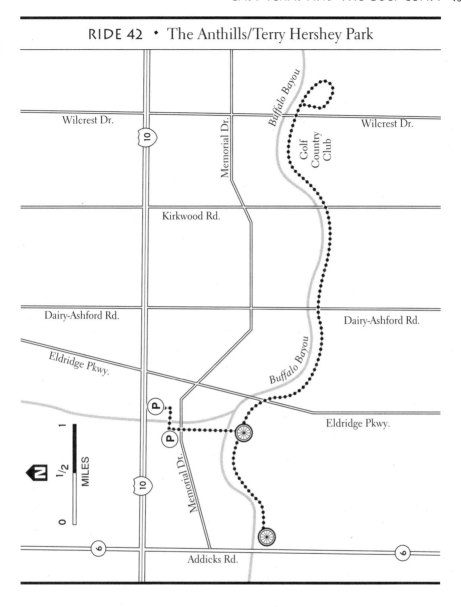

Though some of this trail certainly wouldn't rate as beginner, I'd say this is a 95/95 trail; most riders can handle most of the stuff. But I'd be really careful taking drop-offs that you can't see over. There are definitely several that appear to be where a bike trail used to go, but now simply end in the bottom of the bayou. Be prepared for some deep sand wherever you go here, it gets kind of powdery most of the time. I would probably recommend some mosquito repellent, since this is big game country and they are loaded for griz. I'd also watch real close for poison ivy; this place probably has about a pound per hundred square feet.

General location: Western Houston, Texas.

Elevation change: Slight, you might have 30 or 40 feet between the extremes.

Season: Pretty much year-round. I have ridden here the day after a slight rain and nothing was wet. I wouldn't take off through here in (or after) a heavy rain, however, since we do have flash floods in Texas. This place has all been under water very recently. And don't ride it when it's muddy.

Services: Potty and drinks. Bring whatever else you will need.

Hazards: Poison ivy, hidden drop-offs that lead to the bayou, and there might even be a snake or two. Some of the terrain here is fairly rugged, so you just want to be careful all around.

Rescue index: High. You are in the middle of the city and never very far from major streets. Bring your cell phone and keep a good idea of your location at all times.

Land status: Houston Parks and Recreation Department park.

Maps: The only map I have ever seen of this place is posted on the trailhead kiosk, on the south side of the bayou, west end of the park, around the footbridge.

Finding the trail: The best place to park is on the north side of Memorial Drive, just west of Eldridge Parkway. Take the paved trail south, parallel to the creek, until you cross the main footbridge over Buffalo Bayou. Find a place to get from the paved trail down along the bayou under the bridge and ride gradually eastward. You will cross under several major streets as you go: Eldridge Parkway, Dairy-Ashford Road, Kirkwood Road, and Wilcrest Drive. Slightly past Wilcrest you'll find the end of the trails, and then you can turn around and retrace your steps back to the car.

Sources of additional information:

Greater Houston Off Road Biking
  Association (GHORBA)
3614 Mapleglen Drive
Houston, TX 77345
www.ghorba.org

Houston Parks and Recreation
  Department (HPARD)
2999 S. Wayside Drive

Houston, TX 77023
www.houstonparks.org

Cyclone Cycles
2528 Sheridan Street
Houston, TX 77030
(713) 668-2104

Notes on the trail: A mighty fine job by GHORBA and the city of Houston. This is one of the nicest trails in the state, and I want everyone to know it. Check out the club, they do great work. Also be aware that the city of Houston has big plans. Big plans for new mountain bike trails. As time and the budget will allow, this city will become well known as a great place to cycle.

RIDE 43 · Jack Brooks Park Trail—Hitchcock

AT A GLANCE

Length/configuration: A spider's web of single-track
that winds all around in some trees along the bayou.
There is probably 5 miles of trail here, it's hard to say
exactly.

Aerobic difficulty: The climbing is limited to 5–15
feet at a time, short and steep, so you can work your legs some. This trail is
not really hard, there are no significant aerobicisms.

Technical difficulty: Aye, there's the rub. The tree roots here are evil—
riding this trail can be very tricky. If the mean little things are a little wet,
it is Mr. Bustyerass de Zaster ten times over, holdin' a yard sale, maybe.

Scenery: Mosquitoes, poison ivy, dirt, and trees. Some really cool trees.
Every tree root on this trail looks exactly like a water moccasin. It's spooky,
but you had better check each one for animation.

Special comments: This place can beat you to death on a rigid bike. It is
a constant mass of gnarled tree roots, so managing your machine should
be job one.

I don't need filler, at this point, and if I didn't like riding here I would have left
the Jack Brooks Park out. I dig it, the gumbo reminds me of home, and the
short ups and downs are really exciting if you have the right attitude. The problem is that I know a lot of people who absolutely hate this place.

The trails here are all located in the trees along Highland Bayou. The good
ones anyway. There's some other single-track in the park, but I personally would-
n't bother. I like the parts in the woods. Riding here is like riding around inside
that place with all the snakes in the movie "Raiders of the Lost Ark." Every tree
root looks like the biggest and nastiest water moccasin you ever saw. The scary
part is that you get so used to trying to mentally eliminate each one as a real
threat that pretty soon you miss the real ones. If there ain't snakes here, then I am
not a cyclist. Just 'cause I look stupid don't mean I'm not.

You can forget riding here in or near the rain. It is a slimefest; you'll probably
end up banging your knee or twisting a wrist or something. This is gumbo, boys
and girls. If you think you have quick reflexes, the tree roots at Jack Brooks will
set you free from any misconceptions that you ever want to do this again. In wet
conditions the front and rear of your bike will be slipping every few seconds.
Even if you're Hans Rey, you are gonna go meet Mr. de Zaster here.

I sort of told this story in the first book, but I can give it a go again. Parts of this
place was the Army's Camp Wallace. They had a bunch of troops down here
during WWII, and made 'em crawl around out there in the woods with the
'gators and moccasins and mosquitoes, just to get them ready for action. As Justin
Wilson might say, "Don't that purty?" Yeah baby, sign me up. NOT! You can still

RIDE 43 • Jack Brooks Park Trail

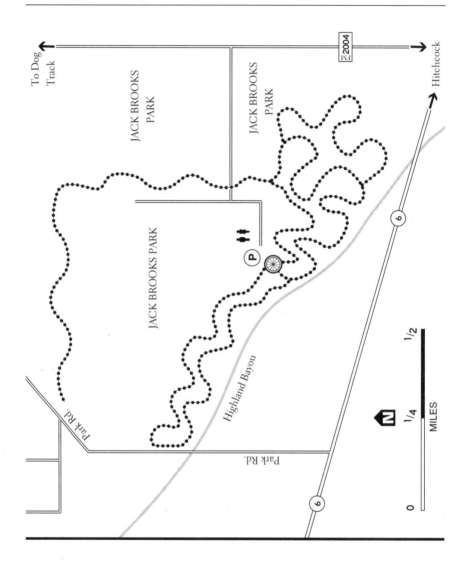

see ruins from old barracks and other stuff from the Army days, if you wander around on the roads here.

General location: Near Hitchcock, Texas, half an hour or so southwest of Houston.

Elevation change: There might be places here that are 20 feet above other places, but they are very few.

Season: Not during or after a rain. If the urge strikes you to ride here in summer, hahaha, I'd bring some mosquito repellent. A gallon or so ought to do it.

Services: You can get a drink and you can go to the bathroom, but that's it. Bring what you need.

Hazards: SNAKES. I've never seen one here, that's what scares me. It's the ones you don't notice that get you. You know something else?—I think they have poison ivy here. I should have put a smiley face after that; this is where the Devil does his research on poisonous plants.

Rescue index: High. You are never far from the parking lot, a mile or so tops, and it's easy to find your way in and out of the trees. Your cell phone will probably work, even.

Land status: This is a Galveston County beach park.

Maps: Not readily available, but you don't need one. You can't get lost out here even if you try. You can get temporarily misplaced, though.

Finding the trail: The entrance to the park is located about three miles south of the intersection of I-45 and FM 2004, near the town of Hitchcock. Enter the park and follow the road to the Veteran's Pavilion. Park here, and you will see the trailhead kiosk. Take a good look at the map. They show lots of trail that doesn't apply to us (we aren't riding the loop, we are riding near the bayou). As far as I can tell, you have to get on the "no bikes" Nature Trail to get down to the trees south of you. Make sure you pay attention to any signs you see, and don't do any riding on trails you're not supposed to enjoy. About a hundred feet from the kiosk you will see where there is single-track going left (east) into the trees, just off the Nature Trail. Follow this around toward the east; you can go as far as the road you came in on. Then curve back toward the bayou and wander around in the trees. There doesn't seem to be any one main trail, there are several main trails. You can punish yourself by gradually meandering west until you hit the other road. Then start back. More of same, there is a lot of trail out there in them trees.

Sources of additional information:

Greater Houston Off Road Biking
  Association (GHORBA)
3614 Mapleglen Drive
Houston, TX 77345
www.ghorba.org

Cyclone Cycles
2528 Sheridan Street

Houston, TX 77030
(713) 668-2104

Parks Department, County of
  Galveston
www.co.galveston.tx.us/Parks_Dept

Notes on the trail: This place gets locked up at night, so don't try to get in beyond the hours of 8 a.m. and dark-thirty. This is a decent beginner trail, maybe not a lot of fun for some riders, but a good place to learn. Hey, is that a snake?

RIDE 44 · North Padre Island— Padre Island National Seashore

AT A GLANCE

Length/configuration: A one-way trip of 30 miles of soft sand ought to about cook us. It always does me. Then someone can haul you back to camp for the night, if you like.

Aerobic difficulty: Tough. The sand sucks your wheels down and the sun burns your body. And your friends—the ones who love you and are carrying you here—the sand and sun will get them too.

Technical difficulty: I don't even use a helmet here, and I am generally the helmet-mafia. With a tailwind and the right tide, it is quite a blast.

Scenery: Excellent. The water along the Gulf of Mexico in Texas is not all nasty like Galveston. The water down here is gorgeous shades of green to blue. The dunes are magnificent. The wildlife is always interesting. The problem is that this ride is through garbage and trash the whole way. Ignore it, just like the people who trash the beach, and you'll love it.

Special comments: This is a fee area; the rangers charge you $10 to get your car in. This ride description covers the area of North Padre from the park entrance to the Mansfield Ship Channel. It could, however, be applied generically to just about any part of North or South Padre Island. Riding on the beach is like that. It is soft and sandy and there are no convenience stores or pay phones. A support vehicle is mandatory.

God might help you out here, but most of the mortals you meet are going to look at you like you're either completely nuts or you're an illegal alien. The only other cyclists I have ever seen on this beach were up from the south, the Mexican south. They ride up the beach as a sneaky way into the U.S. Be nice to them if you see them; they have to ride a hundred miles of this crap to work 12 hours a day or more for pennies, until the INS catches them and sends them home.

Please understand this is not South Padre Island, "the Spring Break island," this is North Padre Island. This ride is near Corpus Christi. But not one you just whip over and do and then go home. You'd better be on a mission. Both your life and your sanity will be at stake. And you had better really love sand. Sand in your eyes and ears, sand in your food/shorts/chain/shifters, sand in your sleeping bag. You gotta love it.

A recon run is not only mandatory but also necessary, logistically. Drive down the island, take a map with you (see the additional information section), and mark it up with points of interest as you go. Theoretically, there is a mile-marker every five miles or so, but the hurricanes eat them so reset your odometer to zero

RIDE 44 · North Padre Island

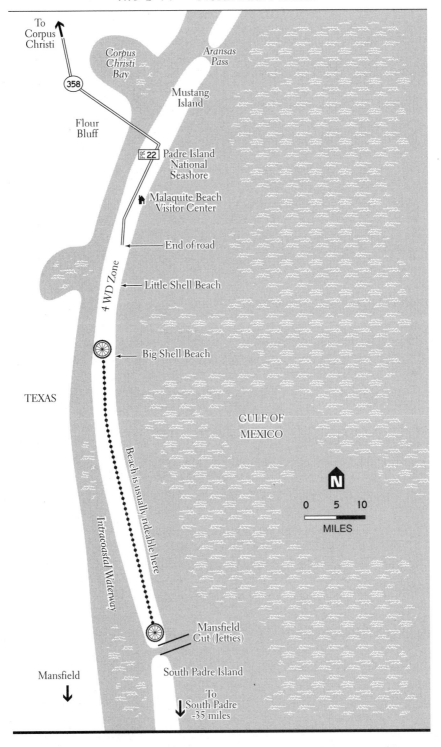

To
Corpus
Christi

Corpus
Christi
Bay

Aransas
Pass

358

Mustang
Island

Flour
Bluff

PR 22 Padre Island
National
Seashore

Malaquite Beach
Visitor Center

End of road

4 WD Zone

Little Shell Beach

Big Shell Beach

TEXAS

GULF OF
MEXICO

N

0   5   10

MILES

Beach is usually rideable here

Intracoastal Waterway

Mansfield
Cut (Jetties)

Mansfield
↓

South Padre Island

To
↓ South Padre
-35 miles

I'd call this a photo-op. Typical scenery along the beach at Padre Island National Seashore.

when you hit the Malachite Beach Visitor Center. A GPS is quite handy here for finding your location, if you have the maps to go with it.

Don't go without a healthy four-wheel-drive. Have a full tank of gas when you start, and plenty of water and guts and fresh underwear. At about ten miles down-island, you pass the "Four-Wheel-Drive Zone" sign, where the nice rangers inform you that you're on your own from here. Nobody is going to come pull you out for less than hundreds of dollars.

You might get up to 50 mph, but mostly you will be driving along at 20 mph or so. About 15 to 20 miles down you start to enter the Big Shell. If you make it through this 20-or-so miles of terrifying beach, it is usually then smooth sailing to the Mansfield cut. Another 30 miles or so of easy driving south will take you as far as you can go. That was the part we will ride, later. Take notes. Seriously. Enjoy the air-conditioning and dry and relatively sand-free conditions inside your vehicle while you can.

At some point during your drive down-island, stop and walk back into the dunes. I must warn you that the mosquitoes are frightening back in there near dusk. Climb some of the tall dunes and gaze up and down the beach. This is a marvelous place, full of wonder and mystery. And sand, lots and lots of fine white sand. And crabs, man, billions of crabs.

When you hit the cut and jetty at the Mansfield ship channel, you have to stop. Then get on your bike and ride back as far as you can. You normally won't be able to ride north more than 30 miles or so. For myself, when I start riding back, I carry a PowerBar and two GU energy packets along with a quart of water or so, per hour. And a can of WD40 for the chain is always nice. The stuff your bike will collect on this ride will make you hate me forever for ever sending you here. Bring lots of sunscreen, and maybe apply some Vaseline before the ride (if you know what I mean, Vaseline). You can leave the helmet at home (for once, and I mean I am the helmet-mafia, but if you can't ride this without dying from a head injury you need to find another sport). Bring a hat and a bandana or two. Long sleeves, and some old shoes instead of your best. A cell phone is useless. On the tallest dune (maybe 40 feet up) you might get a cell if the gods are especially fond of you that day. CB radios are good for five miles or so on a normal day.

OK, now you get someone else to drive the whole 62 miles or so to the cut at the Mansfield ship channel. Then you load up and ride back, right? Yeah, if only it were that simple. You have to hit this beach when the weather and tides are right. I have included URLs to guide you to info on both. Re-supply is better than nice here, so if your buds can sort of ooze along and let you connect every five or so miles you won't have to lug a ton of stuff. But if you're convinced you are capable, you can always just load it all up and ride. Get a nice south wind and a packed beach and just crank.

My point is this: Padre is way better than rideable when it has the right conditions (people do it every day). And death from drowning can happen when it doesn't have them. Like during a hurricane or a bad blow off the gulf. I know the surf gets up to the dunes, because I have walked around back there a few days after this has happened. You definitely need dependable and savvy comrades and a good plan to get out of here and live to laugh about it.

I would expect to average around five miles an hour to consider my pace acceptable. You will often be able to see five miles up the beach, and it will take you an hour or so to reach the event horizon. If you can do 30 miles in this sand and surf and sun and finish in around six hours, and not cry too much, you are a survivor. If you start way down south when the tide is going out pretty good, you will be in excellent condition to make it back to the Big Shell before the tide returns. If you find yourself out on that island with the tides pushing you up against the powder, it will be a death ride. You will be dodging the cycles of waves to find something rideable. All that sand up there toward the dunes, where the four-wheel-drive guys are driving, is not something you will ever average five miles per hour on. More like five miles per day. You must be able to tour the part of the beach packed by the waves from the last high tide, and you have roughly six hours to do it. With a wind from the south it is motor city. With less, it's miserable.

When the tide is out and the wind is from Mexico you can travel. And see shells—I mean seashells—like nice sand dollars and all that (I always see that perfect sand dollar just as it goes under the front wheel and is lost). If you're inclined to photography, like me, you better get your Wheaties for sure. The conditions here are constantly blowing sand from the beach, and salt spray off the gulf. Bring double zip-lock baggies for anything worth anything, maybe a can of aero-duster, and something clean to wipe things off with. Don't forget a polarizer in case you get a really good sky. It happens. I have shot some of my prettiest color here. You ride along until you find a big snag washed up or piece of debris, and then you burn a roll of film.

One thing you won't enjoy photographing, or riding over, or just looking at in general, is the garbage. Totally disgusting. It must wash in from places as far away as New Orleans and Cozumel. The beach is covered with trash. It would take more than a hundred people to carry it all off if they worked eight hours a day for a year. This is the downside. I have seen all that medical syringe crap and milk bottles and morons that abandon campsites full of a week's worth of beer cans. It is quite an embarrassment as far as I'm concerned, as a proud Texan. The only things I ever leave on this beach are footprints and the occasional tent peg that just escaped me. My trash is burned, and what isn't safe to burn is hauled back to the proper receptacles out in the world. In fact, the whole reason I want you to ride here is because I want people to care about this wonderful place. It is an epic ride. When the sky is beautiful and the water is clean and the wind is right you, can fall in love with it. Easier than loving Mike Modano when he scores on a breakaway. I mean it!

And if you like to fish, well you have just guaranteed you will return to this island as often as you can. There are few things in life 'mo betta' than fresh redfish while relaxing in the evening on Padre Island. Add some corn and some fresh shrimp, or some of BBQ Dan's ribs, and a full moon—whoa baby! It pays to have a camping partner who wants to fish and cook while you ride. It is well worth the hassle of hauling them down-island with you. Even BBQ Dan. Just don't drop your corn in the sand like I always do. BBQ Dan never gets tired of reminding me of that.

This is a place where large tires and low air pressures will benefit you greatly. And planning for whatever might happen. And having a crew. If you have a support vehicle, you can ride from a few hundred meters north of the jetty until the beach runs out at Big Shell. But you will seldom ride any farther north than that.

Big Shell is hard to get through in a four-wheel-drive most of the time. The beach is soft and the tides chew it up daily, and you won't want to try to ride through there. The Big Shell is usually bad from about the 15- or 20- mile marker until the 30- or 35-mile marker, heading south. It can be an easy place to lose your vehicle if you get stuck and can't extricate yourself. Sure, guys in other four-wheel-drives will go by. Go by and laugh at your dumb ass for getting stuck. Don't expect people to drag you out of someplace they are barely able to get through themselves.

Carry an air compressor and a tire plug kit, and a good spare tire. And about three cans of Fix-a-flat. I have had people wake me up in the morning because they had a flat and no spare and blah blah blah. (Don't bother me, I'm sleeping.) Bring a shovel and a good jack. Bring one of those solar showers, so you can drain your coolers at night and get semi-clean the next day after your ride. Bring a shortwave radio; the only thing 'mo betta' than beach riding is eating fresh redfish and surfing the long-meter bands, listening to Radio Havana or the BBC from Africa. Plus you can get the weather, always a tidy item to have knowledge of while out on Padre.

Don't try to drive to the cut at Mansfield if your truck is leaking a gallon of coolant an hour or if you haven't checked your spare in a year. Bring tools, some heavy rope or a good long tow strap, jumper cables, and a first aid kit. And lots of beer—I mean, water.

Life is a beach, so this ride is perfectly flat. All sea level. All downhill if you're in a pickup truck. All far from a safe haven if you need emergency help. But at certain times of the year peregrine falcons swoop around, working the dunes and diving the surf, and you'll never forget it. One of the most amazing things I have ever seen was a falcon plunging into the surf and then, in about three flaps of those pointed wings, he comes straight back up. He flutters the wings to shake them dry; then two strokes forward, and he's flying again. You might see an eagle, or you might step on a stingray. It's that kind of place.

Or maybe the pelicans will be zooming up the beach in a pace line of 25 birds; you will see them coming for miles. Or perhaps a coyote will pop out of a cut in the dunes and watch you ride by. You might see dolphins, or sharks, or jellyfish and man-o'-wars, or sea turtles, or deer, or a boat wreck, or maybe the Coast Guard will go by in their chopper or Lear jet. I have seen all of these things on the island (my sea turtle was dead, though). Keep your eyes open, carry some binoculars, lots of film, and a hearty attitude. This is a ride that normal people will not enjoy. Go forth, and don't be normal.

Carry out your trash. Carry out your trash. (Dare I say it again?) There are dumpsters at the entrance. And showers and people and the world of the mundane. Don't leave anything on this beach except for tire tracks and sweat.

General location: Padre Island National Seashore, near Corpus Christi, Texas.

Elevation change: All sea level.

Season: Just about any time there are no weather advisories. The summer heat is tough during the middle of the day, but there is usually a nice breeze. Don't go if there are severe storms in the area. But it can be nice in a gentle rain. Check with the rangers to see what beach conditions are like.

Services: Nothing. Load up in town before you head to the park. There are showers and potties and a store at the park Visitor Center.

Hazards: Maniac drivers, for sure. Stingrays and jellyfish are not uncommon. The weather must be respected here. The soft sand on the beach can swallow your vehicle, and the debris is always laced with boards with nails sticking out of them. Getting stranded down here would suck. Someone will probably happen by every few hours, but you should take a towrope and some tools. Extra gas is good if your can doesn't leak.

Rescue index: Medium. People come down here all the time, but they might be a lot more intent on fishing than pulling you out of the sand. A cell phone is generally useless, but a CB radio wouldn't hurt.

Land status: National seashore, just like a park.

Maps: All sorts of good maps can be had—the rangers will give you a cheapo, but the bait shops around here have some great ones. The Trails Illustrated folks also have a nice one.

Trails Illustrated
P.O. Box 4357
Evergreen, CO 80437-4357

(800) 962-1643 or (303) 670-3457
www.trailsillustrated.com
http://maps.national
geographic.com/trails

Finding the trail: From Corpus Christi, take South Padre Island Drive (TX 358) through town and across the causeway and through Flour Bluff. This is the last stop for supplies, with several convenience stores and hotels and gas stations, stuff like that. Follow the highway until it becomes Park Road #22. In a few miles you will pass the main gate and approach the visitor center. Last chance for water and a shower. Follow the main road until it cuts through the dunes and becomes sand and a hundred miles of beach. Head south until you can't any more and ride back, as far as you can.

Sources of additional information:

Padre Island National Seashore
9405 South Padre Island Drive
Corpus Christi, TX 78418
(361) 949-8173 main number

(361) 949-8175 beach conditions
(361) 949-8068
Malachite beach visitor center
www.nps.gov/pais/index.htm

Notes on the trail: As I mentioned, you can apply the description of this ride generically to any of the beaches of Texas. A lot of people go to South Padre every year for spring break, and you might have some interest in beach riding down there. From South Padre you can ride north to the Mansfield cut and have about 30 miles of open beach to enjoy. Or you might want to explore Matagorda Island, to the north of North Padre Island. This is a state park, and they claim to have nearly 70 miles of beach open to non-motorized travel.

TEXAS PANHANDLE

I grew up out here. I guess you could call it that, spending those pivotal adolescent years here. I camped up in Haynes Canyon, in the snow, and went to rock concerts in Amarillo and Lubbock. Finished high school, and then ran away from home at the age of 21. I'm goofy like that.

There ain't no flat land like they've got here on the High Plains. You can see a town 15 miles away at night, the traffic lights and Allsup's stores and all. We'll go up there to ride some, and we'll wander through to get to some other rides. I want you to think about what it was like up here a couple of hundred years ago. All tall grass and buffalo, a few Indian tribes here and there, and not much else. Maybe a hawk or two.

When the white man invaded this area he had to kill off just about everything that lived there. The Native Americans, the buffalo, and the grass. Now it is huge farming operations and cattle feed lots. Ahhh, the smell of money. Or whatever that scent is wafting on the 40 mph breeze. And believe me, my brothers and sisters, the wind does know how to blow up here. You get a couple of those 70+ mph days a year, where the sky turns brown and opening your car door can be a life-threatening experience.

I have stood in the middle of a wheat field at night, with a huge full moon and the wind whipping the wheat in every direction. The sizzling sound the stalks make and the feeling of energy is better than drugs. Right up there with...well, you know. I love the Panhandle; it has a special beauty that only a few can appreciate. I guarantee those tribesmen had it going on, though. This truly is a beautiful place.

RIDE 45 · Big Loop MTB Trail—
Copper Breaks State Park

AT A GLANCE

Length/configuration: A clockwise loop of mostly rideable single-track, some old dirt roads; about 10 miles per lap.

Aerobic difficulty: Substantial. There are some climbs here; they're loose and tricky and will make you hurt.

Technical difficulty: Some parts are grandma easy and some aren't rideable by yours truly. Some kid on a downhill bike maybe, but not me. I'll definitely walk a few places here. This is not a beginner trail, at least not where it drops off the ridge into Bull Canyon.

Scenery: Quite nice; this is a very pretty park and a couple of the spots along the trail offer sweet views of the Pease River valley. I'd recommend bringing your camera and your best shorts, if you know what I mean.

Special comments: This is another one of those fabulous parks that has grown up a ton since I rode it and wrote about it for the first book. There is a real mountain bike trail here now, a groovy one. A state park entry fee is required ($3) if you don't have a Conservation Passport.

Man, this used to be a tour of the sand, with no markings and no idea where you were. Now it's a top-shelf mountain bike trail, one that you will respect. Some of this is easy and fast and fun, but some of it has to be walked. There are a few drops as you descend into the canyon where it would take several inches of travel on both ends of the bike, and a much younger body, to survive such a rolling assault.

I got excellent directions for riding this thing from my pal Jeff Williams—I think he's an OEF guy, actually. We were going to try and hook up, but I rode the day they had the Hotter'n Hell Hundred over in Wichita Falls. Jeff was racing and figured he should save his legs for Sunday. That's cool—I had a blast, my man, and thanks for all your help.

Let's ride. Start by the headquarters and ride south, down into Bull Canyon. The trail is sandy and rocky, the worst of both worlds. There are some mighty tricky bits as you wander the next couple of miles. There are plenty of trail markers to keep you on the right track, however, so just follow the signs. It is really pretty through here if the sun hasn't sucked all the life out of the plants. You drop off the ridge and cross the creek below the dam for Lake Copper Breaks. There's some fairly technical stuff here, loose and evil in spots. Most of it is rideable, though, and you'll either be bleeding or having fun—or both!—by this point.

Keep following the signs, and you'll ride some old dirt roads and some more cool single-track, and soon you'll be on the far west boundary of the park, near the

RIDE 45 • Big Loop MTB Trail

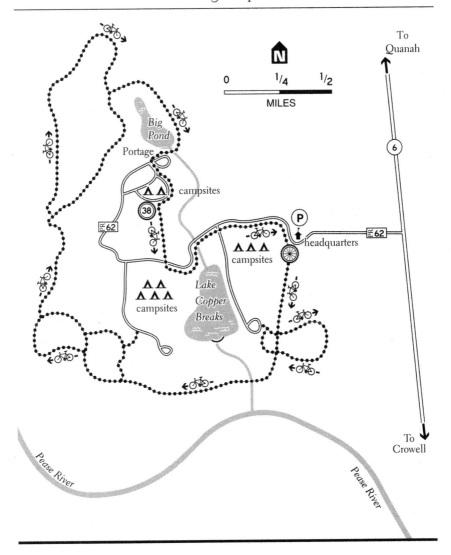

fence. Through here it's like mud flats or something; very fast and smooth and enjoyable. You can fly along and just rip, but watch for softies. You'll wander north for a couple of miles, marking the outer fence on your left from time to time. You will soon curve back and head south, following more old roads and sand.

Pretty soon you'll realize that you're on the north side of Big Pond and you'll hit the spillway, a long piece of concrete. Cross over and climb up the hill to the picnic tables you can see up there. You will have to walk this part, there ain't no ridin' up. Once you get into the camping area (Big Pond), you have to sort of cut across, past the rest rooms, and go southeast looking for campsite #38. The trail

What a pleasant surprise it was to ride at Copper Breaks State Park after so many years. Some serious trail miles out there now, tribe. I mean it.

continues off the hill from the back of site #38. Ride down, being careful because it's got some techies here, and at the bottom of the hill hang a right by the telephone line. Climb up the next hill, a decent one, and when you reach the paved park road at the top, turn left by Comanche Campground and start your final climb of the day.

The climb up the road is one you will remember; it is plenty steep. Follow this pavement back to the headquarters and your car. Whew. Great ride. Let's eat. And then I definitely need a Shiner Bock.

General location: 12 miles south of the tiny town of Quanah, Texas.

Elevation change: There is a pretty solid 100 feet of delta. You start high, ride low, and have to finish back up on the hill.

Season: Year-round. I wouldn't want to be out here in or shortly after a rain, but if the weather has been good I'm sure it's useable.

Services: Normal state park stuff like camping, water, potties and showers, and a pay phone. A safe place to stay, but bring along what you will need out on the trail. Like don't forget your bike or helmet or anything important. It is a long trip back to the rest of the world from down here in Bull Canyon. It's also a long way to the nearest hospital. Keep that in mind as you ride.

Hazards: Some of the terrain here is quite severe—you could crash real easy. I guarantee there are snakes and biting flies here, and the likelihood of a flat tire is high. Your phone is a waste of silicon out here. Be careful and live to ride another day.

Rescue index: Low to medium. Not a lot of people will be out there on that single-track on an average day, and there are plenty of ways to meet your maker, right after you meet Mr. de Zaster. Ride with a partner, and tell the rangers that you're going out to ride the trail. If your car is still sitting there after a day or two, they'll begin to worry and come find whatever is left of you.

Land status: Another fine Texas state park—thank you Texas Parks and Wildlife Department and the people of Quanah.

Maps: The park has an OK one; just ask for it.

Finding the trail: Trail? Hell, finding Quanah is going to be interesting enough for most of you. Start out roughly half-way from Wichita Falls to Amarillo on US 287, and you'll find Quanah. Turn south on TX 6 for about 12 miles. The entrance to the park is on the west side of the road. The trailhead is right by the headquarters building, just to the south, plainly marked by a sign saying "Big Loop MTB Trail." You will return—if you survived—from the northwest on the park road.

Sources of additional information:

Copper Breaks State Park
777 Park Road 62
Quanah, TX 79252-7679
(940) 839-4331
www.tpwd.state.tx.us/park/copper/
copper.htm

Texas Parks and Wildlife Department
4200 Smith School Road
Austin, TX 78744-3291
(800) 792-1112 information
(512) 389-8900 reservations
www.tpwd.state.tx.us

Notes on the trail: There are some locals who built and take care of this place. I'm not sure I know who they all are but, I have heard of 'em, and traded e-mails with some of the players. Thanks, you guys, for some excellent trail. I hope I meet some of you one of these days.

RIDE 46 · Mae Simmons Park Trail—Lubbock

AT A GLANCE

Length/configuration: A winding, wandering loop of single-track, about 8 miles.

Aerobic difficulty: Some pretty decent stuff, not too bad, but it will make you sweat and use your best stuff.

Technical difficulty: There is a lot of loose terrain here, steep and sudden, not real long, but scary. You need to keep your wits when you ride here—it will really work you.

Scenery: Pretty bleak. I'm sorry, but I grew up out here and I can say that. There is nothing to see except mesquite and the occasional vulture.

Special comments: Here in the hometown of Charles Hardin "Buddy"

RIDE 46 • Mae Simmons Park Trail

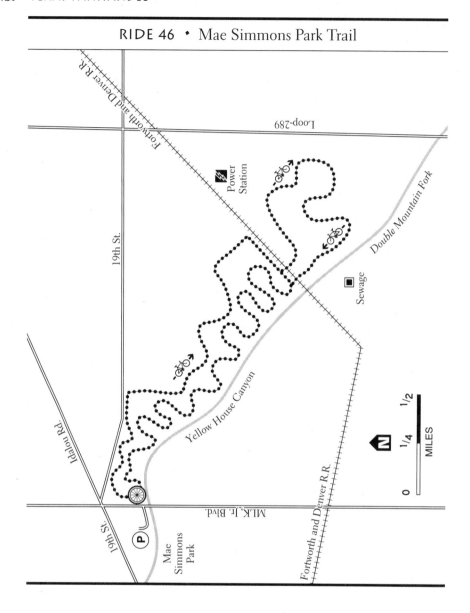

Holly, we ride where we can. Most of the terrain is tabletop flat and in the wind. When you find a cool little place like this here along Yellow House Canyon, you relish it. I don't know who built this, but thanks y'all. This is a place to ride hard.

I had heard of this trail for years before I finally got to ride here. I blew through town one day, headed from Palo Duro to the X-Bar, and found the trail and rode. Down by Dunbar Historic Lake. You know, I grew up north of here, in

Plainview, and I had never been down to this canyon before. I guess I've driven by here a hundred times, but that was long before mountain bikes. I came out here and rode it; I was in a bad mood and it was hot, and I hated this trail. Then, after I came to my senses and thought about it, I realized it is a pretty cool place, after all. I was riding along at one point, and a small hawk came zooming over my shoulder and landed in a tree right in front of me. I fumbled around and tried to get my binoculars out, but he had lunch in his left talon and other ideas. He flew on, I went on up the trail. Stuff like this happens to me.

You start there by Martin Luther King Jr. Boulevard (MLK), where it crosses the lake, and wander around the bluff until you pass a retirement home. Soon you'll find yourself along 19th Street and have to turn right (south) onto an old double-track. Then you ride some more mesquite and start finding forks in the trail. I stayed left to ride the perimeter, dodging the cactus, and sliding through the loose turns. I saw some carsonite signs; they seemed to reflect the typical green/blue/black trail difficulty ratings. If you ride it the way I went, you will get over by the power lines and associated old dirt roads. You can see a power sub-station in the distance to the north, but then you will head south again. The trail here is fast, mostly flat, and very loose.

Then you cross a pipeline and an old railroad grade and go east into some mighty challenging stuff. It is loose and steep and will suck your legs dry. Wander around here some and try to stay upright. This is a maze of trails, more than I was able to trace out completely. Some of the expert sections east of the railroad are almost more than I can do. In the right hands I'm sure it's fast, but I don't like to go around laying down 30-foot skid marks, so I took it easy. Parts of this trail are chewed to crap by abusive riders, I'd have to say.

You loop around and head back west, crossing the old railroad grade again. Here it's slightly saner, but it still has some good tough sections that will test your skills. You wander up and down the bluff on the single-track as it snakes back in on itself in a million places. After a while it evens out a little more and you're back to MLK, where you started.

This is truly a badass trail; it made me fear for my life and lungs in a few places. Check it out.

General location: Far east Lubbock, Texas.

Elevation change: About 50 feet, as far as I can tell, repeated endlessly in spurts.

Season: Pretty much year-round. I wouldn't want to be out here in a tornado, and an ice storm would probably be interesting, but otherwise it seems pretty durable.

Services: Parking, not much else.

Hazards: Mesquite and cactus, loose marbley trail surface. The sun will cook your brain in the summer if you ride here in the middle of the day.

Rescue index: I'll say medium. There probably aren't a lot of people riding out here on a typical day, but your cell phone should work, and you're basically in town.

Land status: City of Lubbock park.

Maps: Not available, as far as I know. I made my own.

Finding the trail: I started at the Mae Simmons Center. Hang a right (south) on

MLK from eastbound 19th Street, just past Avenue A and then the railroad tracks, in eastern Lubbock. This is maybe a mile east of I-27. Turn right just before the lake, and then right into the Mae Simmons Center. From there you ride the pavement back down to the lake and turn east and cross MLK. You can catch the trail there on the northeast corner, over there by that tree. I rode clockwise, because that was how the arrows seemed to point, so hang a left on the single-track by the tree. Follow the trail and you'll be back here in an hour or so.

Sources of additional information:

Lubbock Parks and Recreation
1010 9th Street
Lubbock, Texas 79401
(806) 775-2690
http://parks.ci.lubbock.tx.us/

Lubbock Bicycle Club
5728 76th Street

Lubbock, TX 79424
www.lubbockbicycleclub.org

DFC Cycles & Fitness
6701 Indiana Avenue, # D
Lubbock, TX 79413
(806) 796-2453

Notes on the trail: I rode here in the middle of the day in summer. It was pretty brutal. The surface is white and the sky didn't have a cloud in sight; my eyeballs actually hurt afterward. It worked me pretty good. I was mentally drained when I got back to my truck. I'd really like to see it with some snow; I'll bet it is a completely different ride in winter. I think I could really love this place if I was here in the right conditions and had some more time.

RIDE 47 · Caprock Canyons Trailway—Quitaque

AT A GLANCE

Length/configuration: It depends; the section of this 65-mile trail that I describe is a 15-mile-long point-to-point, or a 30-mile round-trip. You can do the downhill thang and miss the best of how quiet it can be, or you can ride up and back and have it all in your head forever. Figure on 30 miles and 6 hours to really experience Quitaque Canyon.

Aerobic difficulty: Riding up is an easily sustainable steady grind. The ride down is fast and can be scary when you hit the softies. Not much sweat is required if you just ride down.

Technical difficulty: This trail is an old railroad bed, with the tracks and ties removed—I think it is engineered with a 1% maximum grade. That is very gentle. The surface of old railroad ballast will bring stretches of soft gravel in places, but if you have some real tires it's quite enjoyable. Going up is a steady assault, especially when you get the wind in your face, but the ride back down makes it all worthwhile.

RIDE 47 • Caprock Canyons Trailway

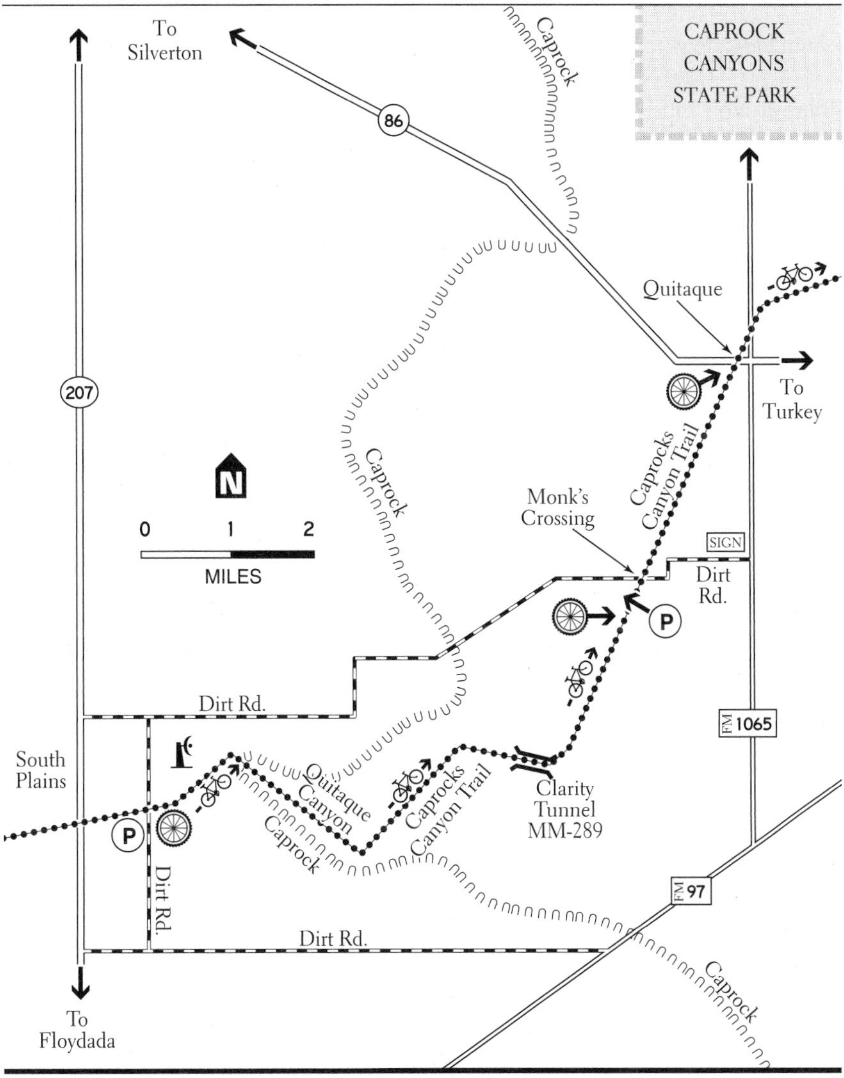

To Silverton

86

CAPROCK
CANYONS
STATE PARK

Caprock Canyon Trail

Quitaque

To Turkey

207

N

Monk's
Crossing

Caprocks Canyon Trail

Caprock

SIGN

Dirt Rd.

P

0 1 2
MILES

FM 1065

South Plains

Dirt Rd.

Quitaque Canyon

Caprocks Canyon Trail

Caprock

Clarity Tunnel MM-289

P

Dirt Rd.

Dirt Rd.

FM 97

Caprock

To Floydada

Scenery: Very, very, very beautiful. You should hear the tapes I made the last time I rode this place. You would believe me. This is the most scenically beautiful ride in this book that anyone can enjoy. My mom could ride this thing. And may, someday, if I ever get a tandem. You are basically riding from the High Plains through beautiful Quitaque Canyon down to the tunnel full of bats. And then you ride a five-mile tunnel of mesquite to where you left the car. It is absolutely stunning, just about any time of year—maybe best when things are green and the temperature is cool.

Special comments: Oh, my God. You suck if you don't ride this some day. You really do. This is the "Trail of Tears," and you should just cry like a little girl if you never ride here. And if you want to know how to say Quitaque correctly, it is generally one of the following: kitta-kway, kitty-kway, or kitty-cue, if you're really from around here.

It is a Tuesday evening, the weather is November perfect in Dallas, and I should be at the DORBA meeting. Problem is that I have this chapter in my head and I have to write it down. I love this ride; it is the best one in this book if you grew up here and know the history and love it the way I do. I have to hike this someday, because I can only imagine what nothing but the sound of my footsteps and the wind would be like. And there's this little cemetery way out there to your east a mile or so, right north of the tunnel. That is where I want to be buried. You can just plant me right there, with the purple canyon under the setting sun. I'll have a smile on my face forever.

I've reached 21 mph on the downhill run out of the tunnel, for a mile or so. You can start up there east of South Plains at Wood's Crossing, and just roll for 15 miles or so down to Monk's. Ride at top speed and have a blast—it's a dream. I like to start at Monk's Crossing and ride up, have some GU and a PowerBar, and then start back. I'll be at the car in an hour-and-a-half with the right wind. Of course, the round-trip is something around four hours, maybe six if I have lots of film and the flowers are doin' their thang. Taking your time going up, stopping for photographs and fun and laughing, and then scream all the way back; that's the way to ride this trail. DORBA certified.

Or you can do it the easy way, start at the top of the hill and get off at the bottom. But you have to shuttle your vehicles and stuff around in order to do that. There isn't always shuttle service, like there used to be. You should ask at the state park headquarters; they will tell you if there is somebody to carry you to the top. Leave your vehicle at Monk's Crossing and get a ride to Wood's on the dirt roads (which are very rideable, by the way). Ride back to Monk's, 15 miles, and see the canyons and the bats and all that. Probably more what the average rider is into. When I do the Hunter's Moon, or Harvest Moon (depending on the timing of that first full moon in fall), we always carry the iron to the top of the hill on a trailer, and leave most of the vehicles at Monk's. We start when the moon is first visible (I am a Moonchild; I can smell it), and we ride down to the tunnel and take a break. Then we head down to Monk's and everyone lives happily ever after. It is one of the best-disorganized rides in the state, in my humble opinion. Which is worth exactly what you paid for it.

Starting from Wood's Crossing, the terrain is as I describe it here. You are on the High Plains. There is a tall radio tower to your northeast. It's windy, the sky is forever, and there's nothing but a gravel road in front of you. You'll ride, normally with a tailwind from here, and try to figure out where the canyon is. You can't really see it. Canyons are sneaky like that around here. Pretty soon you'll notice that the trail is dropping below the surrounding prairie, and then you'll see the first hints of Quitaque Canyon. You pass a gate and there you are. I rode through here once with about a thousand broad-winged hawks swarming all around, 50 feet over our heads. It was like Alfred friggin' Hitchcock. I just wish I'd had a real camera and some Kodak TMZ back then. I probably did, but forgot and left it in the car.

The canyon here is white. Caliche, in the local parlance. Prairie grass, tunnels of mesquite, places blasted into the limestone, and a fence here and there. Soon you'll hit John Farris Station, where you can get a drink if you need it. Somehow, because of the way the trail follows the canyon, you might find a headwind getting to Farris. Then you mount up and blast. Fly. Cruise. Spin them pedals. The canyon turns red somewhere along through here.

Then you'll hit the famous Clarity Tunnel. Thousands and millions of bats. They won't hurt you, but like the signs say, don't touch any of them. If I was a tiny defenseless mammal I would bite you too when you picked me up. It is always cool in the tunnel, and pretty musty smelling. You'll hear the bats squeaking. You can get a drink here, too, if you're so inclined.

After the tunnel, you're pretty much out of the canyons and just blasting along and headed for the car. There's an old cemetery that you won't notice, there to the east. I want to be buried there. I found that place one time by accident. There's a local mountain biker guy buried there who died up in Palo Duro Canyon, when he had taken off for a short ride without his helmet. Not good, trust me—so just don't do it. There's also a rough hand-poured cement marker there that says, "Unknown Cowboy." I want to get buried next to these two guys. My marker can say, "Known Cowboy."

General location: Way out west in the panhandle of Texas, near a tiny town called Quitaque. About 100 miles southeast of Amarillo or 80 miles northeast of Lubbock, as the car drives.

Elevation change: Oh, maybe 800 to 1,000 feet. Not that much really, not the way the trail is graded. I'm kidding; this is far from up to down. But it's spread out so evenly over such a long distance, you will only notice it if you're riding up with the wind in your face.

Season: Year-round. It gets pretty cold up here in the winter and pretty hot in the summer, so use your own judgment. I like the spring and fall best. I often host a ride here as close as I can to the first full moon after the vernal equinox. That would usually be in late September or early October, the Harvest or Hunter's moon. Check my website for more details (www.home.mindspring.com/~ccypert)

Services: There's water and a few chemical potties along the way—thank you, Texas Parks and Wildlife Department. Otherwise I always start prepared. You can load up in Quitaque, it's only a few miles away. There is, however (and this is so weird to me), a pay phone at Monk's Crossing, the downhill trailhead. I called my pal Allan Hetzel from there one time and taunted him because I was there and he and Kenley were not, and I was watching the moon come up. They love it here like I do.

Hazards: Snakes, horse flies, bats. Maybe the occasional black vulture, but he won't hurt you. Watch them damn skunks, though.

Rescue index: Medium-high. You are in the middle of nowhere, but I have a funny feeling that if you stay on the trail you'll be fine. Either the rangers will find you when they do their normal runs, or one of the tour groups from the nearby ranch will report you to the authorities. Either way, they'll find you. It just might take several hours.

Land status: Texas state park, about the best one there is in my opinion—it is a stunning place, and everybody there knows me. Hey y'all, staff of Caprock Canyons State Park (CCSP), I cannot thank you enough for letting me come stay there and ride. Y'all are swell!

Maps: The state park has a mighty fine one, with all the cool stuff marked.

Finding the trail: Well, first you have to find Quitaque. I can drive there without out a map, but a normal person will have to go up US 287 northwest from Dallas, toward Amarillo. About two hours past Wichita Falls, you will be in Quanah and can stop by Copper Breaks State Park for a nice ride, and then continue northwest for another hour. In Killeen you will see signs for the park; hang a left (west) and in half an hour or so you will be in Turkey, Texas. (Hometown of Bob Wills. Bob Wills and the Texas Playboys, ever heard of them? They have a Bob Wills Museum, a Bob Wills Monument, and a big Bob Wills Festival every year. We used to come up here when we were kids in Plainview and wanted to drink beer and drive somewhere. Bad idea, I know, but I did it.)

Anyway, head out of Turkey to the west; you can see the canyon by now, and in 20 minutes you're in Quitaque. "Kitty-kway," as a sign will tell you as you enter town. Turn right (north) by the Allsup's store, following the signs, if you're going to the park. Turn left (south) if you're going to the trailhead. Go a few miles south on FM 1065, until you have crossed Los Lingos Creek, and turn right (west) at the sign. Follow the dirt road for a few miles, and you will turn south for maybe a mile, then a hard right to the west again. Monk's Crossing trailhead is there, on the left (south). Stop and call your friends and taunt them from the pay phone. Then take off up the trail for as far as you can stand. If you want to ride from South Plains down, you will have to ask the rangers how to get a lift up there. Follow this person out to Monk's Crossing to leave your car, and then have them carry you up to Wood's Crossing. Or, have good maps and know how to use them.

Sources of additional information:

Caprock Canyons State Park and
  Trailway
P.O. Box 204
Quitaque TX 79255
(806) 455-1492
www.tpwd.state.tx.us/park/caprock/
  caprock.htm

Texas Parks and Wildlife Department
4200 Smith School Road
Austin, TX 78744-3291
(800) 792-1112 information
(512) 389-8900 reservations
www.tpwd.state.tx.us

Notes on the trail: If you were really a wacko, like me, you might try something like this some day. This whole trail is 65 miles long. I have only described about 15 of them. It would be possible to ride from South Plains to Killeen and have fresh water the whole way, and soft conditions and a 90-pound bike. But it would be an epic ride. The logistics are doable. The thing to do is take several days and throw in a camp at Caprock Canyons State Park. It is only a few miles north of Quitaque, and if you ask them for site #55 down in the South Prong tent area they'll think that you are me. You can do some major hiking (especially if you know your way in these canyons or have a pal) and some biking, and some sitting around. Normal people will camp up at the water/electric area, but I love South Prong. I grew up camping up in Haynes Canyon about a mile west, at an old Boy Scout camp that is now defunct. It was, and still is, beautiferous.

RIDE 48 · The "GSL" and Capitol Peak Trails— Palo Duro Canyon State Park

AT A GLANCE

Length/configuration: A big loop made from pieces of three different trails. About 10 miles in the dirt, and a mile or so back to the car on the paved park road.

Aerobic difficulty: There are some healthy climbs, but it's not like you're going to climb out of the canyon or anything like that. This is no beginner trail, but it is one that all of you should ride someday. Walk the tough sections when you need to.

Technical difficulty: There are some pretty gnarly places on this trail. Most of it is very rideable, but it does have some challenges. Again, this is not a beginner trail.

Scenery: This could be the most scenic ride in the book. Palo Duro Canyon State Park is a beautiful place. I can't even find the words to do it justice; you'll just have to go there some day. The bike trails are in some of the prettiest parts of the canyon, so take plenty of film because there are beaucoup photo-ops.

Special comments: This is one of the best rides in this book. The trails are a blast, the canyon is stunning, and it is just a must if you think you know trails in Texas and Oklahoma. If you are driving from somewhere to somewhere else and your journey brings you up US 287 into the panhandle, you simply have to take a side-trip a few miles south and do this canyon, Grasshopper. Like all the state parks there is an entry fee—a very reasonable $3 if you don't have a Conservation Passport.

G lorious riding, here in the canyon. You have all the weird Texas erosion formations that were left over when the ocean receded, however many million years ago that was. Way before mountain bikes. Check out Lighthouse Peak sometime—it is one of the famous landmarks in the park. I don't like riding up there because of all the horse traffic you can get sometimes, but I have done it. You can make a side-trip from the mountain bike trails and hit it pretty easily; it adds a couple of miles.

But let's ride the real trails. I start in the parking lot at the trailhead for the Givens, Spicer & Lowry (GSL) Running Trail. You climb for a while and then

RIDE 48 • The "GSL" and Capitol Peak Trails

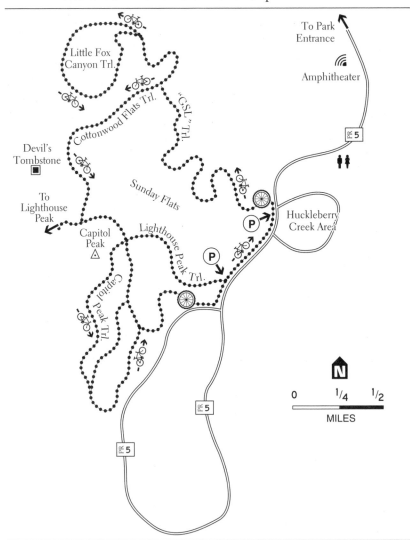

you drop through Givens Gully. If I was Hans Rey, and somebody was paying me all that money to do crazy things with a bike, I would probably be stupid enough to ride this part, but you and I will be walking in this life. No point in punishing the trail, our bikes, or our collar bones. Then you cruise along the edge of the canyon walls until you hit Red Star Ridge. A definite photo-op, and you can take a break here if you're tired. There is some fairly challenging terrain through here; nothing too extreme, but I wouldn't get too carried away on speed or you might get carried away in a chopper. At least one mountain biker has died on this ride because of a crash.

Pretty soon you're crossing creeks, headed out to the fork for Little Fox Canyon Trail. Hang a right at the sign for this outer lollipop. The creek crossings are usually pretty nasty because the approach/exit areas are soft and eroded. Once you get out on the back side of Little Fox, there's a logbook, up under some trees. Stop and say hello by writing your name, and making a few comments, perhaps, if you're a certain mountain biking author. Comments like, "GREAT TRAIL!"

After this, you wind around and back to where Little Fox split off, and you hang a right onto the Cottonwood Flats Trail. There is some interesting terrain here as well: some challenges, some loose rock, and sand. A few spurts of climbing, and then you hit the old horse trail that is Lighthouse Peak Trail. You have gone about seven miles to this point. Turn right to go see the Lighthouse or left to catch the rest of the mountain bike trails. It's OK to ride up to the peak, but you will have to leave your bike at the bottom of the little climb at the end, to get there. Go up and check it out if you never have. Take a break, enjoy the scenery, maybe have a piece of BBQ Dan's jerky or something. Then head back, east on the Lighthouse Peak Trail.

Once you make your way back down from the Lighthouse, you just follow the horse trail until you're all the way to the end of that ridge of land to your right, Capitol Peak. There are places through here where you can be going way too fast. Watch out for hikers and horses and normal people. Don't go running anybody over or I will have to deal with you sternly. Keep your eyes open and you will see where the mountain bike trails—the real ones—cut off to the right and back up into a new part of the canyon, south and east of Capitol Peak. As far as I can tell, there are three or four loops out there, maybe five miles total. It's really hard to say for sure because I always get lost. This is where it gets really fast and fun and confusing. This ain't no jogging trail or horse trail; this is bike trail, swoopy and tricky and very sneaky. I can't keep track of where I am, so I just get out there and ride and take the forks in the trail. You're going to see some more gorgeous terrain and find some pretty groovy little techies. Over here someplace is where that guy died, so be careful.

Ride this stuff as much as you can and enjoy. If you hit the western parts of the Capitol Peak Mountain Bike Trail first and then work your way east, you will gradually find yourself at the original trailhead, on the road. Hang a left on the pavement, and then at the bottom of the hill hang another left at the stop sign. Follow the main road for about a mile-and-a-half and you will be back at the GSL trailhead. Another lap?

General location: About 20 miles southeast of Amarillo, Texas.

Elevation change: Not too much. The canyon is about 700 feet from the floor up to the rim, but this ride only gets you about 100 feet or so down into the floors of the canyon.

Season: Year-round. Not too bad a day or so after light rain; the sand drains pretty well, but I've been trapped out here in a downpour and I don't recommend it. The trail dissolves into something the consistency of greased owl poop.

Services: This is one of the most highly developed and heavily used parks in all of Texas. There's plenty of good camping, a restaurant, an amphitheater with plays and stuff, pay phones—enough to keep the kids occupied and the parents fed. If you just come to ride, bring what you need is always my motto.

Hazards: I have definitely seen rattlesnakes here, more than once. There are dangerous sections of trail; it would be easy to get hurt that way. The weather probably scares me worse than anything else, though. A sudden rainstorm can flood the numerous water crossings on the road, and you could be stranded for a while if this happens. I'd also say a flat tire is something easy to find here, and I always carry my tools.

Rescue index: Medium. You're in a state park, but that park is pretty far from a hospital, like 10 to 15 miles. On the weekend there's a fair amount of traffic along the trails, but during the week it can get pretty lonely. And a cell phone is useless.

Land status: Texas state park.

Maps: The park rangers have a decent one; just ask.

Finding the trail: Palo Duro Canyon State Park is about 12 miles east of Canyon, Texas. Take TX 217 east of I-27 until the road leads you into the front gate. Stop and pay your fee and grab a map. You'll need it. I like to start on the Givens, Spicer & Lowry Running Trail, just west of the Hackberry campground. There is a trailhead parking lot with a kiosk describing the trail.

Sources of additional information:

Palo Duro Canyon State Park
11450 Park Road 5
Canyon, TX 79015
(806) 488-2227
www.tpwd.state.tx.us/park/paloduro/
    paloduro.htm

Hill's Sport Shop
4021 Mockingbird Lane
Amarillo, TX 79109
(806) 355-7224

West Texas Racing Club
www.wtcycling.com

Notes on the trail: This place can be kind of brutal in high summer, and in the winter you'd better have eaten your Wheaties first. I really love riding here—I have been around this canyon on and off for 30 years now. One time I rode my ten-speed down into it and then back out, like it was nothing. I was about 16 at the time. Twenty years later I flew into Amarillo, with my bike in a box, and rode back to Fort Worth. The second morning I left the canyon. The climb out was one of those cycling experiences I will never forget. That road, 60 or 70 pounds of bike and gear, and my big ol' fat butt. I'll bet there are still pieces of my lungs somewhere along the road.

WEST TEXAS

Was that Clint Eastwood, over behind that prickly pear cactus? Or maybe it was Marty Robbins. This is it, brothers and sisters, this is the best. I have saved it until last. We are gonna ride some serious stuff out here. Remote ranches, desert roads, and barren mountains that belong to the Rockies. It may not be fun for the faint of heart. Take heed, mountain bikers, this is serious stuff.

I'm gonna start you up near the Permian Basin, oil country. Then we will wander through a mountain bike haven known as the X-Bar Ranch. We'll have some fun on the ranch, maybe eat a steak or two, and have a memorable ride. Then we're off to el Despoblado (the uninhabitable one) and the land around el Rio Bravo del Norte (the Rio Grande River), the Big Bend Country. You are going to be dipped in history, and fear, and beautiful places.

Then, we'll head for the Franklins. If you don't speak Spanish you'll be in the minority. If you have a problem with latino culture, head the other way. We are going into the heart of Mexican Texas, and our NAFTA brotherland is only a few miles away. Be respectful of the native Latino people; this land was their land before it was ours. If you can dance to salsa you'll be in good stead. Stand up on America and look over to Mexico, it's only a mile or so away.

Let's ride—I'll be needing a good shot of the juice of the agave later. Mas fina. Buenas dias, mi amigos. I don't really speak Español, but I sure wish I did.

RIDE 49 · San Angelo State Park Trails— San Angelo

AT A GLANCE

Length/configuration: A web-like maze that's roughly a series of interconnected loops, 25–30 miles or so total.

Aerobic difficulty: A lot of this is fairly easy, but it's punctuated with sections that are difficult. Difficult like pulling-prickly-pear-needles-out-of-your-butt difficult. There are loose conditions that range from powdery sand to gravel and babyheads. The climbs are all relatively short, but many are steep and tricky.

Technical difficulty: There are some fairly advanced technical challenges here, though they are in the minority. A lot of it is flat and fast. There are lots of places where the trail is loose rock or deep sand, or where it runs over exposed rock surfaces that are rough and treacherous. You could definitely call these techie bits, big time.

Scenery: I guess this ride has some scenic parameters; much of the ride has long views across the lake bottom area toward the dam. The last time I rode here there was a section of big yucca plants in bloom, which was great. Keep your eyes peeled because there's all sorts of wildlife around here in the woods. I saw my first horny toad (not what you're thinkin'!) in 30 years here.

Special comments: Tough ride. Hard to find your way; the maps show names that are different from the markers out in the woods. You'll have to pay attention to where you are and what direction you're going, if you don't take someone with you who knows the way. This is a long serious ride. Typical state park entry fee of $3.

I've met the guy who built a lot of this. I always wanted to come here and ride it. Friends had told me I would need to carry a GPS unit. I made grunting sounds, totally convinced my near Apache-like sense of direction would see me through. Then, about five miles into the ride, it got completely cloudy. That GPS I didn't have was making snotty little remarks in my head, and it took about ten minutes for me to remember I had my compass in my pack. And then all my old Boy Scout bravado came back to me and I found my way. But if you don't know your way, this place can scare you. There are miles and miles and miles of single-track going in several different directions.

But there's no need for terror; you're riding in an area that used to be old parks when O.C. Fisher Lake once had water in it. You're essentially going to ride along a strip of land that is probably no more than a couple of miles wide (east to west) and about ten miles long (north to south). There are many old ruined picnic tables around and even a few parks that may still be active (for equestrian use, I believe).

The ride I describe goes north from Red Arroyo camping area in the southern section of San Angelo State Park. We will ride roughly north on the trails that are farthest to the east until we reach the north end of the park, near the North Concho camping area. Then we will return via the trails on the western side of the park.

Notice: you are going to spend very little time traversing the same trail twice. Some of the ride is on dirt road but most of it is single-track. There are signs out there in the woods, pointing to places like "Flintstones Village," where you will find a rough-hewn picnic table and benches. Pretty neat, so stop and burn some film.

I don't know what the deal is with the maps; they have trail names that are completely different from what the signs out on the trail will tell you. It spooked

RIDE 49 • San Angelo State Park Trails

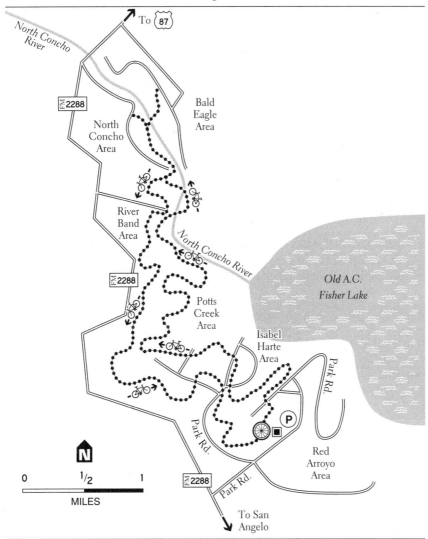

To 87

North Concho River

FM 2288

North Concho Area

Bald Eagle Area

River Band Area

North Concho River

FM 2288

Potts Creek Area

Old A.C. Fisher Lake

Isabel Harte Area

Park Rd.

P

N

0   1/2   1

MILES

Park Rd.

Red Arroyo Area

FM 2288   Park Rd.

To San Angelo

me pretty good, sort of like being in a Twilight Zone episode or something. I am pretty good at this stuff, I tend to take the forks to the right when I find 'em, and I usually know what direction I'm going in and I recognize the same spots I've seen if I find myself riding in circles. In spite of my prowess, I did some repetitious riding here. But the "stick to the right" advice is generally reliable on these trails. Just imagine in your head that you are riding the outer edges of a counterclockwise loop. Keep moving and check out the side trails; they will generally wind around and return you to the main trail or one of the old roads that crisscross this property. Bring liquids, you'll need them.

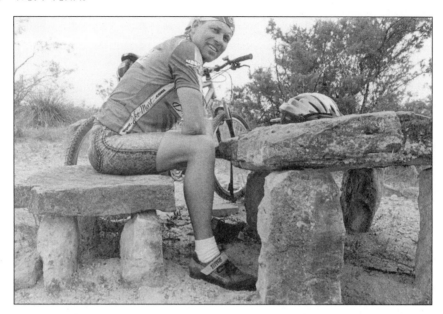

Me taking a break at Flintstone's Village. I wish I could spend enough time in San Angelo State Park to learn my way around better. It can be disorienting on a cloudy day for lost souls like me. Good thing I am 1/128th American Indian.

I saw a horny toad (OK, horned lizard, the Texas state reptile) for the first time in probably 30 years when I rode here; I nearly clipped the little bugger coming around a curve. Then I had a similar experience with several box tortoises. Please be careful and do not harm any of the critters you may meet along this trail. That includes snakes, by the way—don't mess with them. I'd wager there are one or two who call this place home. Also don't mess with any ruins or artifacts you may spot as you cruise along. The state takes a real dim view of that sort of activity.

There are some fun trails here, my friend. I think that once a person has learned his or her way around this beast, it would be a blast to ride hard for times. I want you to have fun when you ride here, but maybe it would be best to find a friend to take along. Someone who has ridden here before. Check in town at the bike shops, or get on the web and sniff around for people in the area. I'd be a jerk if I didn't warn you about all this; all my nervousness is out of genuine concern for your safety and happiness. Don't wander too far off the main trails until you know what you're doing, carry your map and a compass, lots of water, and enjoy a nice long hard ride.

General location: North of San Angelo, Texas, by a few miles.

Elevation change: The maps show the lake level at around 1,900 feet, but I didn't see much water when I was here. I think the lake dried up. Still, I don't think you ever get any lower than that level. The highest point along the way appears to run around 2,000 feet, so we can call the elevation change 100 feet. It's really spread out pretty good so you don't spend the whole time going up and down; the worst climbing is maybe 50 to 60 feet at a time.

Season: I'd imagine you can ride here nearly any time. I saw signs of mud in a few spots, so riding in the rain is a bad idea, but there's probably enough sand that it'll drain pretty quick. I'll bet it is blistering in the summer; you might want to get an early start if you're here in July.

Services: The park has several nice camping areas, most with showers and electricity and all that. There are pay phones, and a little store near Red Arroyo, where I start. As usual though, I recommend getting here with everything you will need to hit the trail.

Hazards: Man, this place is practically desert. Almost all the plants would love to leave something stuck in your leg, and you had better believe there are some serious snakes around here. This place would probably be fun, but dangerous, at night. Much of the trails have loose surfaces—sand and broken limestone with babyheads thrown in for garnish. You might not meet a lot of other folks out here; it gets pretty lonely if you have a flat and can't fix it yourself. There's equestrian traffic in much of this park, so be careful if you see any horses. They need a wider berth than rattlesnakes, and some of them scare pretty easily. Mr. Bustyerass de Zaster has cousins around here.

Rescue index: Medium. Your cell phone is probably reliable from some of the trail areas, and you're never more than a mile or two from FM 2288, if you took one of the old roads westward as an escape. I'm just not sure how much traffic this place gets. There are quite a few mountain bikers in San Angelo, as the tracks in the sand will attest, but it might take a while before somebody found you if you weren't able to get out under your own steam. I'd definitely recommend taking a biking partner.

Land status: A Texas Parks and Wildlife Department state park.

Maps: The rangers will give you one for the price of entry into the park, but as I mentioned, some of the information contained in them may have no use in the field. I think the lines showing approximate locations of the trails are probably OK, but the names are totally confusing.

Finding the trail: Head southwest on US 67 from San Angelo and turn north on FM 2288, just past the Wal-Mart. Continue north on FM 2288; soon you will cross FM 853, and very soon after that you will see the San Angelo State Park South Entrance sign. Turn right (east) into the park and pay "The Man." Follow the main road into the Red Arroyo area and park in front of the rest rooms, across from the park store. Now it gets interesting. Head north from the rest rooms, across the grass toward the vicinity of the cabins. Soon you will see single-track heading north through the park. Follow this, as best you can. What you are trying to do is get to the northwest end of the camping areas and then head off cross-country. There is so much trail here that finding the right one is just a matter of staying on the one that heads sort of north. Take the forks to the right as you find them, keep going, and watch the terrain around you. Go the direction that lets you read the signs; that's the best advice I can offer. If you find yourself coming up behind some signs, you're probably going backwards on the trail.

Sources of additional information:

San Angelo State Park
3900 - 2 Mercedes
San Angelo, TX 76901
(915) 949-4757
www.tpwd.state.tx.us/park/sanangel/s
anangel.htm

Texas Parks and Wildlife Department
4200 Smith School Road
Austin, TX 78744-3291

(800) 792-1112 information
(512) 389-8900 reservations
www.tpwd.state.tx.us

Bike Pro Bicycles
4134 Sherwood Way
San Angelo, TX 76901
(915) 223-2453

Notes on the trail: The dam is to the east of the trailhead; you can see it most of the way on the first part of the ride. As you go you will cross old roads that head to defunct camps along what used to be the beaches, I guess. There's sort of a main dirt road that runs due north and south through here. You can use this as a reference—it bisects this part of the park. Keep going north, taking the forks to the right, and eventually you will find the equestrian areas near the River Bend camping area. The trail only goes another mile or so before it pops out of the woods into the North Concho group area. This is an RV park, and you can potty or get water here. Rest for a few minutes and return on the same trail that got you here.

Once you're back around River Bend, you will get some more forks; go to the right and you're in a whole new section of the park. Follow the single-track as it winds around in the trees, and pretty soon you're back by the old north/south road and should see some stuff you recognize. From here, fork right again and you'll travel through a bunch more rough terrain that you haven't seen yet. You will wind around and find yourself in sight of the housing development to the south (just north of where you left the car). There are several side loops here that may confuse you—they did me; just try to keep going south and east and you will be back in the camping areas of the southern park site. Before you know it, like a miracle, you will pop out just west of the store and your car. That was about 25 miles, by my computer.

In several places the trail splits and a sign directs horses one way and bikes the other. This is actually pretty cool—if everybody obeys the rules, they stay on their stuff and we have ours, free of hoof prints. Not that I have anything at all against horses, they just tear the crap out of a good mountain bike trail most times. And they always bite me—I can't understand it.

RIDE 50 · X-Bar Ranch—Eldorado

AT A GLANCE

Length/configuration: Counterclockwise loops, mostly rigorous single-track with some old roads thrown in here and there, about 12 miles if you do the big loop.

Aerobic difficulty: This place is a pretty good workout; the miles of trail here are fairly tough. This is no beginner trail.

Technical difficulty: The X-Bar starts out with a mile or so of pretty good rock gardens. After that it's not so bad, but you will find some more technical spots with regularity. This is an advanced intermediate trail in a lot of places, not pure beginner but not impossible either.

Scenery: I love it here. You can sit on the back porch of the Live Oak Lodge, look out across the valley and forget the world. It is quite a beautiful place, and hasn't changed much in a couple hundred years. The birding is super, if you're into that—there are bird feeders everywhere.

Special comments: This is a fee area—$5 to ride, with camping and cabins available for additional fees. Please be aware that you don't just drive over here and ride; they want to know you are coming. Call ahead to check trail conditions and availability. Say hey to Stan or whoever, and make arrangements for being let into the property, because the gate is normally locked. Also, this is an active ranch, so any gates you have to open must be closed behind you as you ride. This is one of those wonderful places that you should all visit someday—you'll never forget an afternoon on the X-Bar Ranch. If you're lucky the way I was, you might find yourself on this 7,100 acres all by your lonesome. It is a truly memorable experience to sit out there on the porch and watch the buzzards fly around; you'll never forget it. And they have a pool.

This place is awesome. The trails will whip you and the people will give you a taste of fine Texas hospitality. The Meador family are such Texas folks, I strongly urge you to obey the rules and take care of the facilities like they were your own. We have been blessed with access to this property, so leave them with a feeling that you love this land as much as they do. One thing I thought was really cool was the sort of livestock I saw on this ranch. None of it seemed to be raised for slaughter. All I saw were sheep. Even though they allow hunting here, I don't think they're into killing animals. This is a real ranch, but it belongs to really kind and thoughtful folks. God bless 'em.

You start right behind the lodge and have a very tough rock garden for nearly a mile. At one point you pass the white-blazed cutoff for the hiking trail—stay off it. Then you hit the fork to the left for the beginner trail, the Green Loop. From here on it's not so bad, but you have some riding to do before you get back up to the lodge. If you continue on the Red/Blue Loop you'll wander down through the

RIDE 50 • X - Bar Ranch

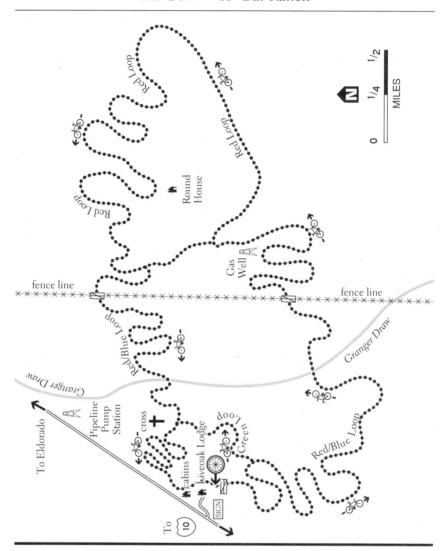

valley, have to cross a couple of gates, and soon you're on the far side of the property. Out by Lookout Junction the Red Loop and Blue Trail split; Blue takes a shortcut that leads you down a road and back onto the trail where Red joins. If you take the Red Loop, you'll wander to the right (east) around to the back of the property, mostly on old roads but soon you'll hit some more serious single-track.

The single-track out on this part of the property is rideable, but there will probably be a few spots you'll fail to negotiate and you'll have to dismount and walk. The trail out here is very nice; tricky and tough in spots, but a load of fun. You wind around the trees and soon cross a road. Stay on the single-track and you will presently cross another road, Blue Trail's reunion spot, and then you'll descend into the floor of the valley again. You will have to cross some gates—be sure to close them behind you—and there's another road to cut over. Then you ride by the big white cross, the cross you can see northeast of the lodge lit up at night. The grandfather built this—no one recalls exactly why—and it lights up at night. Pretty cool; out there on the hill at night there's this big white cross, glowing in the distance.

The trail winds around a bunch here, and has some ledges and loose rock interspersed with dirt. And some climbing—you have to get back up on the hill to the lodge. A lot of the drops are sneaky and most of the terrain is evil. This is truly an outstanding mountain bike ride, but you need to have some skills and a dependable bike. And some conditioning, it's a fairly hard trail.

The last time I was here is a pretty good story. It was the week after the World Trade Center disaster—that part is easy to recall. I had Stan and his dad show me out to the ranch and get me all set up in a cabin. They gave me full run of the place, and went home. How cool is that? I got all rigged up, got on my bike, and when I was about as far from the lodge as you can get, it started raining. A downpour of biblical proportions. I am standing there, looking across the valley at the lodge and trying to imagine how I will survive this calamity. Stan had marked some of the ranch buildings on the map for me and I managed to find the grandfather's cabin. I stood on the porch for a while and it just kept raining harder. I tried the door, and thankfully it was unlocked. I sat there for an hour or so, thinking of mud. Finally it stopped raining. I took some very muddy roads along the pipeline back to the highway, and that back to the front gate. By the time I made the gate there was this huge grand thunderhead to the east. One of those classically beautiful anvil clouds that you just stare at in awe. Like a huge mushroom up in the sky, silvery white on top with an orange stem and a purple base. Stunning.

I tried to ride again the next morning, but the trail was about as wet and dangerous as anything I have ever ridden. I turned around after a half a mile or so and went back to the lodge. The rest of the day and into the evening I sat on the back porch, grilled a steak and had some Shiner Bocks, and just reflected on my camping trip. And the fact that it had rained on me four of the last five days. It is so quiet out there; the occasional pickup truck rolls by on the road out front, but otherwise you could hear your eyes blink. By the next morning it was dry enough to make a third attempt. I got it done that time. It was still wet in a few spots, but not the nasty muddy-tires-on-limestone death ride it had been the day before. I started early in the morning, before the sun, and just rolled along, unintentionally scaring the sheep I passed along the way. When I was through, I loaded up and headed over to San Antonio. My first visit to the X-Bar Ranch was something to cherish for the rest of my life.

General location: Way out west, about 3 hours west of San Antonio, Texas, near the small town of Eldorado.

Elevation change: Topo maps show there is about 150 feet of elevation across this property.

Season: Closed during hunting season, roughly October through January.

Services: Camping, cabins, a marvelous lodge building with a full kitchen, a swimming pool (nice on a hot day), a phone, and a Coke machine. If you hit this place fully prepared, you can stay a couple of days and have a great time. But bring what you need—town is far away.

Hazards: Lots of techie bits; rock gardens, ledges, loose rock, tight trees, and short climbs. It would not surprise me a bit to see a big old rattler along this trail. You can flat easily, and mesquite and cactus are SOP. You can crash easily, and it won't be pretty; ride with the greatest care. You are in a very remote area—the nearest hospital is far away. Again, be very careful.

Rescue index: Low to medium. There aren't a lot of people out there on the trail most times, so if you get hurt there won't be anyone to help you if you left all your mates at home. A cell phone is fairly dependable, but if you can't tell them where you are because you forgot your map, well, you may have a big problem, in the form of a major risk to your life. Stan and them will notice your abandoned car and get concerned and have to come find you, and they will, but don't let it happen.

Land status: Private property.

Maps: The ranch has good ones; ask at the lodge.

Finding the trail: The X-Bar Ranch is located north of I-10, just west of Sonora. Headed west from Sonora, take Exit 388 and go north on FM 2129 about 8 miles, and you'll see the entrance to the ranch on the east side of the road, plainly marked by a big gate with flags. The lodge is just through the gate, at the end of the road. The trail starts just behind the lodge; hang a right onto the single-track and go through the gate. Ride until you're back here.

Sources of additional information:

X-Bar Ranch
5 North Divide
P.O. Box 696
Eldorado, TX 76936-0696
(915) 853-2688
www.xbarranch.com

South Texas Off Road Mountain-
  Bikers (STORM)
P.O. Box 12371
San Antonio, TX 78212-0371
www.storm-web.org

Notes on the trail: White markers are for the hiking trail, green for the beginner loop (which unfortunately runs you through one of the toughest stretches on the ranch), blue marks the intermediate loop, and red is the expert or outer loop. Trail ratings are more related to distance than difficulty. Choose your route based on how far you want to go.

I have to take a moment to thank the Meador family for their fine Texas hospitality. This is a fabulous place, and another one of those places I found while working on this book that just made me fall in love with Texans and Texas mountain biking all over again. A ride here can be terrifying, but it is an epic trip. Thank you, X-Bar Ranch and ranchers, for the experience of a lifetime.

RIDE 51 · Glenn Springs and Black Gap—Big Bend National Park

AT A GLANCE

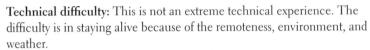

Length/configuration: A counterclockwise loop of old dirt roads, about 35 miles.

Aerobic difficulty: It don't get a lot tougher. The roads are loose and soft in places, and there is some climbing involved. If you do the loop counterclockwise, the climbing involves as little stress as is possible.

Technical difficulty: This is not an extreme technical experience. The difficulty is in staying alive because of the remoteness, environment, and weather.

Scenery: If you're from Texas or Oklahoma, you'd call this stunning. The mountains and desert are magnificent. There are only one or two rides in this book that are equal or better.

Special comments: Get your Wheaties, chilluns, 'cause we are headed straight into the belly of the Chihuahuan Desert, and it is not necessarily a friendly place, most times. Still, this is one of the most interesting rides in the book, partly from the historical significance of the area and partly from its ability to test of your mountain bike metal. Yeah, it's old road and not single-track, but this is a superb ride.

This is your typical gorgeous ride through the desert and mountains. You have the Chisos Mountains to the north as you make your way down Glenn Springs Road and then as you ride down Black Gap Road to the old mine area of Mariscal. When the desert is blooming and beautiful this is truly a joyous ride. When you reach the vista west of Glenn Springs, you will be offered a view of all the badlands you are about to traverse, a view that will never fade from memory. The area around the mine is neat—full of abandoned buildings and ruins—a veritable ghost town. As you depart the mine area and wind along the River Road, you will catch glimpses of mountains in Mexico, such as the Sierra del Carmen (the famous "Bacon Strip" of local fame). From there you hit more high desert as you head back to Glenn Springs, and then you will have the Chisos Mountains again to your north. Beautiferous!

This is a ride that requires extreme preparation and a full complement of equipment and supplies. About the only way you can do it is either to pack a ton of stuff along, or have a four-wheel-drive support vehicle tagging along with refreshments. Packing in enough stuff to survive a day in the desert is possible—I've done it—but having support is the cherry on the cupcake. As well as the only hope you have of rescue if something goes wrong.

We should keep our eyes open and our senses sharp, ready to both absorb the surroundings and keep us alive. We should also keep ourselves hydrated and

RIDE 51 • Glenn Springs and Black Gap Road

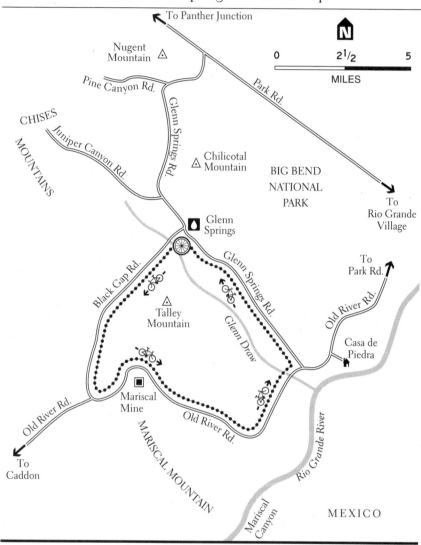

carbo-loaded, 'cause it will be a long, arduous day. Road signs may or may not be in place—these pesky things have a tendency to wander—so you need to watch for the other roads and turns on this ride because they can be tough to spot sometimes. The jaunt from Glenn Springs down to Mariscal is just desert, but the area around the old mine near Fresno camp is a cool place to take a break and wander some of the old ruins. Get the park brochures so you can find everything, and their map fits nicely in the pocket of a Camelbak. Speaking of refreshment, a one-hundred-ounce water container is maybe half what you will need. My bike has four water bottle cages; I have them loaded at the start and I also bring my rear

My friends, that right there is the closest thing you will find to a 7-11 on the Glenn Springs Loop. I give you some of the ruins at Mariscal, with the Chisos Mountains in the background.

panniers with a couple of extra bottles of water. I ran out down here once, and it has happened to a couple of buds of mine—it ain't pretty. After a while you're so tired of your legs cramping that getting bit by a snake seems a minor inconvenience.

I wouldn't count on seeing anyone else along the way, though you might, and a cell phone is useless. Good wits, a map, and twice the water you would need to ride this far at home is what I call being a good Boy Scout. Or Girl Scout—I ain't leaving anybody with ovaries out.

General location: Big Bend National Park, Texas.

Elevation change: You start around 2,600 feet in Glenn Springs, and the river is around 1,900. That 700 feet will not only turn your legs into butter, it will also suck a gallon of water out of your body and a few tanks of oxygen out of your lungs.

Season: Definitely not summer. Laugh about it while you lounge around the pool back home, but 120° in the shade (there is no shade) is quite capable of killing you and me. The weather varies in any season, but this area of my state is comfortably attacked when cool (sub-90°), roughly from October until early April. The rains vary from year to year, but March through May are often the wettest months. The busy season is in the late fall and early spring. Don't even think about Spring Break, unless you get there early, because the sites all fill every day. Better to call ahead and check the status of this park before driving all the way there.

Services: There are stores in Panther Junction and Rio Grande Village. Load up before you head out into the desert and don't ask if there's a potty, 'cause there are potties everywhere. If you're a guy.

Hazards: Everything. This environment is as tough as they come. The weather will just about always punish you a little; sometimes it has absolutely no sense of humor. You may never see a drop of rain, but while blasting through a turn you might find the road ahead (and probably behind, as well) washing away from a flash flood pouring out of the mountains.

Body armor would not be out of the question. All the plants are exceedingly well armed to do harm. What blood they don't draw from your body is balanced by the air they take from your tires. You are so far from help that any of several ways to die can find you. There are poisonous snakes and insects for sure that would love to send you to heaven. The road is so loose and rough and poorly maintained that it might as well be the scariest single-track you ever saw; it is that severe.

There will occasionally be four-wheel-drive vehicles with drivers of question-able helpfulness and/or sobriety—watch out for them. To top it all off, the desert will suck moisture out of you at a rate that is frightening, and there is nowhere to get fresh water. Water is often seen flowing across Black Gap Road in Glenn Springs, but I wouldn't drink it without normal precautions such as a filtration system, chemicals, and/or boiling. Oh, boy, go have fun. Say hello to Mr. de Zaster here, and you might not make it back home.

Rescue index: Very, very poor. The only way you'll get out of here is to pedal or to spend several bumpy hours in your support vehicle, if you bring one. Cell phones are useless and you might, just might, find someone in a vehicle to carry you out, but I wouldn't bet on it. The nearest pay phone is at least 30 miles away, the nearest ambulance about 50 miles, and the nearest hospital about 100 miles away, in Alpine.

Land status: One of Teddy Roosevelt's finest national parks.

Maps: Park headquarters at Panther Junction will sell you anything you need, or free ones are available at the entrances. I personally recommend the Trails Illus-trated map of Big Bend National Park (1:100,000 scale), and the National Park Service publication "Road guide to the backcountry dirt roads of Big Bend National Park." Or you could try One Map Place (www.onemapplace.com) or REI (www.rei.com).

Finding the trail: From Panther Junction, head east toward Rio Grande Village. About five miles down the pavement you will see the sign for Glenn Springs Road (south), pointing you down a rocky, bumpy, old dirt road. Follow this, not taking any of the side roads unless you know what you're doing, and about eight miles later you will find the cutoff for Black Gap Road. Park here or keep going past for a short ways until you find somewhere you are comfortable leaving your vehicle. Head west on Black Gap Road until you reach the old River Road, about nine miles (three miles past the trailhead for the Elephant Tusk Pack Trail). Hang a left onto the old River Road and proceed until you start seeing old buildings—the Mariscal Mine area. From there, stay on the old River Road for another four miles or so, until you get to where Glenn Springs Road hits it. Hang a left and head north about seven miles to where you started.

Sources of additional information:

National Park Service
www.nps.gov/index.htm

Big Bend National Park
Big Bend National Park, TX 79834
(915) 477-2251
www.big.bend.national-park.com

Big Bend Natural History Association
P.O. Box 196
Big Bend National Park, TX 79834
(915) 477-2236

Desert Sports "Your Big Bend
  Adventure Connection"
P.O. Box 448
Terlingua, TX 79852
(915) 371-2727
www.desertsportstx.com

Trails Illustrated
P.O. Box 4357
Evergreen, CO 80437-4357
(800) 962-1643
(303) 670-3457
www.trailsillustrated.com or
http://maps.nationalgeographic.
  com/trails

GORP Big Bend guide
www.gorp.com/gorp/resource/US_
  National_Park/tx_big_b.HTM

Weather in the Big Bend
www.intellicast.com/LocalWeather/
  World/UnitedStates/SouthCentral/
  Texas/BigBend/Forecast/

Notes on the trail: When they say this is a four-wheel-drive road, they mean it. You might horse a two-wheel-drive truck through here; it's been done, but I wouldn't recommend it. Don't try to go ride this thing without a map. I can't stress enough how remote and lonely these rides can be, and often are. You can't just run down and hit this thing and go home. It is far to drive, far to ride, far to experience, and far to survive. Take a buddy, slime your tubes, have a healthy machine and a stout heart, and take that extra two bottles of water. How about an extra tube and lots of film as well? This is truly a ride to die for, but not one to die on. People have died here, lots of people, and they all found their special means of becoming lifeless. Banditos are not out of the question — the park rangers and the border patrol folks are around, but you won't see them out here on in the desert. You're on your own. Just you, me, and Jesus.

RIDE 52 · The Old Ore Road—
Big Bend National Park

AT A GLANCE

Length/configuration: This old gravel road is 27 miles long and is best ridden from north to south. This orientation will often bring you a head wind but it is much cooler that way. Trust me.

Aerobic difficulty: This is an extremely adventurous ride. Everything from easy cruising to long hard climbs. This old road has about a half-dozen serious assaults on steep double-track that is covered with everything from babyheads to solid rock outcroppings that resemble partially buried boulders. The ascents are hard and the descents sides border on lethal.

Technical difficulty: Well, you better eat your Wheaties, 'cause this ride will work you. The climbs require proper weight distribution for finding traction, and the drops will exercise your suspension, hands, eyesight, and courage/foolhardiness. The last climb headed south, right before the finish, always makes me feel like hammered dog meat.

Scenery: There's not a better ride in this book. Some are as good, maybe, but when the weather is right and the desert is in bloom you will be ready to die and go on from here. It is a beautiful ride that all Texas and Oklahoma mountain bikers should see at least once in their lives.

Special comments: This is a ride that requires extreme preparation and a full complement of equipment and supplies. About the only way you can do it is either to get dropped off at one end and picked up at the other, or have a four-wheel-drive support vehicle tagging along with refreshments. Packing in enough stuff to survive a day in the desert is possible—I've done it—but having support is the cherry on the cupcake, as well as the only hope you have of rescue if something goes wrong.

Well, here you go. Off into the high Chihuahuan Desert and the mountains and scenery of Big Bend National Park. It will make you think about why in the heck you're out here in the middle of nowhere riding your bike. Why? Sometimes it ain't a lot of fun, sometimes it hurts and makes you bleed. But when the conditions are right, and when your attitude is right, it is a journey to the center of your mind.

The Old Ore Road is called that because the miners used to haul ore up this thing to Marathon, long ago. If you ride this course the way I try to, you will start to the north on a huge flat desert full of yucca plants all around. They call them Mexican daggers here, and the name Dagger Flats will be forever burned into your memory if you ever see this area in bloom.

You gradually wind over and around on an old gravel road toward a vista that looks out on some magnificent badlands. On the way you gradually leave the high flats and ride along a ridge—mountains to your left, mountains to your right, mountains ahead. You reach the vista above McKinney Springs, and you can see out across the badlands toward Panther Junction and the Chisos Mountains, and you may spot a vehicle on the park road, several miles to the west.

From the vista, you drop into McKinney Springs and then climb back into the hills and Roy's Camp. After Roy's you'll wind around and ride parallel to the Alto Relex for a few miles. This is always one of the most glorious parts of this ride. The sheer cliffs show you much about the geology and biology of the Big Bend; old eroded cliffs and cactus that grows from chunks of solid rock. Keep moving; the lowlands along Tornillo Creek and Ernst Tinaja are next.

Having enough time and energy to explore some of the camping areas and sites that cut off the main road will yield some more awesome geology, if you know where to look. Definitely check out Ernst Tinaja, if you can. This is a site of striated rock outcroppings formed long ago from layered mud. It hides a water

RIDE 52 • Old Ore Road

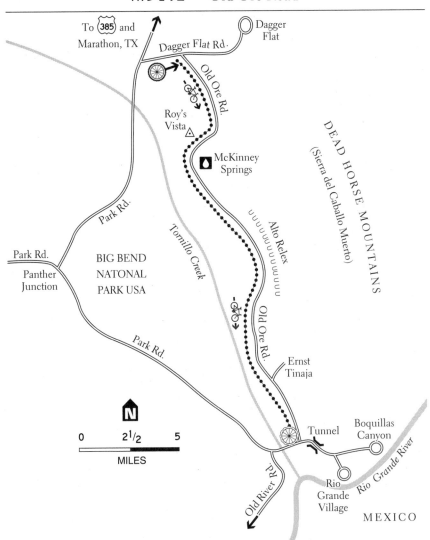

tank (tinaja) that has supplied water to the inhabitants of this area for many centuries.

Then you climb, hard and long, back into some hills. Wind around the desert for a few more miles and then, finally, the last climb (guaranteed to make you wonder what it was about mountain biking that seemed so sexy back home). Ride it, or walk it, and the finish is at hand, above the campsite at Candelilla. There is a small parking area here, and right down the hill is the pavement. The left will take you to Rio Grande Village and the campground and store there; the right is back to Panther Junction.

Me and my Cimarron along the Old Ore Road, the Alto Relex in the background. This is, in my humble opinion, the most magnificent ride in my book. If you leave your camera at home, I will never speak to you again. Photo by Daniel Haynes.

General location: Big Bend National Park, Texas.

Elevation change: The start, off Dagger Flat Auto Trail, is about 3,150 feet. You gradually wind up and down and around to end up halfway between McKinney Springs and Roy's Camp, back up to about 3,000 feet. Where the southern end of Old Ore Road meets the pavement of the park road the elevation is almost exactly 2,050 feet. So, call it a net loss of about 1,100 feet. Neat, huh?

Season: Definitely not summer. Laugh about it while you lounge around the pool back home, but 120° temperatures can kill you. The weather varies in any season, but it's best to ride here when the mercury is below 90°, roughly from October until early April. The rains vary from year to year, but March through May are often the wettest months. The busy season is in the late fall and early spring, especially around Spring Break. Better to call ahead and check the status of this park before driving all the way there.

Services: Not much. The closest little stores with gas and stuff are nearest Panther Junction from the start, and in Rio Grande Village, nearest the finish. There are no ambulances, paramedics, hospitals, or doctors. Not for many miles. Cell phones are useless here. You will only have access to what you bring, both in the way of supplies and your general resourcefulness.

Hazards: Everything. This environment is as tough as they come. The weather will just about always punish you a little; sometimes it has absolutely no sense of humor. You may never see a drop of rain, but while blasting through a turn you might find the road ahead (and probably behind as well) washing away from a flash flood pouring out of the mountains.

The cacti and other hardy vegetation here are ready to stick and scrape you, and they'll settle for deflating your tires if you manage to dodge 'em. Poisonous snakes and insects are almost as prevelant. The unmaintained roads are so rough as to rival any Texas single-track. Additionally, four-wheel-drive vehicles can pose a danger if the driver is reckless.

To top it all off, the desert will suck moisture out of you at a rate that is frightening, and there is nowhere to get fresh water. Stagnant water is often found up in Ernst Tinaja, but I wouldn't drink it without normal precautions such as a filtration system, chemicals, and/or boiling. Oh boy, go have fun. Our old pal Mr. de Zaster was born here.

Rescue index: Very, very poor. The only way you'll get out of here is to pedal or to spend several bumpy hours in your support vehicle, if you bring one. Cell phones are useless, and you might, just might, find someone in a vehicle to carry you out, but I wouldn't bet on it. The nearest pay phone is at least 30 miles away, the nearest ambulance about 50 miles, and the nearest hospital about 100 miles away, in Alpine.

Land status: One of Teddy Roosevelt's finest National Parks.

Maps: Park headquarters at Panther Junction will sell you anything you need, or free maps are available at the entrances. I personally recommend the Trails Illustrated map of Big Bend National Park (1:100,000 scale) and the National Park Service publication, "Road guide to the backcountry dirt roads of Big Bend National Park." You can also try Maps for the Big Bend (One Map Place; www.onemapplace.com) or REI (www.rei.com).

Finding the trail: Roughly 13 miles north of Panther Junction on US 385 is the cutoff called "Dagger Flat Auto Trail." Turn east, and go about two miles to the cutoff for "Old Ore Road." This is traditionally the starting point. The southern end is about 15 miles southeast of Panther Junction, right before the tunnel to Rio Grande Village. There is a small parking area about a quarter-mile north of the pavement. This is the finish area.

Sources of additional information:

National Park Service
www.nps.gov/index.htm

Big Bend National Park
Big Bend National Park, TX 79834
(915) 477-2251
www.big.bend.national-park.com

Big Bend Natural History Association
P.O. Box 196
Big Bend National Park, TX 79834
(915) 477-2236

Desert Sports "Your Big Bend
  Adventure Connection"
P.O. Box 448

Terlingua, TX 79852
(915) 371-2727
www.desertsportstx.com

Trails Illustrated
P.O. Box 4357
Evergreen, CO 80437-4357
(800) 962-1643
(303) 670-3457
www.trailsillustrated.com or
http://maps.nationalgeographic.
  com/trails

GORP Big Bend guide
www.gorp.com/gorp/resource/US_
  National_Park/tx_big_b.HTM

Weather in the Big Bend
www.intellicast.com/LocalWeather
  World/UnitedStates/SouthCentral/
  Texas/BigBend/Forecast/

Notes on the trail: To say this is a four-wheel-drive road may be an understatement. Two-wheel-drive trucks have made it before, but I wouldn't recommend it. Don't try this ride without a map. You are in the middle of the dessert; I can't overstate the remoteness of this ride. You can't just run down, do the ride, and go home. Besides the remote location, you must account for the length of the ride and its arduous nature. Bring a friend. Be sure your bike is in good shape before you come, and carry a patch kit and some tools. And lots and lots of water. Of course, carry a camera too. If you make certain to stay hydrated, you'll have a blast stopping to shoot the native flora and fauna along the way. Again, banditos aren't entirely out of the question here. The park rangers and the border patrol folks are around, but you won't see them on Ore Road. You're on your own. Just you, me, and Mr. de Zaster.

RIDE 53 · The Monk's Trail—Crazy Cat Arroyo

AT A GLANCE

Length/configuration: There are sections that are roughly the main trail, with many side trails and loops that wind around the area between the developed part of the city and the Franklin Mountains. I would estimate there's around 8–10 miles of fine single-track to enjoy here, but you've got to know your way around to get the most out of this place.

Aerobic difficulty: There is an easy 600–700 feet of climbing from the lowest spots to the highest. The trails are steep and loose and pretty tough. This is a fairly hard trail—at least it was to this flatlander.

Technical difficulty: Get your Wheaties. You will ride on loose gravel with scattered babyheads and a forecast for deep sand. Anyone who is just learning how to ride a mountain bike will be in way over their head on these trails.

Scenery: In the evening, with the city lights spread out around you, it's beautiful. In the day it offers fascinating views—Mexico just right over there, and the mountains behind and around you. The Franklin Mountains are situated like a finger stuck against the Rio Grande River, and the city of El Paso is shaped like a horseshoe, fitting nicely between the mountains and the river.

RIDE 53 • The Monk's Trail

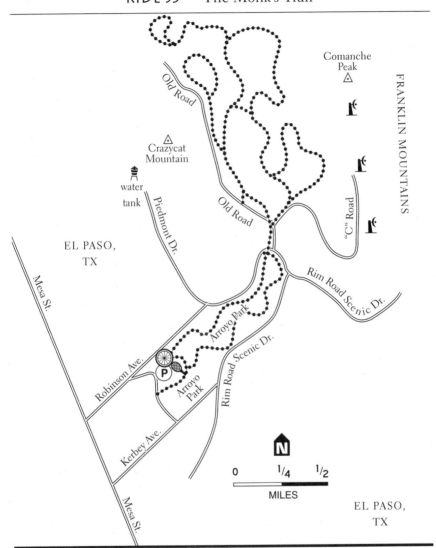

Special comments: I was so fortunate to find the guys at Crazy Cat Cyclery; they hauled me around and showed me where to ride. Their shop is less than a mile from the start at Crazy Cat Arroyo, so stop by. Tell 'em Chuck said "hi," and maybe they'll be nice to you anyway. This is one place where a guide will get you to the finer parts of the park and keep you out of the nastier bits. Some other trails connect into the main area from the tops of the mountains; ride 'em if you want, but they're really more hiking than biking trails.

I want to tell you about the Monk's Trail. This is gonna be most people's favorite trail in the Franklin Mountains. Even though they'll probably have to buy new tires every couple of months or so (this places chews the lugs right off).

This is all fine, high desert single-track; steep, loose, treacherous, wicked, and fun. The area in question is actually part of Crazy Cat Arroyo Park and the surrounding Franklin Mountains. Start at the tennis center, then ride the arroyo, then cross Robinson into the areas of Monk's. If you know where to look you will find Anna's Trail, the Colombian Connection, Spanish Fly, and all the mysterious treats of Monk's.

You can ride some fast, steep stuff on single-track, and blast through the arroyos on all that loose rock. We are talking major babyheads here, folks. You had better chow down your Wheaties, because you will use every inch of suspension you have and all the skills you thought you had. In typical Franklin Mountain fashion, there are connectors to side-loops all along the way. I would say the whole area probably has over ten miles of super-challenging single-track.

It also has some monster-steep old double-track up to the radio and TV towers, a beast called the "C" Road. This is a service road for the equipment up there, and it has signs saying "DON'T," but the gate was open when I was there so I went for it. Actually, I missed the cut to Monk's and rode up to the top of the mountain. Climb to the ridge if you too are dumb enough. The wind really blows up there—like 50 to 60 mph most days. That ridge has more of a hiking trail than a mountain biking trail, but I am told some folks ride it. I can't say for certain, because I chickened out, but it appears to be connected to Monk's by some sort of single-track. To get there you have a two-mile gravel road that rises about 1,700 feet to Ranger Peak. They call it "C" Road, and it is all you can handle. Or you can do the easier hard stuff and stay down on the side of the mountain, far below the radio and TV towers. There's everything here you can stand, and then some more.

I was told the name Monk's comes from a guy or some guys; they live quiet lonely lives. They love mountain biking and they built these trails. The main one got married, apparently, to a girl named Anna—hence the loop called Anna's. What you do is go out and ride everywhere you see trail, and you'll find all the spicy challenges that are the Monk's Trails.

Accurate maps are hard to come by, because the trails here cover a lot of territory. You can ride five miles, or you can ride ten. It all depends on the route you take around the areas of Monk's. Stop by Crazy Cat Cyclery and ask about riding in the park. This is one of those super-good bike shops where the people are friendly and the bikes are fast. They might even take you for a ride if you show up at the right time. Hell, we did a night ride when I was there. Talk about being scared witless. I flatted and was walking through Crazy Cat Arroyo, at night, singing to the rattlesnakes. The guys all laughed at me, but I don't care what they say. I could just feel those beady little rattlesnake eyes using their infrared to target my legs. Creepy.

Go on and get yourself some of the Monk's, Pilgrim. 'Nuff said.

General location: The middle of El Paso, Texas.

Elevation change: Boy, you can ride to the tops of some mountains that are more than 5,600 feet high—Ranger Peak is at the end of the "C" Road. The start at Crazy Cat Arroyo Park is around 3,900 feet. The main Monk's trails probably get up to around 4,600 feet at the highest point.

Season: I'd get there early during the summer; this is the high Chihuahuan Desert, and it can be a balmy 110° on a typical day in the summer. There are times the wind blows so hard you won't want to be out here in the flying dirt. Other than that I would say it's groovy any time of year.

Services: Since the park is basically in the middle of town, you'll have plenty of opportunity to get set before you go to the trailhead. There's nothing there but parking and the tennis center.

Hazards: Cell phones are a good idea out here. This is not a beginner trail. It has just about every hazard you might expect. Flats are common, so run some sealant in your tires or bring flat stuff. The Crazy Cats kept telling me that there's so much traffic that snakes are not a big problem—not like they are up in the mountains—but I would be careful just the same. The conditions are harsh and loose and you'd better be prepared for survival when you ride here.

Rescue index: High, if you can get word to someone that you need a rescue. This is one of the larger cities in Texas and you're right in the middle of town.

Land status: Arroyo Park is a nature preserve—I never did figure out if the city or county maintains it. I presume the City of El Paso. The main area of the trails is probably on some private land and might be developed some day, but some of it appears to be part of Franklin Mountains State Park.

Maps: There aren't a lot of maps of this area; city maps and USGS topos are about it. The quads for this area are Smeltertown and El Paso.

Finding the trail: From Mesa Street in El Paso, take Robinson Avenue east, toward the mountains, until you see the tennis center (maybe a mile). Park at the tennis center and catch the trail along the north side of the tennis courts. Follow the trail up into Arroyo Park until you reach Robinson Avenue again, and cross to the gate on the dirt road heading back toward the mountains. Go around the gate and follow the dirt road a short distance until it forks. There are entry points for the single-track here, going in several directions. Grab a trail and ride the loops around until you're tired. Return to the tennis center, either on the road or back the way you came on the park single-track.

Sources of additional information:

Crazy Cat Cyclery
2625 N Mesa Street
Suite B
El Paso, TX 79902-3100
(915) 577-9666

Notes on the trail: Just go out there and explore. The trails in Arroyo Park wind around behind the tennis center in the park. The trails up around the mountains wind around between the developments and the mountains and generally loop back into the main trail until you're back at the dirt road that leads from Robinson Avenue. You can go north for a couple of miles or so, but the east/west borders are the developments and the mountains, and the southern border is Robinson Avenue/Rim Road.

RIDE 54 · Gilbert's Trail (The Southside)— Franklin Mountains State Park

AT A GLANCE

Length/configuration: Various loops of single-track in an area between the city and the mountains and Trans Mountain Drive. There's probably 10–12 miles of trail, total.

Aerobic difficulty: This place is not that hard, but it is open desert. There are some loose spots and some climbing, but not as severe as the other trails in the El Paso area.

Technical difficulty: There's everything here from easy and fairly flat trail to some short steep climbs with rock ledges and babyheads. There's a place or two you will probably have to walk. The drops are too much or too scary to attempt while you're clipped in. Overall, I would give this a medium technicality rating.

Scenery: This is a neat place. You have the mountains to the east, the river valley to the west. You can see for a long ways, but this is not the most scenic ride in this area.

Special comments: At present I fear that some of the trails are on private land and may disappear under the hob-nailed boot of urban sprawl, but most of it is part of Franklin Mountains State Park and should be here for a long, long time.

At one point, out there in the desert, you pass a shrine. In typical Catholic style it is often adorned with candles and flowers, but the neat thing is how it is just carved into solid rock on the side of a hill, right by the trail. Stop and pay your respects, even if you're not the religious kind.

As I sit here in Tyler State Park, trying to use my old piece-of-crap laptop, in the dark, to make notes on Gilbert's Trail, I wonder at the world. It is raining like a big dog. We were supposed to have a race this weekend, but I blew that off for another day and headed east. I fired up my old tape of the ride on Gilbert's and tried to start a fire. That's when the rain began to fall in earnest. And that's where I will begin to

RIDE 54 • Gilbert's Trail (The Southside)

tell you about the best trail in El Paso. I don't know for sure who Gilbert is, but my thanks to him for his labors. This is the best trail in El Paso County.

I sort of blew into town after a wicked sandstorm and then got to enjoy beautiful weather while I enjoyed several beautiful trails. This single-track is more fun than a barrel of monkeys. It goes this way, and that way, and the whole time you can see for miles. You can see the mountains, the cities, the rest of the single-track, the housing development encroaching to the south. You can't really get lost here unless you have no wits. In which case, I can help you not at all. You

A nice shady spot along Gilbert's Trail. The beautiful Chihuahuan Desert and Franklin Mountains of El Paso.

see, I too am witless part of the time, but I don't get lost very often. Not near often enough, some will say. But if you want a ride you can take just about any of your mountain biking pals on, this is it.

I started on the end of Redd Road, when I rode this. I am told that the lady who owns the house there is cool, but the parking area I used was obviously about to be an entrance to some new exclusive/excessive housing development, so at this point I have some advice for you: go see the people at the state park. Much of this is private and is about to be consumed by the beast, but the state of Texas has a bunch of it in their/our pockets. Talk to the rangers, they can set you up with an annual pass to the park parts that will always be there.

This fine desert single-track, you see, this "best trail in El Paso," is mostly on public property. The trail I learned was Gilbert's is actually what the Franklin Mountains State Park employees call "the Southside." They will sell you an annual pass to ride this, and the Sunset Loop, for $25. That's about $2 a month for some of the best riding west of the Pecos. Cool.

I would estimate there are about a dozen miles of good trail here. I rode about half of it. Most is quite well established and rideable, but some is only walkable. But it is fairly easy, as trails go here, and about what I would call a good trail for beginners with at least a little bit of sand. I think I could take my friend Marty and his son Ryan, and Ryan is only nine years old. But he has a pretty good bike. I would definitely get Ryan a Camelbak first, slime in his tires, and a patch kit under his seat. He probably would need all these things—or at least, I think any-one should have them before attempting a trail like this.

There's nothing but cactus and ocotillo for miles. And sharp rocks and deep sand. And tricky bits. Just don't push it, and you'll do fine. Ryan will probably kick both our butts, anyway.

General location: The far north end of El Paso, Texas.

Elevation change: This one is relatively flat, compared to some in the area. The start on Redd Road is around 4,100 feet and the start over by the state park entrance is around 4,500 feet. The highest you will get is in the neighborhood of 4,800 feet, and the lowest is probably about 4,000 feet. You'll be able to enjoy 600 to 800 feet of delta, if you ride the whole enchilada.

Season: Any time there isn't a major sandstorm should be nice. This is the high Chihuahuan desert, so summer afternoons will hover anywhere from 100° to 120°, in the shady sections. Oh, by the way—there are no shady sections.

Services: Nothing at present. If you start at the state park entrance, you'll have a place to park. Nothing else. Bring what you need from town.

Hazards: A cell phone would probably not be useless here, since you're right next to the city. As has been observed by Texan desert residents, "everything here sticks, stabs, stinks, or bites." This trail is a flat tire waiting to happen if you don't use sealant. The surfaces are loose and tricky, and it would be too easy to go OTB if you get too rambunctious on a drop or around a curve and get a boo boo. I wouldn't be shocked if I saw rattlesnake, not even if I saw one that was six feet long. So keep your eyes open, especially around dawn and dusk.

Rescue index: High. This place has lots of traffic; it's probably ridden every day by someone, but you are in the middle of the desert. If you can pinpoint your location you could summon help on the phone. Since you can see a long ways, you would be able to spot another rider or emergency personnel from most points if you needed help.

Land status: The land on the southern areas is under constant development, being turned into fancy homes at a frightening rate, but most of it is property of the Texas Parks and Wildlife Department (under the auspices of Franklin Mountains State Park). It is, therefore, not going anywhere. Plus, the rangers here love mountain bikers. Just realize you are on their land, and they can ticket you if you ride here without a permit. They swear that they patrol the roads here, and I believe 'em.

Maps: Not generally available. The USGS quads for this area are Smeltertown and Canutillo.

Finding the trail: Most people will tell you it's all right to park at the end of Redd Road and ride from there. I have absolutely no confidence, however, that this will always be the case. Nevertheless, since this is currently the main "trailhead," I describe riding from there. Follow Redd Road until it ends at the construction area. Park carefully, allowing construction vehicles substantial passage around your vehicle, and ride off northeast into the desert on the first single-track you see. Then just wind around on the various trails until you're tired, and head back to your vehicle. Visibility here is in the range of many miles, so as you wander try to keep tabs on where you are in relation to the housing area, and you can only get just so lost.

Sources of additional information:

Franklin Mountains State Park
1331 McKelligon Canyon Road
El Paso, TX 79930
(915) 566-6441
www.tpwd.state.tx.us/park/franklin/
    franklin.htm

Texas Parks and Wildlife Department
4200 Smith School Road
Austin, TX 78744-3291

(800) 792-1112 information
(512) 389-8900 reservations
www.tpwd.state.tx.us

Crazy Cat Cyclery
2625 N Mesa Street
Suite B
El Paso, TX 79902-3100
(915) 577-9666

Notes on the trail: Wide-open riding under a big sky is what you will enjoy here. Bring whatever you will need—don't leave your patch kit and pump in the car— and bring some pals. I would recommend that you check with the folks at the state park or Crazy Cat Cyclery on current trail conditions before you drive all the way over to the Redd Road trailhead, just in case anything has changed since I was there. Good luck, have fun, pay the rangers their entrance fee, and keep the rubber side down.

RIDE 55 · The Sunset Loop—Franklin Mountains State Park

AT A GLANCE

Length/configuration: This trail is a clockwise loop with about 15 miles of single-track and old roads. There are several bailouts that allow you to go from the Lower Sunset Trail to the Upper Sunset Trail and avoid the more remote sections.

Aerobic difficulty: The Sunset Loop is a pretty darn hard trail. The surface is loose sand in many places, and some of it is gravel so soft and deep it's tough to pedal through. And then there's the elevation-exchange process. A few of the climbs are steep, and the very last climb, up into the park, is very steep, especially after the last 15 miles of hard trail.

Technical difficulty: Due to the loose surface and tricky climbing sections I would have to rate Sunset as a trail where your technical abilities will all be used and abused. This is a ride that will show you what you got.

Scenery: You are basically running out through open desert and then returning along the base of the Franklin Mountains. If you are someone

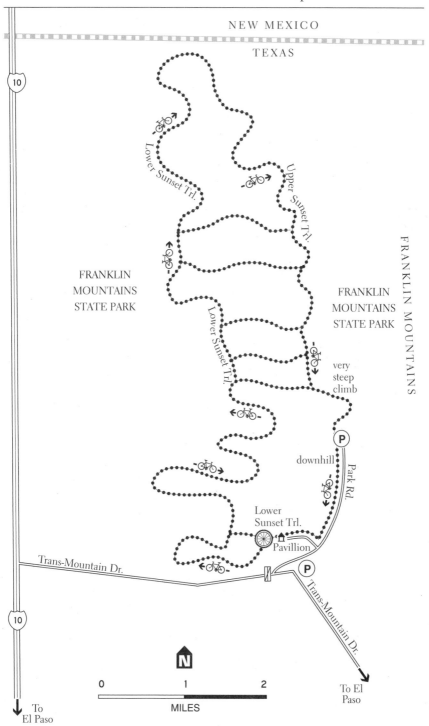

NEW MEXICO

TEXAS

FRANKLIN
MOUNTAINS
STATE PARK

FRANKLIN
MOUNTAINS
STATE PARK

FRANKLIN MOUNTAINS

Lower Sunset Trl.

Upper Sunset Trl.

Lower Sunset Trl.

very
steep
climb

P

downhill

Park Rd.

Lower
Sunset Trl.

Pavillion

P

Trans-Mountain Dr.

Trans-Mountain Dr.

To El
Paso

N

0   1   2

MILES

10

10

To
El Paso

like me who loves this sort of stuff, then you will think this is a beautiful ride, like I do. The mountains stretch to the north, into New Mexico, and the Rio Grande River valley is just a few miles west. You can see far into Mexico and New Mexico, and they don't call it the Sunset Trail for nothing. Take a hint from that and plan your day accordingly.

Special comments: Franklin Mountains State Park is the largest urban park in the nation, covering around 37 square miles of the foothills and mountains of the Franklin Range. In addition to the fine mountain bike trails, there are hiking trails and rock climbing activities, if you like that sort of thing. When the state has this place fully online there will be over 50 miles of trail for bikes, alone. Believe it—there is a lot of serious property out there.

This is a long, hard, treacherous ride through difficult terrain, a test for any mountain biker. Or it is a fairly routine, straightforward hour or so in the desert, if you bail onto one of the shortcut routes. But it is one of those world-class bike trails they ought to have the friggin' Olympics on someday, it is that tough.

The ride I describe for you starts with the Lower Sunset Trail and then connects with the Upper Sunset Trail to return you to the parking lot at the start. The rangers will tell you, as will the maps, that the full loop is 16 miles. I would say that the whole enchilada is about a three-hour ride. Unless you're one of those racerheads that can ride something like this in an hour-and-a-half. It is what you make of it—easy or hard, or something in between. This is one awesome ride, either way. It can be tailored to just what you want to ride today. Some easy, some hard, some monster. And that last climb as you return to the park is, well, steep. It will definitely get your attention. But once you get up there it is fast downhill pavement back to the parking area near the start.

Some stretches through the arroyos are steep, loose, and desperately difficult. Some stretches are long and flat, but on loose ankle-deep gravel that I can barely ride, if at all. Some stretches are barely marked by bike tracks; you will only find your way because the trails are so well signed by the state of Texas. There are signs every half-mile or so that correspond to points on the map, and without them you are basically buzzard-bait. Take a map, take plenty of liquid, and sun screen up before you start. Screen up heavy, it will be a long day.

When the rangers are through building this thing it will stretch about 25 miles to the north, all the way into New Mexico. Man, I'd like to see that. When these guys are done they will have one of the best trail systems anywhere, at least anywhere this side of Colorado and Utah. I am told the labor to construct this animal is all coming from chain-gangs. I think that's a worthy use of leisure (jail) time. Thanks, convicts, you do good work. And you build wicked trail. Come back with a bike when you get out of the slammer. We'll hammer.

What a fun and difficult trail. You think you have it licked? Carry on, mountain biker; you'll earn your scrapes and scratches on this single-track. If you have the sand.

General location: In El Paso, Texas, the heel of the Texas boot.

Elevation change: The trailhead area is about 4,800 feet above the Gulf of Mexico, and the finish area is around 5,000 feet. In between you will find the lowest point along the trail to be around 4,300 feet, and you never get any higher than the 5,000 feet at the finish. The range is a solid 700 feet, but you will never have more than, say, 400 feet to climb at once (right in the final couple of miles). You will definitely be feeling this for a few days after the ride.

Season: Winter, spring, summer, or fall, like the song says. The weather is to be respected here—some days the wind may blow 80 mph and you probably don't want to be out in the desert in that. You definitely don't want to be on any of the mountains when it's like that. The heat in the summer is about what you would expect, 100° to 120° in the shade. And there ain't no shade, by the way.

Services: Load up in town. There is a convenience store/gas station at the turnoff from I-10 as you head up toward the park, so get what you need here or do without. There are chemical toilets (oh goody!), but no running water in the park.

Hazards: Getting dead without wanting to. In so many ways. Rattlesnakes, dangerous plants, treacherous conditions; just about anything dangerous you can imagine except large wild beasts. Wait, the riders count there, I guess, but they are a pretty friendly lot so don't be scared. I've heard it said that everything that lives in the desert either sticks, stabs, stinks, or bites. Again, about snakes, be careful in the twilight times, early and late, because there are snakes around. Don't stop and mess with them or try to take a picture. You're gonna feel pretty dumb if you take a picture of a snake biting you.

Rescue index: A cell phone should be good around some of this trail. If you can get word out that you have trouble, people will come find you. The trail is very well marked, and if you carry a map you can simply report your approximate location. If you're unconscious, however, you better hope your partner can find your cell phone and map and call in for you. This place gets some traffic, although it can be pretty lonely on the outer sections, and you might not see another human for a couple of days or weeks.

Land status: Texas Parks and Wildlife Department state park.

Maps: The rangers have one that's pretty good, it shows all the trail markers and side trails. Don't leave home without it.

Finding the trail: From I-10 in El Paso, proceed north to the northwest part of town and exit at Trans Mountain Drive, heading east toward the mountains. The main entrance to the park will be on your left (north), about a mile or so up the road. Pull into the park and pay your fee, and pull on up the road until you see the sign for the Lower Sunset Trail. Turn left and park. You will find marker #51 here, the last spot on the map. Jump on the trail and follow the markers as they are shown on the map. You will wind around in the desert, passing points on the map, until you are about eight miles north. From there you are very near the New Mexico border. Head east on the old jeep road, around the ridge, and then you will return to the park riding between the mountains and the ridge. Once you are in site of the pavilion on the north end of the park road, you climb back into the main park area and you can take the pavement back to where you parked, about a mile of mostly downhill. You'll be glad for that last part.

Sources of additional information:

Franklin Mountains State Park
1331 McKelligon Canyon Road
El Paso, TX 79930
(915) 566-6441
www.tpwd.state.tx.us/park/franklin/
    franklin.htm

Texas Parks and Wildlife Department
4200 Smith School Road
Austin, TX 78744-3291

(800) 792-1112 information
(512) 389-8900 reservations
www.tpwd.state.tx.us

Crazy Cat Cyclery
2625 N Mesa Street
Suite B
El Paso, TX 79902-3100
(915) 577-9666

Notes on the trail: Franklin Mountains State Park is a primitive facility; there's no water and only chemical toilets. There is no phone, but the rangers are usually somewhere around the property as long as the gate is open. There is a fee of $3 to $5 per head to enter. The park is closed and the gate is locked from 5 p.m. until 8 a.m. the next day. There are usually tons of good places to have a picnic before or after the ride, and quite honestly I don't think this place gets enough visitors. If you camp up here you may not have neighbors, anywhere. That was like my last night at Franklin Mountains State Park—it was quiet and I had a big old juicy steak with a baked potato and field peas, and then listened to some short-wave from Mexico. It was grand. But then, I'm goofy for stuff like that. I'd definitely have to buy that annual pass if I lived here.

AFTERWORD

"No reason to get excited," the thief, he kindly spoke,
"There are many here among us who feel that life is but a joke.
But you and I, we've been through that, and this is not our fate,
So let us not talk falsely now, the hour is getting late."
— Bob Dylan, singer and songwriter,
"All Along the Watchtower"

It is not by accident that the first chapter in the book and the last one are where they are. I chose them that way on purpose. I started you in the dawn of the history of these areas, and I left you with the sunset. I'm goofy like that.

I hope you have enjoyed riding with me. I can ride anywhere—any trail that's new, or that I've seen before—and fall in love again. It's just like I was nine years old again sometimes; I melt into the woods.

I can go out when it's 100 degrees and laugh, or when it's 10 degrees and act completely silly. I don't care, I just love to ride. I love the woods and the trails. That's why I take certain things personally. Like people who abuse or disrespect my trails.

If I have griped about things you do, then I am sorry for you. Get a grip. I ride like it matters. It only matters to me, but I do it anyway. I love my bikes, I love my dirt, and I love my pals. We know how to have fun. If all you do in the woods is bitch or shred, then you've got a hard row to hoe, Pilgrim.

If you don't really love mountain biking, then give it up. You don't have to be John Tomac or Ned Overend—it doesn't matter to me; all I care about is that you love this silly sport. Do you ride the dirt because you love the dirt, and maybe a little because you fear the blue hairs, or do you just do it because it's trendy? Or because you have an expensive DH bike? Well, dude, if that's all it means to you, then go jump in the lake. It means a lot more to me. It means being a responsible citizen, being a caring trail steward, and being someone who loves riding a bike so much that if I meet my maker on the trail, you'll know that the smile I'm wearing in the casket was not put there by the undertaker.

God bless America. Nam myoho renge kyo. Death before dishonor, and "Duty Honor Country." Let's roll!

International Mountain Bicycling Association (IMBA)
1121 Broadway
Suite 203
P.O. Box 7578
Boulder, CO 80306
(303) 545-9011
(888) 442-4622
www.imba.com

GLOSSARY

This short list of terms does not contain all the words used by mountain bike enthusiasts when discussing their sport. But it should serve as an introduction to the lingo you'll hear on the trails.

Air	What's between you and Mother Earth when you jump your bike.
AKA	Also Known As.
Auger	Gathering soil samples with a part of your body, typically the face, but the knees and elbows are common implements used to perform this maneuver as well.
Automorons	People who think bicycles are toys and have no business being on "their" street or road. People who roll up to a traffic light and turn right without looking to see if some woman might be pushing her baby carriage across the intersection.
Backscratcher	Low hanging stuff on the trail that will try to snag the back of your jersey or your Camelbak.
Baggies	Those loose-fitting cycling shorts worn by many mountain bikers.
Babyheads	Rocks the size of your fist, typically strewn loose along the trail.
Bacon	Scabs and contusions.
Bail	To leap from your steed in an (often useless) attempt to prevent injury because a crash is imminent.
Bayou	A small river or large creek.
Berm	A banked turn. Opposite of off-camber. Like the inside of a bowl.
Big ring	The largest sprocket of the front gears on your bike. Good for high-speed flat cruising.

Bike panties The more traditional cycling shorts, typically form-fitting Lycra.

Blaze Marks painted onto trees along a trail to mark the route. Might be arrows, rectangles, or just indistinct splotches, depending on the person doing the blazing.

Blue hair An old person in an automobile exhibiting either a complete lack of awareness of their surroundings, or a lack of ability to see over the dashboard.

Bluehole A deep spot in a creek or river, suitable for swimming in. When you see one, you'll know why they are called that.

BMX A kids' bike. Hey, lots of mountain bikers started out as kids, and they were doing off-roading before there was mountain biking. BMX is the style of off-road riding done with very durable single-speed bikes like you see the kids riding. They do some amazing tricks with those machines.

Bomb Sort of like Gonzo, but not quite so reckless—going too fast, though.

Bonk A state of total exhaustion. This happens when you have consumed all the energy stored in your legs and liver. Your only recourse is to eat something, or enter the death march phase of the ride.

Booboo An owie. An injury sustained from riding.

Boot To vomit/hurl/purge, also known as the Big Spit.

Brain bucket Bike helmet.

Bridge Any construction allowing you to cross a stream or ditch and not get your tires wet; i.e. a bridge passes over a creek so you're not required to go all the way to the bottom of the ditch to get to the other side.

Bunny hop Lifting the entire bicycle off the ground by using either the suspension or sheer muscular strength. Often used to clear deadfalls.

Camber Any slope to the trail, maybe in a turn or maybe just along the side of a hill, that runs perpendicular to your direction of travel. Sometimes it requires you to lean in toward the side of the hill, putting only the very edge of your tire in contact with the ground. Like riding on the outside of a bowl.

Camelbak A personal hydration system invented by a guy from Texas. It consists of a poly-bladder that can be filled with

	ice and drink, then fitted into a small insulated backpack arrangement. The flexible straw that feeds you from the bladder has a bite-valve, and fits nicely under a helmet strap to be easily accessible for a quick slurp.
Caliche	Very fine white dirt, common in parts of Texas.
Carsonite	That weird flat plastic-looking stuff that is often used for trail markers.
Carve	To fly through twisty trail, expertly using the machine and your skills.
CCOSP	Collin County Open Spaces Commission.
Clay	Real fine dirt, any color from black to red to light tan. A bitch when wet.
Clean	To successfully negotiate a technical piece of trail.
Climbing turn	Sort of like an uphill switchback. These are often very tight and require proper gear selection, weight distribution, and steering input.
Clock	Bike computer or odometer.
Corduroy	Those trail repair materials that are laid down perpendicular across the trail in order to keep bike tires out of the mud when a bridge is not appropriate. Typically landscape timers, fence posts, or two-by-four's.
CR	County Road. Usually gravel or dirt.
Cross country/XC	This refers to the sort of riding where you ride many miles across the land. It's not just downhill; you have to have a bike that's realistic. Perfect bikes for this type of riding will be relatively lightweight and have at least some squish in the front, and often an inch or two in back. My Ripley is awesome for this type of riding—it's my style.
Cruise	And easy ride, usually pretty flat.
Cruiser	A bicycle in the old style, typically having only one gear, balloon tires, and a big fat seat with springs.
Crumblies	Those little flakes of dirt that dry clay turns into when it has been ridden on a lot.
C-store	Convenience store, like Seven-Eleven or Allsup's or any little "mom and pop" grocery.
Dab	Touching something besides your seat, pedals, and handlebars in a technical section. Best done with the foot, but knees, forearms, hands, and heads have been used with great efficacy.

Deadfall	Anything resembling a tree which is laying across the trail because it fell there and then was left as a technical obstacle. Either by God or the local crew.
Death march	A ride that starts out as a fairly straightforward affair but soon turns into a miserable and exhaustive day of horrors. This may be caused by weather, bugs, terrain, or an unexpected obstacle that makes you turn around and retrace your whole journey when you're a substantial distance into a long ride. This usually starts with the words, "Man, my Camelback is already empty, you got any extra water?"
Delta	Change of elevation.
Dip	A depression in the trail large enough to get both your whole bike into with neither wheel out of.
DORBA	The Dallas Off-Road Bicycle Association. North Texas mountain bike club with roughly 300 members. DORBA builds and maintains almost all of the mountain bike trails in the Dallas–Fort Worth metropolis.
Downhill/DH	A relatively recent development in the mountain biking world, it consists of riding as fast as possible down a hill, strangely enough. The bikes used in this activity usually have several inches of suspension travel in front and back, and disc brakes. This allows the highest possible speed over the roughest available terrain. A lot of the riders of these things wear body armor and full coverage helmets because crashes are gonna happen. The bikes these people use are usually way too heavy to be decent XC machines.
DPARD	Dallas Parks and Recreation Department. The agency that operates City of Dallas park facilities.
Double-track	The dirt road type of two-lane. Might be a four-wheel-drive road or utility access on a closed piece of property.
Endo	When you hit something with the front wheel of the bike, or when you lock the front brake and the rider flies over the handlebars. Sometimes their bicycle follows them in a gentle arc and hits them in the back or some other unprotected body part.
Epic	A long, hard ride through remote and difficult terrain that was so much fun the last time you rode it you can hardly wait to do it again. Often accompanied by countryside of great scenic beauty. Often accompanied by unexpected mechanical or physiological failure of the participants.

Should only be pursued by groups of competent riders with tools and tubes, and plenty of water. Often turns into a death march.

First blood	A badge of honor earned by the first injury of a ride.
Flags	Pieces of surveyor's tape tied to trees and objects along a trail to mark the route.
FM	Farm-to-Market Road. Texas is crisscrossed with paved two lane roads that were built to allow farmers and ranchers to have roads they can use to get—like the name says—from farm to market. Generally well maintained, though may not be heavily trafficked. Might even have a shoulder sometimes.
Free-ride/FR	As far as I can tell, this involves jumping off things with total disregard for personal safety or longevity of equipment. This style of riding finds its participants riding their bikes off buildings, walls, big rocks; just whatever that will allow them the maximum amount of air. I think these people finally got too old to ride skateboards and bought bikes that weigh as much as two normal bikes. Total silliness in the context of Texas and Oklahoma mountain biking.
Full-suspension/FS	A bike with a suspension fork in front and some sort of linkage-style spring-and-shock rear suspension. Sort of a generic term in a lot of ways considering all the advanced rear suspension technologies available today.
Gnarlies	Trail obstacles that involve bike handling skills. Might simply involve technical intrusions, or throwing a speeding bike through a section of trail that requires accurate placement of both machine and body parts.
Gonzo	Foolishness. Devil-may-care riding. Looking for Mr. Bustyerass de Zaster. I think this term originally dates to Hunter S. Thompson and his "gonzo journalism."
GPS	Global Positioning System. Great way to find where you are, if you have the maps that go with it.
Granny ring	The smallest front sprocket on your bike. Good for that low-speed grind up a long difficult hill. Whew, I'm tired. Are we there yet?
Gravel	Chunks of rock sized between marbles and golf balls.
Grunt	A tough climb, may be short or long.

GU	Brand name of a line of energy packets, a hundred grams of quick carbs in a swallow. Available at most bike shops. I swear by this stuff, easy to carry and quick to ingest. There are some really off-color pseudonyms for this product.
Gully	A dry stream bed or other type of wash where the water runs during rain. Dry otherwise.
Gumbo	Sticky black dirt that works like plaster when it's wet. It sticks to your bike tires and pretty soon they weigh more than five bikes and cease to revolve. This stuff is mighty nasty when it has been rained on any time in the previous several days.
Hairpin	A very tight turn of more than 90 degrees of arc, usually more like 180 degrees.
Hard right or left hander	An immediate turn of the slightly more or less than 90 degrees variety.
Hardtail	A bike with a rigid frame, no rear suspension, but has a suspension fork on the front.
Hike-a-bike	A section of trail—maybe short, maybe lengthy—where you simply cannot ride and have to drag/push/fling the bike to get anywhere.
Hammer	To ride hard. Hard enough to boot.
Hybrid	An on- or off-road bicycle having 700C or 27" wheels.
I-	Interstate highway. The Green Stamp, as the truckers say.
IMBA	International Mountain Bicycling Association, the world-wide organization dedicated to promoting responsible mountain bike activities.
Involuntary dismount	A nice term for crashing or falling off your bike.
Kiosk	A big sign at the trailhead that often has maps and other nifty bits of data available.
Lagniappe	A word from Louisiana, Cajun maybe? It means "that little something extra." Like a mint at a restaurant or a little bag of bath salts like my girlfriend throws in at her craft shows. Or a loose stick you did not see but your rear tire found it. Say it like "LAN-yap."
Line	The preferred place to put your wheels when riding, or the path your bike takes through a turn or a techie bit. If

you know how to see the line before you get there you can look really cool when you sail over something hard and make it look easy. If you don't see it in time, or mess up as you hit the tough stuff, you can have a yard sale.

Lollipop	A trail that goes out, then has a loop, and then you ride the first part back to the start. Think about it.
Loop trail	Any trail that will bring you back to your starting place without having to turn around at any point.
Loppers	Pruning tool used to clear tree branches from the trail.
Marbles	Small pebbles or pieces of rock, smaller than gravel sometimes, that lie on the trail and send you to see Mr. Bustyerbutt sometimes.
M-dolphins	Chemical enzymes your glands produce to make pain feel good. Known to medical science as endorphins.
Meander	A slow ride on a cool trail, a ride where you forget about time. Or the way a trail will sometimes seem to be designed with no real intention of providing a direct route.
Mechanical	A failure of a machine caused by broken parts.
Metromess	The Dallas/Fort Worth Metroplex area.
Mister Bustyerass de Zaster	The ground where you fall, a rock you leave a knee on, a tree that tears your jersey. Anything dangerous or abrasive or just plain not soft along the trail.
Mo/momentum	More important on a suspension bike than a rigid, sometimes. When you have squish, you have to keep enough speed that the suspension doesn't rebound and throw you backwards or sideways into your riding partner.
Mo betta	Very good. Muy bueno. Pleasantly acceptable.
Moguls	Short, spaced, small dips in the surface of a trail. Not to be confused with washboard. More like a quick series of hard, large bumps.
Mojo	A good luck charm or toy worn by a mountain biker or attached to the bike.
Mountain bike/ MTB	A bicycle specifically designed to be ridden off-road, typically having 26" wheels.
Mountains	Those really big piles of rock. Texas and Oklahoma have some of these, but don't try to sell that to someone from Colorado.
NORBA	The National Off-Road Bicycle Association, the sanctioning body for American mountain bike racing.

Northshore	Apparently there are these people in British Columbia who have invented their own style of riding. Some of it is DH and some is FR, and then they build these crazy looking structures out of two-by-four's to ride on. Totally radical. Very hard on both equipment and bodies.
Ooze-along	A slow easy ride with no timetable.
Organ donor	A rider with no helmet.
OTB	Over The Bars. As the name implies, this athletic maneuver relates to a particularly nasty form of involuntary dismount. This separation of rider and bike is achieved by one of two methods: the good one and the bad one. The good one involves landing feet first, while the other often includes a serious headache. Not to be confused with any Olympic events.
Out-and-back-trail	Any trail that runs like a line from point A to point B. Requires you to turn around at point B to return to point A.
Overcook	Going so fast that you cannot negotiate the next turn and you get a booboo.
Peds	Pedestrians; mountain bikers who either did not bring their bikes, or have given said steed a mechanical.
Point-to-point trail	A trail that connects two points, A and B. Same as an out-and-back.
Portage	A canoeing term, it means carrying your bike.
Porta-potty	A chemical toilet like you see around construction sites.
Powder	Very loose and very fine material making up the surface of a trail. May be several inches deep. Not sand exactly, more like dust.
PR	Park Road. The roads in parks, strangely enough. They are usually paved.
Quads	Quadriceps, if I'm talking about legs, or quadrangles if I'm talking about maps.
Radius	The rate of directional change relating to a turn or bend in the trail. If the turn gets tighter through its course, the radius is decreasing. If the turn starts tight and bends less and less through its course, its radius is increasing.
Relief	Terrain contour or elevation change.

Retro-grouch	A rider who prefers an old bike with old components and doesn't need a fancy new bike with loads of technology to have fun. Me, perhaps.
Rigid	A bike with a solid front fork, no suspension.
Roadie	A rider who only rides the street.
Road rash	Contact dermatitis; an allergic reaction of skin to moving asphalt.
Rock garden	Where the rocks grow up out of the ground. Don't water them with your blood.
Rose rocks	There are places in Oklahoma where you will find these little golf balls of sandstone that have been shaped by erosion to have weirdly contoured surfaces, and they resemble rose blooms.
RR	A Ranch Road, related to Farm-to-Market roads, only in a different part of Texas.
Rut	A small ditch across or on the trail. Not a purposeful construction, usually caused by water erosion or tire tracks.
Sand	Crystals of dirt, roughly the size of sugar granules.
Screw the pooch	To have a booboo, often involves humiliation or personal injury.
Shredding	Riding like hell. I define it as ripping the dirt with your tires. Not a good thing.
Shred-head	Someone who would rather see the dirt fly than leave it where they found it.
Single-speed	A really cool trend in the mountain biking world. A mountain bike with only one gear, suitable for a lot more trails than you might think. Most have a front suspension fork, but there are a few out there that are totally traditional. A throwback to the good old days.
Single-track	A one-lane trail in the woods, not any narrower than your tire but might be up to a foot wide.
Skeeters	Them pesky mosquitoes. What God was thinking, I don't know.
Slalom	S-turns in the trail that are roughly parallel to the direction of the trail.
SNA	State or Scenic Natural Area. Sort of like a state park without all the appurtenances of state park infrastructure; i.e. nothing but primitive camping facilities.

Snake bite	Hopefully this only relates to your tires. If you smash down on a tire so hard that the edges of the rim cut the tube, you have given the tube a "snake bite" flat.
Soft-tail	An odd type of mountain bike having a small amount of rear suspension travel because the frame itself flexes; there are no moving parts other than a rear shock of some sort. Like my Ripley.
Softies	Powdery spots in the trail that might drag you into Mr. de Zaster's living room. Against your will.
Squish	Suspension. Some amount of travel on at least the front of your bike.
Steed	The machine. The bike. The tool.
S-*turn*	Left right left right left right, etc. Looks like an exaggerated letter **S** from the air.
Swag	Free stuff you get at a trail workday, and sometimes at the races.
Sweeper	A gradual turn in the trail, less than 90 degrees—not so tight to prevent it from being taken at speed.
Switchback	In order to make a very steep incline rideable, it may be necessary to build the trail so that it zigzags in a series of hairpins up the face of the incline. Normally involve some off-camber and bermed places where the direction reversals occur.
Tabletop	A maneuver made while getting air. Consists of pulling the bike as parallel to the ground as possible and then getting the wheels on the ground, and making it look cool. This last part is important.
Tall Cotton	As good as life gets; euphoria.
Tank	A pond is typically called a tank in the southern Midwest.
Techies/techie bits	Those special places along the trail that make you use your skills. See technical.
Technical	This relates to pieces of trail that are difficult to negotiate because of several factors. There might be loose rocks to deal with, or tree roots you have to part hop and part finesse the bike over. You might have to use your best weight distribution and steering skills, and balance is often required. Not something that is just hard because it is steep; it has to have an obstacle or series of obstacles. You will understand technical the first time you almost

make it through a rock garden.

Topo/topographical map	Maps that show contour lines which indicate elevation changes in terrain. Typically, this will be the USGS-variety 7.5-minute quadrangles, available from the U.S. Department of the Interior, or a map store near you.
TPWD	Texas Parks and Wildlife Department. The agency responsible for operating state parks in Texas.
Trail-nut or trail-nazi	The more militant members of the trail building and maintenance community who aren't afraid to tell you when you're being an idiot. Like when you ride with no helmet, or when you abuse the rest of us by disrespecting the trails or other trail users.
TTN	Texas Trails Network. A group of concerned trail users dedicated to acquiring and protecting lands that will be used for public trails.
Tweak	This might be minor damage to your steed that makes something like the gears quit working just right, or it might be an injury to some part of your body that gives you moderate discomfort for the rest of the ride. And for a few days after, when you get over about 35 or so.
Twisties/ Twisty-turnies	Any series of fast turns that requires pitching the bike around expertly, if you want to shave seconds from a lap time. See **S**-turn.
UFO	Unlucky Fall Originator.
US	Federal Highway, not an Interstate.
USACE	United States Army Corps of Engineers. Those kind folks with the United States Army who build bridges and reservoirs and levees.
USGS	United States Geological Survey. Used in this manuscript to refer to topographical maps produced by the Federal government's surveyors.
Wander	Ride with no clear sense of direction, or the way some trails seem to reflect this philosophy.
Washboard	When the surface of a trail or road has a series of small undulations, like tiny whoop-de-do's. These would be the smallest of bumps, and will put you sideways quick. A bitch when you're riding, even if you have squish.
Washout	A rut or ditch caused by erosion. Way too common in some places.

Wash out	To have the front tire lose traction, especially while going around a corner.
Water bar	A small ditch cut across the trail to drain water, or any construction to divert the flow of water rushing down a hill. Sometimes takes the form of landscaping timbers buried in the trail to form a step perpendicular to the direction of travel. This keeps the water from rushing full-speed down an otherwise unprotected erosion zone. Also serves to keep the mountain bikers honest on fast downhills.
Water crossing	Any place you cross the actual bed of a stream and your tires can get wet. If it's dry it's not a water crossing, only a dry stream bed or gully, but it may revert at any time.
Wheelie-drop	A way to negotiate ledges and steep drop-offs. You roll up to the drop and slow, pull the bike vertical, and then launch. If done properly, the rear wheel lands below first and you can set the front wheel down, allowing you to ride off steep drops that have small landing zones. When done poorly, you break your bike or get to meet Mr. Bustyerballs.
Whoop-de-do	Dips in the trail that are like a series of small hills, one placed immediately after another. Big enough to catch some air on.
Wildernut or wildernazi	People who care more for the woods than for other people. I get like that sometimes, but I'm trying to cut down.
WMA	Wildlife Management Area. A parcel of land set aside for hunting and/or fishing, often crisscrossed with trails and unpaved roads. Outside of hunting season, many of these facilities are practically abandoned except for the casual camper, and may offer miles of mountain bike trails to the hearty enthusiast.
Yard sale	A crash, or near-crash, where you scatter bits and pieces of your personal items. Stuff like water bottles and pumps and bike computers, etc. A really good one may see your stuff spread out over an area several yards in diameter, or larger.
Zone	The way you ride when you have that perfect euphoric feeling that connects you with everything in the universe, and you are carving and life is good. This is the ultimate goal of all real mountain bikers; sort of a biking nirvana. Or when you completely lose it and cheerfully ride off the trail into the arms of Mr. Bustyerass de Zaster.

INDEX

Alto Relex, The Old Ore Road, TX, 208

The Anthills/Terry Hershey Park — Houston, TX, 164–66

Arbor Hills Nature Preserve Mountain Bike Trail — Plano, TX, 67–70

Arcadia Lake Trail — Edmond, OK, 30–33

Austin, TX, 115–26

Bar-H Ranch — Saint Jo, TX, 95–99

Barton Creek Greenbelt, Austin, TX, 115–18

Bee Caves, TX, 126–29

Benny's Trail — Guthrie, OK, 27–29

Big Bend National Park, TX, 203–12

Big Loop MTB Trail — Copper Breaks State Park, TX, 178–81

Big Pond, Big Loop MTB Trail, TX, 178–81

Big Shell Beach, North Padre Island, TX, 170–76

Black Gap — Big Bend National Park, TX, 203–7

Bluff Creek Ranch — Warda, TX, 129–33

Bluff Creek Trail — Oklahoma City, OK, 40–43

Bonham State Park Trail — Bonham, TX, 149–51

Boulder Park Trail — Dallas, TX, 70–73

Braggs, OK, 16–19

Bryan, TX, 155–58

Buffalo Bayou, The Anthills/Terry Hershey Park, TX, 164–66

Bull Canyon, Big Loop MTB Trail, TX, 178–81

Burnout Hill, Arcadia Lake Trail, OK, 31

Cameron Park Trails — Waco, TX, 112–15

Camping
  Arcadia Lake Trail, 32
  Big Loop MTB Trail, 179–80
  Bonham State Park Trail, 149
  Cedar Brake Trail, 105
  DORBA Trail, 80
  Double Lake Park Mountain Bike Trail, 160
  The "GSL" and Capitol Peak Trails, 191
  Lake McMurtry Trails, 26
  NuDraper Mountain Bike Park, 39
  Oklahoma "Ankle Express" Hiking Trail, 18
  The Old Ore Road, 208, 209
  Rocky Hill Ranch, 135
  Roman Nose State Park Trail, 46
  San Angelo State Park Trails, 197
  The Seven Mile Loop, 110
  "The Breaks" at Bar — H Ranch, 98
  Tyler State Park Trail, 153, 154
  Wolf Mountain Trail, 138
  X-Bar Ranch, 202

Capitol Peak Trail — Palo Duro Canyon State Park, TX, 189–92

Caprock Canyons Trailway—
    Quitaque, TX, 184–89
Cedar Brake Trail—Dinosaur Valley
    State Park, TX, 104–7
Cedar Hill State Park, TX, 77–81
Cellular phones, 9–10
Chihuahuan Desert, TX, 203–24
Clarity Tunnel, Caprock Canyons
    Trailway, TX, 187
Clear Bay Trail—Lake Thunderbird
    State Park, OK, 37–40
Cleburne State Park, TX, 108–11
Coldspring, TX, 158–61
Combination ride, 3
Comfort, TX, 143–47
Copper Breaks State Park, TX,
    178–81
Corpus Christi, TX, 170–76
Cottonwood Flats Trail, The "GSL"
    and Capitol Peak Trails, TX, 191
Crazy Cat Arroyo Park, TX, 212–16
Cryptosporidium, 8

Dallas, TX, 64–66, 70–73
Dead Man's Vista, Old Military
    Road, OK, 15
Denio Creek, Cedar Brake Trail, TX,
    104–7
Denton Creek, Knob Hills Trail, TX,
    57
DeSoto, TX, 74–77
Devil's Backbone, "The Breaks" at
    Bar-H Ranch, TX, 97
Dinosaur Valley State Park, TX,
    104–7
DORBA Trail—Cedar Hill State
    Park, TX, 77–81
Double Lake Park Mountain Bike
    Trail—Coldspring, TX, 158–61

East Recreation Area, Lake
    McMurtry Trails, OK, 24, 26
Edmond, OK, 30–33
Eldorado, TX, 199–202
El Paso, TX, 212–24

Emma Long Motorcycle Park,
    Austin, TX, 119–22
Ernst Tinaja, The Old Ore Road, TX,
    208–9
Erwin Park Trail—McKinney, TX,
    88–91
Etiquette, trail, 4–7

First-aid kit, 9
Flat Rock Ranch—Comfort, TX,
    143–47
Flintstones Village, San Angelo State
    Park Trails, TX, 195–96
Flower Mound, TX, 52–57
Fossil Rim Wildlife Center—Glen
    Rose, TX, 100–104
Franklin Mountains State Park, TX,
    216–24

Garland, TX, 81–84
Gas Pass, Bluff Creek Ranch, TX,
    129–33
Giardia, 8
Gilbert's Trail (The Southside)—
    Franklin Mountains State Park,
    TX, 216–20
Givens Gully, The "GSL" and Capi-
    tol Peak Trails, TX, 190
Glenn Springs and Black Gap—Big
    Bend National Park, TX, 203–7
Glen Rose, TX, 100–107
Grapevine, TX, 61–63
Greenleaf State Park, OK, 16–19
The "GSL" and Capitol Peak
    Trails—Palo Duro Canyon
    State Park, TX, 189–92
Guthrie, OK, 27–29

Highland Bayou, Jack Brooks Park
    Trail, TX, 167–69
Hill of Life, Barton Creek Greenbelt,
    TX, 115, 117
Hitchcock, TX, 167–69
Horseshoe Trail—Grapevine, TX,
    61–63

Houston, TX, 161–66

International Mountain Bicycling
    Association (IMBA)
    address, 5
    Rules of the Trail, 5

Jack Brooks Park Trail—Hitchcock,
    TX, 167–69
Johnson Branch Trail—Ray Roberts
    Lake State Park, TX, 92–95

Knob Hills Trail—Grapevine Lake,
    TX, 57–60

L. B. Houston Nature Trail—Dallas,
    TX, 64–66
Lake Bryan Trails—Bryan, TX,
    155–58
Lake McMurtry Trails—Stillwater,
    OK, 23–26
Lakes
    Arcadia, 30–33
    Bryan, 155–58
    Double, 158–61
    Dunbar Historic, 181–84
    Grapevine, 52–63
    Hefner, 40–43
    Joe Pool, 77–81
    Lake Copper Breaks, 178–81
    Lavon, 84–88
    McMurtry, 23–26
    Old A. C. Fisher, 194–98
    Stanley Draper, 33–36
    Thunderbird, 37–40
    Watonga, 43–47
Lake Thunderbird State Park, OK,
    37–40
Lighthouse Peak, The "GSL" and
    Capitol Peak Trails, TX, 189,
    191
Little Fox Canyon Trail, The "GSL"
    and Capitol Peak Trails, TX, 191
Little Pete's Trailhead, The
    Northshore Trail, TX, 54, 56

Loop ride, 3
Lubbock, TX, 181–84

Mae Simmons Park Trail—Lubbock,
    TX, 181–84
Mansfield Cut, North Padre Island,
    TX, 170–76
Maps
    legend, ix
    Texas and Oklahoma, x–xi
    topographic, 3–4
Mariscal Mine, Glenn Springs and
    Black Gap, TX, 203, 204
Mary's Cove, Oklahoma "Ankle
    Express" Hiking Trail, OK,
    18–19
Matagorda Island, TX, 176
McAllister Park Trails—San Antonio,
    TX, 140–43
McKinney, TX, 88–91
McKinney Springs, The Old Ore
    Road, TX, 208
Memorial Park Trails—Houston, TX,
    161–64
Midwest City, OK, 33–36
Monk's Crossing, Caprock Canyons
    Trailway, TX, 184–89
The Monk's Trail—Crazy Cat
    Arroyo, TX, 212–16
Mountains
    Chisos, 203–12
    Franklin, 212–24
    Sierra del Carmen, 203–7
    Turkey, 20–23
    Winding Stair, 12–16
Muleshoe Bend Trail—Bee Caves,
    TX, 126–29

National Off-Road Biking Association
    (NORBA), Code of Ethics, 5–12
Norman, OK, 37–40
Northeast Trail, Lake McMurtry
    Trails, OK, 24
North Padre Island—Padre Island
    National Seashore, TX, 170–76

The Northshore Trail—Grapevine Lake, TX, 52–57

Northwest Trail, Lake McMurtry Trails, OK, 24

NuDraper Mountain Bike Park—Stanley Draper Lake, OK, 33–36

Oklahoma
overview, 11–12
rides, 12–47

Oklahoma "Ankle Express" Hiking Trail—Greenleaf State Park, OK, 16–19

Oklahoma City, OK, 40–43

Old Military Road—Talihina, OK, 12–16

The Old Ore Road—Big Bend National Park, TX, 207–12

Ouachita National Forest, Old Military Road, OK, 12–16

Out-and-back ride, 3

Padre Island National Seashore, TX, 170–76

Palo Duro Canyon State Park, TX, 189–92

Pedernales Falls State Park, TX, 137–39

Plano, TX, 67–70

Point-to-point ride, 3

Quanah, TX, 178–81

Quitaque, TX, 184–89

Ray Roberts Lake State Park, TX, 92–95

Red Star Ridge, The "GSL" and Capitol Peak Trails, TX, 190

Ride configurations, 3

Ride recommendations, xxvi–xxviii

Rivers
Arkansas, 20–23
Bosque, 112–15
Brazoz, 104–112
Colorado, 126–29

Paluxy, 104–7

Pedernales, 137–39

Trinity, 64–66

Rockledge Park, The Northshore Trail, TX, 55, 56

Rocky Hill Ranch—Smithville, TX, 133–36

Roman Nose State Park Trail—Lake Watonga, OK, 43–47

Rowlett Creek Nature Preserve Trails—Garland, TX, 81–84

R.R. "Pat" Murphy Park, Bluff Creek Trail, OK, 41

Saint Jo, TX, 95–99

San Angelo State Park Trails—San Angelo, TX, 194–98

San Antonio, TX, 140–43

The Seven Mile Loop—Cleburne State Park, TX, 108–11

Sister Grove Park Trail—Lake Lavon, TX, 84–88

Smithville, TX, 133–36

Southeast Trail (Race Loop), Lake McMurtry Trails, OK, 24, 26

Southwest Trail, Lake McMurtry Trails, OK, 24–25

Spring Creek Trail, Arcadia Lake Trail, OK, 30–33

Spur ride, 3

Stevie Ray Vaughn Memorial Bridge, Windmill Hill Nature Preserve Trail, TX, 74

Stillwater, OK, 23–26

The Sunset Loop—Franklin Mountains State Park, TX, 220–24

Talihina, OK, 12–16

Talimena Scenic Drive, Old Military Road, OK, 14, 15

Talimena State Park, Old Military Road, OK, 16

Terry Hershey Park—Houston, TX, 164–66

Texas, 49–51

Central
  overview, 100
  rides, 100–47
East and the Gulf Coast
  overview, 148
  rides, 149–76
North
  overview, 52
  rides, 52–99
Panhandle
  overview, 177
  rides, 178–92
West
  overview, 193
  rides, 194–224
Texas A&M University, TX, 158
Texas Stadium, Dallas, TX, 64
"The Breaks" at Bar-H Ranch—Saint
  Jo, TX, 95–99
Tools, 8–9
Topographic maps, 3–4
Tornillo Creek, The Old Ore Road,
  TX, 208
Tulsa, OK, 20–23
Turkey Mountain Park Trails—Tulsa,
  OK, 20–23
Tyler State Park Trail—Tyler, TX,
  151–55

Waco, TX, 112–15
Walnut Creek Trails—Austin, TX,
  122–26
Warda, TX, 129–33
Water, 7–8
West Recreation Area, Lake
  McMurtry Trails, OK, 24, 26
Windmill Hill Nature Preserve
  Trail—DeSoto, TX, 74–77
Wolf Mountain Trail—Pedernales
  Falls State Park, TX, 137–39
Wood's Crossing, Caprock Canyons
  Trailway, TX, 184–89

X-Bar Ranch—Eldorado, TX,
  199–202

Yellow House Canyon, Mae Simmons Park Trail, TX, 181–84

Zilker Park, Barton Creek Greenbelt,
  TX, 115–18

ABOUT THE AUTHOR

"I'd rather wake up in the middle of nowhere, than in any city on earth."
—Steve McQueen

It is OK to have more than one bicycle. I mean, would you go on a trip with only one change of clothes? No way, right? So having seven or eight bikes sort of makes sense, on a certain level? Good, my friends, we understand each other.

Hi, I'm Chuck. I have a real job—I break things for a living. Other people's software, mostly. I love my job; I am much better at breaking things than I ever was at fixing them. And my company (InterVoice-BRITE) was way beyond understanding when they gave me enough vacation days to finish this manuscript. Thank you.

I still remember my first tricycle—thanks, Dad. I still have most of the bicycles I have ever owned. In 1980 I spent $1,500 on a custom bicycle, and I didn't even own a car. In Dallas, even! My friends thought I was a nut. I still am.

Some of you might wonder how the heck I ever got into writing books on mountain bike trails. It's actually a pretty good story. This guy in Utah was the editor of a series of books for the whole U.S., and he was looking for some pigeon to do Texas and Oklahoma. He found me because I had written a few articles for the local mountain bike club newsletter! I came home from work one day to this answering machine message from Dennis Coello, with this perfect FM radio voice, asking me if I would like to tackle this project. Duh, sure dude, what's in it for me? The first edition of this tome was finished about 14 months later, in late 1994. Now it's time for an update, and here we are, in 2002.

I've never been married, no kids, but I have a wonderful girlfriend. Susan had so much patience while I was working on this project. It's probably a miracle that I still have this beautiful, skinny, Japanese girl in my life. Thanks for hanging on, baby—I'm finished now, and we can have a normal life (whatever that means?), starting tomorrow. I promise.

I have had the same female roommate, Kennis Ketchum, for a bunch of years, her and her silly birds and cats. I'm practically a member of her family, we've lived together for so long. Sometimes I think my mom loves her more than me. Our relationship is a blast.

So that's who I am. I hope you enjoy the pages of this mess as much as I did getting rained on and dragging a muddy bike around while I created them for you. OK, maybe it would be better if you liked 'em more than that. Just don't

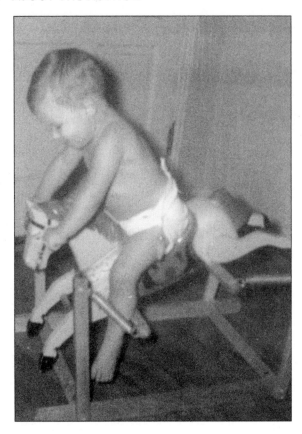

Long ago, in a galaxy far far away from clipless pedals. How about those early bike shorts and full-suspension ride?

get hurt or eaten by bugs on any of these rides, and I will be made whole. The fun-level responsibility is on you.

Buena suerta, mi amigos. Remember to wear clean underwear. And love your mom. She's worth it because she birthed you.

"Pain is life is pain is life is pain is life, ad nauseum."

—Me

Chuck in Dallas:
www.home.mindspring.com/~ccypert
ccypert@mindspring.com